Yale Romanic Studies, Second Series, 24

REASON AFLAME

Unamuno and the Heroic Will

VICTOR OUIMETTE

New Haven and London, Yale University Press, 1974

Copyright © 1974 by Yale University.
All rights reserved. This book may not be
reproduced, in whole or in part, in any form
(except by reviewers for the public press),
without written permission from the publishers.
Library of Congress catalog card number: 73–86914
International standard book number: 0–300–01666–2

Designed by Sally Sullivan
and set in Fairfield type.
Printed in the United States of America by
The Colonial Press Inc., Clinton, Massachusetts.

Published in Great Britain, Europe, and Africa by
Yale University Press, Ltd., London.
Distributed in Latin America by Kaiman & Polon,
Inc., New York City; in Australasia and Southeast
Asia by John Wiley & Sons Australasia Pty. Ltd.,
Sydney; in India by UBS Publishers' Distributors Pvt.,
Ltd., Delhi; in Japan by John Weatherhill, Inc., Tokyo.

For C.S.O.:

. . . pour célébrer le souvenir
d'un grand homme

Contents

Foreword

"I say to you in all sadness of conviction, that to think great thoughts you must be heroes as well as idealists," Justice Oliver Wendell Holmes wrote in 1886. His sentence has a lofty ring, a Romantic aura, that brings us back to the nineteenth century. We live now in an era of technocrats, bureaucrats, statisticians, and spies—obviously not the best vantage point from which to perceive the role of heroes as essential to our survival. Heroes, and specifically intellectual heroes, as seen and defined by a great intellectual hero in his own right, Miguel de Unamuno, make up the list of characters of this book. Yet for some time our attitude toward heroes, intellectual or otherwise, has been ambivalent, diffident, often negative. Could it be that in a "post-Industrial society," according to the formula of Daniel Bell, we no longer need heroes? Our time has seen, according to Raymond Aron and Bell, "the end of ideologies" and also, hopefully and for the immediate future, the end of major wars. We are all becoming, East and West, less like Athens, Sparta, or even Rome, and more like Carthage. This may be a new Punic Age, one in which trade, production, reinvestment, the gross national product, and the balance of payments replace in our minds every other value. Can Ralph Nader replace Themistocles?

We should not necessarily become alarmed when we hear our adolescents claim that they have no heroes. They may admire certain people and be reticent about their admiration. It has happened before. It happened all over Europe after the Religious Wars and the Thirty Years War had produced a crop of fanatic heroes and devastated most of the civilized world. The end of the Cold War will probably witness another swing of the pendulum away from fanaticism and toward cynicism. This change seems to have taken place for some influential portions of the Western intelligentsia as early as the twenties, when the Cold War had not yet come into being. The results might be another eighteenth century, another era of elegance, skepticism, and selfishness. The signs are all around us. On the stage — whether in New York, London, Paris, or elsewhere — comedy outnumbers tragedy ten to one. *Catch 22* is perhaps the great antiepic of our time. Humor and satire thrive, as they did in the eighteenth century. If no major disaster takes place, we are headed toward a new Enlightenment — duller perhaps, with almost no elegance and a surfeit of pornography, but able to be compared in many ways to the age of Johnson and of Voltaire. It will be an era of wits and antiheroes: the picaresque will always survive. Humor is our daily sustenance; Russell Baker and Art Buchwald are certainly more widely read, perhaps more influential, than our best poets or fiction writers.

I think it is possible that the right moment to compensate for this drift toward witty cynicism has come. Once more the theme of the hero should reappear, as a necessary counterpoint, much more useful than any other current antidote — more valid, more noble, than the present vogue of the occult. The hero, as an embodiment of selflessness and vision, is the only human type that can revitalize our societies. Yet heroes, just like ghosts or elves, have a stubborn habit: they do not appear to those who do not believe in them. We must pave the way, learn to understand and appreciate them, make ourselves worthy of their efforts, before they condescend to come back to us.

There are two main reasons why this book is an important one. First, Miguel de Unamuno is the perfect bridge between an era that still understood heroes and our present time. Second, Victor Ouimette, as a scholar, has fused thoroughness to brilliance and brought to us the passion, the vision, the drama of Unamuno's encounter with heroes and the meaning of being a hero.

Stubborn, gifted, a thinker though also a man of action, Unamuno, born in 1864, belongs fully, through background and intellectual attitudes, to the nineteenth century; yet his Existentialist philosophy and his keen observation of social change bring him close to our time. The great Romantic writers Kierkegaard, Nietzsche, Tolstoy, and Dostoevski are ingredients in his melting-pot; yet his life and his copious writings — whether poetry, philosophical essays, novels, or dramas — are always oriented toward the present — his present no doubt, but in many respects our own present — which he mapped and defined with accuracy. A loner, a rebel, he withstood the pressures of his particular Establishment and sought to redefine the future of his country as an epic fight to the finish between the king and himself. (Who would nowadays attempt a similar task? What intellectual in the Western world would dare to dream Unamuno's dream? Norman Mailer may come to the mind, but he can be dismissed after one or two seconds. Unamuno's fight lasted half his life — it was the king who lost the battle.)

Looking for a shortcut, we might define Unamuno as a Spanish Emerson. Yet this will not do. Unamuno had the same rebellious spirit and passionate communion with nature as Thoreau, the same poetic breadth as Walt Whitman — and some ironic touches bring him close to Mark Twain. Let us add a few intellectual flourishes: he could read Leopardi in Italian, Camoens or Antero de Quental in Portuguese, was familiar with major and minor French and English writers in their original texts (his essay on Izaac Walton's *The Compleat Angler* is a delight), did not need any translations — often none were available — to understand German philosophers and theologians, and learned enough Danish to deal with Kierkegaard in the original language. As a professor of Classics in the University of Salamanca he was at home with Greek and Latin sources and quoted them with a minimum of pedantry, when needed. Our admiration grows when we realize he was one of the few "rounded" men ever produced by our Western civilization: he was physically strong, could endure ten or twelve hours of continuous physical exercise without flinching; he walked the highways and byways of Spain and Portugal in search of cultural understanding and for the love of the outdoors. He was the "healthy artist" Van Gogh had hoped for as the best answer to our uncertain world, a durable man who could be both strong and sensitive. He was also a capable administrator, a political and intellectual leader, a passionate believer — almost a mystic at times — who nevertheless harbored an indestructible kernel of skepticism.

A tragic man, no doubt, since the struggle between his heart and his rational self could never be resolved. Yet also a man of contemplation and peace, a man capable of finding solace in beauty, in space, in his own hard work. If we add that he was a perfect husband and father, a devoted family-man who wrote love poems inspired by his wife and whose most poignant lyrics lamented the death of one of his children, we catch a glimpse of his complexity and his stability in the face of constant inner turmoil. Three key words in his life and his works are *contradiction, passion,* and *agony.* Unamuno was always contradicting himself, changing his moods and his viewpoints: there is nothing frozen or static about his rôle and his ideas. Sometimes he plunged into action, into politics, and saw himself as a powerful bell or alarm clock whose historic mission it was to wake up his country, to inspire Spain and the whole Western culture to a more ethical and sensitive way of life. At other times he found his constant confrontations with himself almost unendurable. He sought, and found, shelter in the beauty of nature or in the serene continuity of everyday family life.

Since he recognized and accepted his essence as being made of struggle and contradiction, Unamuno's work had, perforce, to become permeated by duality, antinomy, contrast: light and shadow, reality and dream, action and contemplation, faith and doubt. A modern Don Quixote, he was by turns a practical man and a dreamer of impossible dreams. He walked the sunny Spanish roads fighting for his ideals, striking his enemies with all the might of his pen and thought, being struck in turn. He was often harassed, arrested, several times exiled. His goal was the most ambitious a dreamer has ever dreamed: to make eternity out of what is fleeting, the present moment; to see eternity in a grain of sand or in a glimpse of a tree, a mountain, the self. His quest led him to moments of glory and also into blind alleys — hence the melancholy that pervades some of his later works. Unamuno can be, and often is, irritating, even exasperating to a modern young reader. We are compelled to disagree violently with him time and time again. Yet he is never boring. Passion never is.

His labyrinth of contradictions and his experimental use of language make him thoroughly at home in our era. Joyce, Proust, and Kafka may have fashioned our sensitivity, and in many ways Unamuno shares the goals of their art. He tries, like Joyce, to re-create language through puns, philology, made-up words. Like Kafka, he places us in a labyrinth hedged in by anguish and ambiguity. Like Proust, he plunges into childhood memories and subtle nuances in order to make the fleeting moment into an eternal work of art. Moreover, his constant use of a binary approach, such as the dichotomies of being and nothingness or faith and doubt, place him in tune with our contemporary Structuralist currents. A philosopher and an artist for all seasons, he is both annoyingly old-fashioned and startlingly modern.

The bibliography on Unamuno is very extensive, as befits the work of a major writer. It is almost as extensive as the criticism on Cervantes, whose *Don Quixote* inspired Unamuno in a central way. Yet it remained for Victor Ouimette, a young yet remarkably mature Canadian scholar, to bring order and light out of chaos in an important aspect of Unamuno's works: the theme of the hero, the rôle played by heroes in Unamuno's writings. Unamuno has been, for Ouimette, a fruitful obsession, a sort of intellectual Moby Dick to be captured at all costs. First begun in Montreal, later pursued during his graduate studies at Yale where he was one of our most gifted students, his study of Unamuno continued in Salamanca, where Ouimette worked with his personal library and papers. The quest has been successful: a unifying theme for Unamuno's complex works has been found at last. Ouimette's patience, thoroughness, and powers of analysis are worthy of a modern Ahab. His synthetic approach, his summing up, is, I think, decisive: at last Unamuno begins to fall into place, not despite his contradictions but because of them. This book will be invaluable to Unamuno's numerous devotees — and to those who are convinced that the theme of the hero can enrich our jaded ear.

Manuel Durán

Preface

There is an inner logic in the works of Miguel de Unamuno that makes an exploration of any aspect of his thought a revelatory experience. In tracing his concept of heroism, I have based the beginning of my discussion upon the essays and philosophical works containing theoretical comments that cast light upon his ideas. Starting principally with *Del sentimiento trágico de la vida* and the book that presents the most specific development of the topic, *Vida de Don Quijote y Sancho,* I have attempted to give precision to attitudes dispersed across the entire body of his work and to systematize them, at least to the extent of making the concept a cogent and workable facet of his thought, especially in regard to the "mystery of the personality," which was certainly the nucleus of Unamuno's preoccupation. In order to clarify the more difficult or obscure points, I have filled out these aspects with the poetry, essays, and other philosophical works. Such an attempt at systematization and classification is at best presumptuous, but since Unamuno never provided any sort of scheme for his philosophy and since almost every work reveals a variety of general concerns, not limited by the title or avowed intent of the work, it seems necessary to extract his comments and reorganize them in order to examine a specific problem.

The second part of the work deals with the fiction of Unamuno and is an attempt to see to what extent his theories of heroism affect his characters, and their success or failure at achieving reality. Unamuno frequently insisted upon the need for concrete proof of abstract theories, and for this reason I try to show the relationship between theory and practice in his own work.

Since heroism is the subject of this book, it is of course my main concern. Hopefully, however, it will not seem to be either Unamuno's only concern or the solution to all the quandaries into which his writing thrusts us. It is merely intended as a sort of philosophical cross-section of his thinking which, aside from having its own justification, will also be useful in the interpretation of other problems. Heroism is not Unamuno's panacea, but since it is his term for maximum fulfillment in the individual and for the greatest degree of reality a person can achieve, it seems reasonable to look upon it as an enlightening approach to his attitude toward the individual in general, and himself in particular.

Both a teacher of the Classics and a voracious reader of all literature, Unamuno is an extremely difficult subject in whom to look for the roots of any of his ideas. However, there are certain fundamental concepts of heroism that provide either an unconscious basis for his own ideas or that are specifically mentioned by him in his work.

Unamuno never made any definitive statements regarding the various forms of heroism, as did Carlyle and Nietzsche, nor did he see in the hero the salvation of a people, as Nietzsche saw in his own *Übermensch*. Throughout his works, though, the words *héroe, heroísmo,* and *heroicidad* occur with such frequency that it becomes clear that, although he left no systematic explanation of his views, Unamuno did indeed have a very definite and concrete idea of what these terms meant within the context of his interpretation of the problem of the personality.

In order to make the works of Unamuno accessible to as broad a public as possible, I have translated all quotations in this study into English, except where another translator is indicated. In the interests of clarity, I have preferred literal translations to more colloquial ones and have attempted, where possible, to preserve Unamuno's neologisms. All references are to the original Spanish versions.

This study in its original form was prepared as part of the requirements for the degree of Doctor of Philosophy at Yale University. In the years since, it has undergone many changes in which suggestions from many people have been incorporated. Anyone who is at all familiar with the Unamuno bibliography and who would nonetheless try to add something new to it, is probably simultaneously demonstrating a mental incompetence that should bar him from the task. Unamuno is, all the same, a pleasant — although occasionally rugged — pasture in which to wander, and the temptation is irresistible; but I am fortunate in having good guides. It is consistent, then, that whatever strengths this work may have are largely due to them, while its weaknesses are recognizably my own.

Above all else, it is to the forebearance, good humor, and encyclopaedic knowledge of Manuel Durán of Yale University that I am most indebted. He has followed this undertaking since the beginning, and his encouragement and advice have been beyond calculation.

To Gustavo Correa, also of Yale, I express sincere thanks for many lucid comments that were essential to this final version, and to Monica Harvey of McGill University I express my gratitude not only for preparing the way but for helping to pave a bit of it.

Along with an entire generation of Unamuno students, I am also grateful to Felisa de Unamuno for her help with my work in Salamanca.

To both Yale and McGill universities I am indebted for their generous financial support throughout this venture, as I am to María Black and Barbara Folsom for their help with the final drafts.

And of course, always, to María Elena.

V. O.

McGill University
Montreal
December 1971

1. Unamuno and Nineteenth-Century Concepts of Heroism

In historical events, where the actions of men form the subject of observation, the most primitive conception of a cause was the will of the gods, succeeded later on by the will of those men who stand in the historical foreground — the heroes of history.

Leo Tolstoy

Surrounded by apparently incomprehensible cosmic phenomena and besieged by a confusion of purpose, man has constantly searched for evidence of some explanation within a divine power. He has tried to explain the mysteries of the universe by deifying nature, and to extend his own powers through the creation of anthropomorphic gods and a mythology designed to stand between the tyranny of his own limitations and the abyss of oblivion. This need has translated itself since the earliest beginnings into a consistent search for clearly superior men who might serve as examples of the ideal expression of human potential. Such a man may be historically real, imaginary, or a combination of both, but his image impresses itself upon the popular mind in a way that makes him both exceptional and accessible. It is possible for ordinary men to see enough of themselves in him to believe that his greater qualities may also be theirs. He is a source of hope and inspiration for lesser men, is especially blessed with the attributes of soul, and his feats tend to outlive him. He is the hero.

In Western thought, the concept of heroism has its immediate roots in pre-Homeric Greece, where it referred principally to the distinguished dead, who were revered as demigods who had to be appeased in order to ensure the successful outcome of any enterprise. They

occupied a middle ground between ordinary mortals and the anthropomorphic gods with whom the Greeks felt at home. The cult of
hero worship was largely promoted by the oracle at Delphi, and temples and cenotaphs were erected upon the sites of the heroes' graves,
which were believed to be the continuing center of their existence
and of their future acts. In classical Greece, however, the attitude
changed considerably, as reverence gave way to fear and sacrifices
were made at their temples. Distinctions were not particularly precise,
and some heroes were thought to be the issue of unions between
mortals and gods and thus to possess the qualities of both worlds.
Consequently, they were endowed with immortality: even if they
died, they were generally believed to have profound influence over
earthly matters from beyond the tomb or, as in the case of Hercules,
to continue as heroes among the gods after death.

With the passage of time, however, the importance of magical elements diminished, and in the age of Homer the hero became more
humanized until the term came to represent all great or outstanding
men, almost without regard to their social position or the divinity
of their origin. They were especially blessed with the virtues of wisdom, justice, temperance, and courage, but their exceptional gifts
were rather a matter of quantity: they possessed in abundance physical and spiritual abilities that ordinary men had only to a lesser extent. This made greater identification possible and gave their exploits
a degree of plausibility and immediacy that had not been attained in
tales with a strong supernatural basis. The heroes are the logical and
ideal extension of Everyman. In the epics they included all the
bravest soldiers, and indeed valor has been the most consistent criterion for heroism. Heroes were the men who represented the hopes
of the common people, since one important aspect of their superiority
was to relieve some of the mysteries of life, through which they
seemed to pass with greater ease than most.[1]

The hero becomes man's hope because he has gone before and "is

1. See Will Durant, The Story of Civilization (New York, 1939), 2: 180;
C. M. Bowra, Heroic Poetry (London, 1964), chap. 3; Charles Baudoin, Le
Triomphe du héros (Paris, 1952), Introduction. Especially useful is the article
of Pedro Salinas, "El 'héroe' literario y la novela picaresca española: semántica
e historia literaria," Ensayos de literatura hispánica (Madrid, 1967), pp. 58–74.

always the figure endowed with magical power, who makes the impossible possible." [2] He must somehow return from his trials to enlighten man, and his deeds must be reflected in mankind. In other words, the hero needs an audience. Joseph Campbell describes the heroic experience as follows: "A hero ventures forth from the world of common day into a region of supernatural wonder: fabulous forces are there encountered and a decisive victory is won: the hero comes back from this mysterious adventure with the power to bestow boons on his fellow man." [3] Power and the unknown — the hero's accomplishment lies largely in his success in approaching the ultimate truth of existence, which, within the Platonic tradition, is not communicable. He can show the way, but he cannot reveal the truth, and this concept will be fundamental for Unamuno. The hero may be accepted and hailed by the society he serves, or he may be scorned and ridiculed; but he is, when finally recognized, symbolic of some sort of divine revelation that each man must experience for himself.

In most cultures the hero represents the liberator, the redeemer who can free a land or a people from any sort of enslavement by means of a mighty blow intended to wreak destruction upon the tyrannical forces that inspired the popular imagination to create the heroic myth in the first place. As Joseph Campbell explains: "In a word: the first work of a hero is to retreat from the world scene of secondary effects to those causal zones of the psyche where the difficulties really reside, and there to clarify the difficulties, eradicate them in his own case (i.e., give battle to the nursery demons of his local culture) and break through to the undistorted, direct experience and assimilation of what C. G. Jung has called 'the archetypal images.'" [4] This attitude will develop into Unamuno's distinction, based on readings of Kant, between substance and appearance. This is, perhaps, the essential point — that the creation of the hero is largely the result of external effects and is not an absolute quality with which a man is or is not endowed, depending upon his birth. Throughout history and up to the age of

2. C. G. Jung, *Psychological Types*, trans. H. Godwin Baynes (London, 1923), p. 324.
3. Joseph Campbell, *The Hero with a Thousand Faces* (Cleveland and New York, 1956), p. 30.
4. Ibid., pp. 18–19.

Nietzsche, heroism is a heightened state of being that must be achieved, although it is seldom done consciously but rather as the indirect outcome of some other goal.

Indeed, much of the encouragement the hero brings to mankind arises from his death, which serves as proof of his superiority since his inspiration — and, in ideal instances, his powers — continue beyond the tomb of his image and into his afterlife or, occasionally, resurrection. Man is loath to relinquish his hold over the hero and throughout the ages has felt compelled to fabricate some belief in his everlasting strength, often in the form of his continuing protection or as a defense against the death of man himself. In the words of Stephen Spender, man chooses to view them and their exploits as, "Legendary heroes, plumed with flame like pyres, / Whose flesh-winged day was that bewildering island / The timeless sea engulfed" ("Seascape"). They vanish but they continue nonetheless. For this reason, there is attached to the great heroes from ancient times to the Middle Ages the belief that after their departure from earth in human form they will continue to demonstrate powers equal, if not far superior, to those they employed during their purely human existence. This is evident not only in the hero worship of the Greeks, but in the tenets of Christianity and in much of the popular literature of the European Middle Ages. Curtius gives one of the most adequate definitions of the modern concept:

> The idea of the hero is connected with the basic value of nobility. The hero is the ideal personal type whose being is centered upon nobility and its realization — hence upon "pure," not technical, values — and whose basic virtue is natural nobility in body and soul. The hero is distinguished by a superabundance of intellectual will and by its concentration against instincts. It is this which constitutes his greatness of character. The specific virtue of the hero is self-control. But the hero's will does not rest here, it presses on into power, responsibility, daring. Hence the hero can play the role of statesman or general, as in earlier times he played the role of warrior.[5]

The heroic literature of modern Europe is contained principally in the epics. Siegfried, Sigurd, Roland, and El Cid are among the rulers

5. Ernst Robert Curtius, *European Literature and the Latin Middle Ages* (New York, 1953), p. 167.

of the medieval hierarchy, and miraculous powers from the tomb are not lacking in this literature either. El Cid, it is said, won his last battle while dead and strapped to Babieca on the beach of Valencia.[6] France's Roland is resurrected, in spirit at least, through his famous sword, which becomes converted in the popular Spanish mentality into the almost equally noteworthy hero, Durandarte, whose immortality is attested to by Don Quixote himself (pt. 2, chap. 23). The epic hero is really not an individual with a clearly defined personality, but rather a representative of the culture that created the myth surrounding him, as Lukács explains: "Strictly speaking, the hero of an epic is never an individual. At all times the fact that the object of the epic is not the fate of a person but rather that of a community has been considered to be an essential characteristic." [7] In the late Middle Ages all levels of society allowed themselves to be inspired and moved by tales of knights rescuing fair virgins and extending hope through the gloom of everyday life.

In the chivalric romances of the fifteenth and sixteenth centuries the hero was placed in an aura of enchantment and beauty, the very unreality of which was its charm and inspiration. According to Huizinga, it was precisely the feeling of despair from which the romances lifted men that gave rise to the great heroes of the times: "Still this very pessimism is the ground whence their soul will soar up to the aspiration of a life of beauty and serenity. For at all times the vision of a sublime life has haunted the souls of men, and the gloomier the present is, the more strongly this aspiration will make itself felt." [8] The appearance of the hero is, then, a strongly social phenomenon. He is the product of all his surroundings and will provide an example for imitation; yet it will not be considered the duty of every man, but only of the aristocracy, to respond to the call of heroism. Their example will filter down through society. In 1422, Alain Chartier addressed himself to all of France, when in the *Quadrilogue invectif* he said: "And yet I say that little should he esteem his birth and less

6. See the ballads, "Mientras se apresta Jimena," no. 528 of the *Romancero general*, ed. Angel González Palencia (Madrid, 1947), and "Muerto yace ese buen Cid," no. 149 of the *Romancero del Cid*, ed. F[ederico] S[ainz de] R[obles] (Madrid, 1962).

7. Georg Lukács, *La Théorie du roman* (Lausanne, 1963), p. 60.

8. J. Huizinga, *The Waning of the Middle Ages* (New York, 1954), p. 37.

desire the continuation of his life both he who spends his days as a man born only for himself, without enriching the common usefulness, as well as he whose memory is extinguished with his life." [9] It is the duty of the nobles to show the way so that the other levels of society may take hope and follow.

Heroism as a historical concept is much too widespread for the scope of this work, and to trace any significant path leading directly to Unamuno would be audacious indeed. Heroes are found in all the popular literatures of Europe, and while they all form the basis upon which future concepts must be built, the direct influences for the thought of Unamuno came much later. Throughout Unamuno's thought there are traces of the principal European thinkers, especially from the seventeenth to the twentieth centuries; all his ideas, including heroism, are supported, regardless of the most immediate influences, by a foundation that has absorbed aspects of the thought of Pascal, Spinoza, Kant, Hegel, Schopenhauer, Spencer, Haeckel, and Bergson, as well as Balmes and the Spanish mystics, and his friend and contemporary, Angel Ganivet.

The influences of both Søren Kierkegaard and Etienne Pivert de Senancour are also of great importance in any critical study of the thought of Unamuno, although neither of them had any substantial effect on his concept of heroism as such. Nevertheless, Kierkegaard's beliefs that man must find his truth within his own personality and that life is a state of tension between temporal existence and eternal truth are basic to Unamuno's idea of personality. Unamuno found a "brother" in Kierkegaard, whom he discovered by way of Ibsen. Both the Dane and the Spaniard felt the agony of their ontological peril and chose to take an intuitive leap toward God rather than a rational one. Kierkegaard was to abstract from the deepest recesses of his life the guiding principles for his future activity, and Unamuno did essentially the same thing in his concept of heroism. For both men, that is the only hope man has of attaining truth, which for Unamuno in particular became an increasingly problematic concept. This need for commitment before God is essential for all men

9. Alain Chartier, *Le Quadrilogue invectif*, in *Jeux et sapience du Moyen Age*, ed. Albert Pauphilet (Paris, 1951), p. 868.

who wish to live to the full; and this God must be living also, not a mere abstraction. The risk is the same for Unamuno's hero.[10]

Senancour presents Unamuno with a man, Obermann, whose very name is significant. He is a character in a book, to be sure, but perhaps is more real than his creator, as he suffers the anguish of his existence with stoic heroism. Like Kierkegaard, Obermann bases his life upon his own inner tensions. In the words of Van Wyck Brooks: "He resolves, that is, to hold fast to nature by means of the only touchstone within reach, the sum-total of his own intuitions." [11] *Obermann* (1804) is a journal of Romantic introspection. The incurable melancholy of the protagonist, however, differs greatly from the encouragement that Unamuno tries to offer his readers. The soul-searching and the so-called *désordre des ennuis* is akin to the inner anguish that is the springboard for the hero's actions, as is the attitude that man must not deserve death—that is, that he must resist annihilation. Life is a difficult experience and must not be accepted blindly: "In the perpetual uncertainty of an existence that is always eventful, precarious, servile, you all, blind and docile, follow the traces beaten out by the established order; thus abandoning your life to your habits, and losing it painlessly as you might lose a day." [12]

This idea will find an echo in Unamuno, who urges men on to greater extensions of their capabilities while resisting the confinements of established attitudes. Senancour saw the great potential that lay within mankind, and much of his melancholy is due to his awareness of the abyss between what man can do and what he is content to do:

> Man's moral sense, and his enthusiasm, the restlessness of his wishes, the need for extension which is a habit in him, seem to indicate that his purpose is not in fleeting things; that his action is not limited to visible specters; that his thought has as its object necessary and eternal concepts; that his business is to work for the betterment or repair of the world; that his final purpose is,

---

10. See especially Luis Farré, "Unamuno, William James y Kierkegaard," *Cuadernos Hispanoamericanos* 20 (1954): 279–99 and 21: 64–90. Also Jesús-Antonio Collado, *Kierkegaard y Unamuno* (Madrid, 1962).

11. Van Wyck Brooks, *The Malady of the Ideal* (London, 1913), p. 56.

12. Etienne Pivert de Senancour, *Obermann* (Paris, 1913), p. 166.

in a way, to elaborate, refine, organize, to give matter more energy, beings more power, organs more perfection, seeds more fruitfulness, to give greater soundness to the relationships between things and greater dominion to order.[13]

This is a manifesto of truly heroic proportions, and while Senancour, like Unamuno, did not create a work based on a clear systematization of heroism, many of his attitudes regarding the scope of mankind developed into Unamuno's faith in the potential of the individual in his striving toward immortality.

Unamuno's references to heroism are not limited to any single period of his life, although the one work in which he is most specifically concerned with heroism is the *Vida de Don Quijote y Sancho*, published in 1905 and deeply influenced, as Gonzalo Sobejano has pointed out,[14] by Nietzsche's *Also sprach Zarathustra*, published between 1883 and 1885. Unamuno's debt to Nietzsche has still not been studied in sufficient depth, and much of what he did learn from Nietzsche was greatly altered as he adapted aspects of it to conform to his own views of life. First, however, came the influence of Thomas Carlyle, which is probably far more important and dates from the earliest part of the twentieth century.

In 1840, the somber Scot delivered a series of lectures in London that were later published in book form under the title *On Heroes, Hero-Worship and the Heroic in History* and translated into Spanish in 1893. The immense importance of Carlyle's thought and style to Unamuno's work has been documented by Carlos Clavería, who points out: "In Carlyle's pages on heroes, Unamuno must have sought the answer to his anguished questions and, in any case, avoided falling into acceptance of the popular and current interpretations superficially revealing themselves in the book by Carlyle which has done most to make its author's name known throughout the world." [15]

13. Ibid., 1: 176. This passage is marked in pencil in the edition (cat. no. 644), in Unamuno's library in Salamanca: *Obermann*, preface by George Sand, Bibliothèque Charpentier (Paris, n.d.), new ed., letter 42, p. 171.

14. Gonzalo Sobejano, *Nietzsche en España* (Madrid, 1967).

15. Carlos Clavería, "Unamuno y Carlyle," *Cuadernos Hispanoamericanos* 10 (1949): 62. It is worthy of note that in Unamuno's collection there are the following volumes by Carlyle: *Sartor Resartus, Heroes and Hero-Worship, and Past and Present* (London: George Routledge and Sons, 1888), cat. no. 0557; *Past and Present* (Chicago and New York: The Henneberry Company,

There is no doubt that Unamuno was familiar with the book, as he was with most of Carlyle's writings, and indeed this may well have been the first of Carlyle's works that he read. Around the beginning of the century, in fact, he was at work on a translation of Carlyle's *The French Revolution: A History* which, as he admits in his essay "Maese Pedro," written in 1902, left him thinking in a Carlylean manner for some time.

The principles of Carlyle's approach to heroism are, like a great deal of his work, rigid and often contradictory, but his basic tenet is that the hero is a divinely inspired leader of men whose word is a sort of revelation. He is the model and mold for history and has it in his power to save society, whose duty it is to listen, with a Government of the Wise as its ultimate goal. It was an idea of enormous influence, as was most of Carlyle's thought, and represented the fulfillment of a mission which Carlyle felt had to be carried out in an age that worshipped Mud-Gods and Mammon and turned its back on a spiritual renascence. He felt that Hero-worship offered religious possibilities that were far more convincing than traditional Christianity, and presented a historical analysis based on six representative moments in man's submission to those who seemed to incarnate a truth or vision more far-reaching than was normally realizable.

From the pagan worship of the Norse god, Odin, in whom his fellow men recognize a spark of divinity, the hero metamorphoses into a prophet. Carlyle, with his deep admiration of action and power and his sympathy for the sincerity of Islam, chose the example of the militant Mohammed rather than that of the meek Christ, whose teachings were deeply troubling him. In the third stage, he sees the hero as poet, a comparison he believes to be applicable to all ages, especially since he sees the prophet in the poet and feels that each has inseparable elements of the other. His examples are Dante and Shakespeare, in whom he sees embodied the Spirit and the Flesh, respectively. In the fourth stage of his evolution the hero is priest and

---

n.d.); *English and Other Critical Essays* (London: Everyman's Library, J. M. Dent and Sons, n.d.), cat. no. 5181; *Scottish and Other Miscellanies* (London: Everyman's Library, J. M. Dent and Sons, 1923), cat. no. 5175; *The French Revolution: A History* (Leipzig: Tauchnitz, 1851), 3 vols., cat. nos. 4762–3–4; *Oliver Cromwell's Letters and Speeches with Elucidations*, Chapman and Hall (London: n.d.), 3d ed., 4 vols., cat. nos. 4793–96.

reformer, as exemplified by Martin Luther and John Knox. Next, he is discussed as man of letters and product of the new age that began in the middle of the eighteenth century and was still continuing in 1840. His examples, for startlingly different reasons, are Samuel Johnson, Jean-Jacques Rousseau, and Robert Burns. Finally, he discusses the hero as king, referring specifically to Oliver Cromwell, whom he admired, and to Napoleon, whom he did not.

Essentially, Carlyle's concept is rooted in the idea that might makes right and that he who holds power is a hero.[16] Nevertheless, the need for a superior intellect is repeatedly stated, as Louis Cazamian stresses: "Therefore the characteristic attitude of the hero, face to face with this obscure realm of appearances, is one of energetic intuition, inspired and directed by a moral need of superiority." [17] Few aspects could be further removed from the thought of Unamuno who does, however, consider at least to some extent the heroic elements in each of the fields suggested by Carlyle, adding an important nuance, the hero as saint. This is a division Carlyle could scarcely have appreciated since, to a large degree, for him the hero replaces the saint. Like Unamuno, however, Carlyle demands of his hero an almost religious sincerity and honesty of insight: "I should say sincerity, a deep, great, genuine sincerity, is the first characteristic of all men in any way heroic"; and he adds, "Sincerity, I think, is better than Grace." [18]

Hero-worship is Carlyle's new religion, and it is this sincerity that gives the hero the ability to penetrate the mysteries of life and to work beyond the appearances that baffle the lesser man. Unlike Unamuno's hero, however, he is a public, history-making, and often political figure, for whom justice is conceived of as action, earnestness, courage, and hard work. Carlyle, ever suspicious of the new democratic trends, asserts that all men are not equal and that the hero will prevail by divine right. Individualism is a heroic quality, and it is in this most fundamental aspect that Unamuno will part

16. See an intriguing examination of the character of the hero in Ernst Kretschmer, *The Psychology of Men of Genius,* trans. R. B. Cattell (New York, 1931), especially chap. 9.

17. Louis Cazamian, *Carlyle* (Hamden, Conn.: Archon Books, 1966), p. 175.

18. William Carlyle, *On Heroes, Hero-Worship and the Heroic in History* (Lincoln, Neb., 1966), pp. 45, 30.

company with both Nietzsche and Carlyle. Carlyle's hero, much like Unamuno's, is an instrument of a superior will, but his vision is far less a product of his own will and his own efforts to extend personal gifts; and because of Carlyle's struggles with Christianity, the forces moving his hero are scarcely distinguishable from those of Nature itself. Unamuno also struggled with Christianity, but the conflict manifested itself in a totally different way.

Carlyle sees the emergence of great men as part of the cyclical evolution of history leading to one of two results: either the hero will answer the call of his epoch and deal specifically with its problems, as did Cromwell; or there will be a sort of *Gotterdämmerung* (Carlyle uses the word frequently) at periodic intervals in history, which will represent the opportunity for a fresh beginning, as was the case in the late eighteenth and early nineteenth centuries. The hero's sincerity, coupled with a clear awareness of his mission of revelation, permits him to act with determination and boldness and to lead others on toward progress.

The historical nature of Carlyle's idea is evident when he states that "Universal History, the history of what man has accomplished in this world, is at bottom the history of the Great Men who have worked here," and that Hero-worship is sure to last as long as mankind exists. He sees the world as a monument, therefore, to those who have fulfilled their duties in faith and sincerity and with the support of the society that both spawned and formed them: "Society everywhere is some representation, not *in*supportably inaccurate, of a graduated Worship of Heroes; — reverence and obedience done to men really great and wise." These men are dictatorial figures whom he is loath to define, but who have appeared with the specific mission of preserving their moment in time through their ability to render concrete what all men were on the verge of saying at that very instant. They are in the forefront of a general awareness because, "The Hero is he who lives in the inward sphere of things, in the True, Divine and Eternal which exists always, unseen to most, under the Temporary, Trivial." [19]

This is not a metaphysical approach, and although much of what is in Carlyle also appears in Unamuno, the insistence upon the his-

19. Ibid., pp. 1, 12, 155.

torical dimension does not seep into Unamuno's writings at all. Indeed, the most fundamental distinction to be drawn between the
ideas of the two men is that Carlyle believed in the hero as a unique
figure conforming to the demands of the moment, while Unamuno
conceived of him as the best of any individual and saw heroism in
every action directed toward a sincere cause. For Carlyle, the social
significance was compensation for a wavering religious belief; in
Unamuno it is replaced by emphasis on individual evolution: he
substitutes the plenitude of a personality for the progress of a people.
In other words, the grandiose and epic in Carlyle becomes intimate
in Unamuno. Therefore, Carlyle stresses action to eliminate doubt
and asserts that the great man would be heroic in almost any endeavor,
while Unamuno sees heroism in supreme achievements consonant
with each man's vision.

The concept of Hero-worship in Carlyle is almost as important as
heroism itself, for he feels that it is a noble attempt for any man
who is not a leader and a relief for more mediocre men. As Eric
Bentley explains: "Hero-worship (in Nietzsche, too, who was infatu-
ated with the histories of his friend Burckhardt) partakes of nineteenth-century antiquarianism (cult of the Middle Ages, cult of the
Renaissance) which is a projection on to the page of history, now one
of the chief outlets for personal fantasy, of the escapist yearning." [20]
This explains not only the interest felt by the nineteenth-century
philosophers, but also their encouragement of their own followers'
admiration (particularly Carlyle's appreciation of the fawning of his
friend, John Sterling). Unamuno rejects the principle of Hero-worship and replaces it with an insistence upon the necessity of realizing
one's own needs and following another man only insofar as he can
help to fill them; but he will not support the adulation of the hero
simply because of his apparently superhuman qualities, since for him
the hero is not merely a lucky recipient of outstanding qualities, but
a deeply agonizing victim of the struggle for immortality — something
Carlyle's atheism could not see.

Carlyle, however, did prepare the way for the coming of Nietzsche's *Übermensch*, a superior being bred by events rather than created out of himself. Bentley summarizes:

20. Eric Bentley, *A Century of Hero-Worship* (Boston, 1957), p. 61.

By nature both worldly and religious, Carlyle tries to reconcile the two elements in his nature through a philosophy of heroism. He postulates the hero because, in the first place, the hero is human, fleshly, successful, the highest product of the evolutionary process, and because, in the second place, men may transfer to the hero the feelings they had associated with God. The hero is an instrument of progress and a justification of life. His achievements are substantial, the hope he holds out unbounded. Through him body and spirit, time and eternity, policy and religion, are reconciled, Carlyle thinks, in a new *Weltanschauung*.[21]

Carlyle's hero is the product of social needs and forces. He supersedes Christianity and himself becomes an object for adoration. He can save the individual by saving society — unlike Unamuno's hero, who is the maximum extension of the individual himself.

One of the men deeply influenced by the thought of Carlyle was Friedrich Nietzsche, many of whose writings on the Superman reveal the effect of Carlyle's concept of heroism. It would be foolish to try to cite Carlyle as a truly fundamental source of the thought of Nietzsche; the German thinker was far more of a philosopher than the historian Carlyle, and his work shows a polish and a profundity that Carlyle could never have achieved. Moreover, Nietzsche's prejudices, though sometimes no less extravagant than those of Carlyle, did not impede his judgment and the clarity of his conclusions to the same extent. In one specific concept, however, the two men found themselves in close contact. Both of them saw the very salvation of society in the hero.

Nietzsche's *Übermensch* is the hero of the future, a combination of both the heavenly and the diabolic, the product of breeding, power, and intellect. Nietzsche and Carlyle both agree that power makes the hero right; but, unlike Unamuno, neither sees the hero as a compassionate being, but rather as a magnanimous overlord well adapted to the specific needs of the times. That is to say that Nietzsche's Superman is to be the direct outcome of the moral decay of society at the end of the nineteenth century and will represent the start of a superior race that will rule the slave mentality. He will be born out of man's chaos and the despair of contemporary civilization. The

21. Ibid., p. 67.

influence of Rousseau (which may also be seen in Carlyle) is important, since Nietzsche sees mankind as essentially innocent and perverted in its natural impulses, and the select few who will be the Supermen will represent man's new goal and the object of his yearning. This will be the new form of love, and is a highly aristocratic attitude, since Nietzsche sees democracy as harmful to man and places greater emphasis upon the division into and inevitability of two races: the superrace and the slave mentality.

Also like Carlyle, Nietzsche reveals great ambivalence in his attitude toward individual personal immortality, although he definitely insists upon the existence of eternity, exemplified especially in the doctrine of Eternal Recurrence. This is intended as a substitute for man's desire for personal immortality, but it is an idea that Unamuno could never have accepted.[22]

It is interesting to note, however, that Zarathustra, like Unamuno, stresses the need for disciples of his teachings. For Unamuno this is another source of self-perpetuation on earth, but Zarathustra sees the Higher Men who will spread his teachings as New Evangelists who will preach the Gospel of the Superman. This leads to a certain amount of praise on Nietzsche's part for the saint in history, especially as an active human being. (For this reason it seems he cannot accept Schopenhauer's saint, whom he finds too passive.) A similar respect will be shown by Unamuno, but in his case the roots are to be found in his traditionalism and his affinity for the great Spanish mystics.

For Unamuno, heroism is a struggle, but with oneself first and then, in a secondary way, with outside elements. For Nietzsche, however, life is a struggle to attain power, and this brings individuals into conflict with each other before all else. Man becomes predatory, since *der Wille zur Macht* becomes the first law of Nature and the basis upon which the state will be constructed. It is the process of becoming and is the only true value — instinct and passion. If we are to

22. It is noteworthy that in *La agonía del cristianismo,* Unamuno writes: "The doctrine of progress is the doctrine of Nietzsche's Superman; but a Christian must believe that he must not become a Superman, but rather an immortal man, that is, a Christian." *Obras completas,* ed. Manuel García Blanco (Madrid, 1951), 16: 524. All quotations from Unamuno, except when otherwise indicated, refer to the edition of *Obras completas* edited by Manuel García Blanco (Madrid, 1950–58), hereafter cited as O.C.

accept Adler's interpretation, this is merely the psychological camouflage of one who is essentially weak. However, this seems inadequate. Nietzsche's idea is similar in some ways to concepts in both Bergson and Unamuno, but it leads to nothing concrete and has no goal. Unamuno's goals are always very clear, and the predatory aspect of this becoming does not appear at all except in the Cain and Abel works.

Thus it is that the hero comes to be an absolute value for both Carlyle and Nietzsche. Certainly for Nietzsche this is a direct outgrowth of his discovery of Hellenistic culture, and it seems that this could be at least partly true for the professor of Greek at Salamanca. For Nietzsche, however, the Superman represents man's zenith, just as the heroes did for the Greeks, whereas for Unamuno the hero represents individual man's zenith and his most immediate goal. Unamuno sees in the hero — much as Carlyle did, but without the sociohistoric grandiosity — a leader, whether of one man or of a people.

The Superman is not a moral concept; Nietzsche envisions him as being beyond all our traditional scales of values, which he wants to see transformed (Umwerthung aller Werthe). He will be able to make his own interpretations of values on the basis of whether a thing is harmful or useful to him. Thus is it bad or good. The will is the important aspect and continues to be so through William James and Unamuno, but Nietzsche sees it less as a question of free will than as a matter dependent upon the will-to-power specifically, without which the will cannot function. Henri Lichtenberger explains it as follows: "In reality, there is no soul separate from the body; neither is there such a thing as free-will, nor yet is there non-free-will. There are only strong wills which show themselves by their great deeds, and weak wills whose actions are considerably less. . . . This illusion of free-will, once created and admitted, the slave was able — at least in imagination — to become the equal of his master, or even to surpass him. If the value of an individual is contained not in the strength he controls, but in the use he makes of his free-will, there is nothing to hinder the weak from excelling the strong."[23]

23. Henri Lichtenberger, The Gospel of Superman, trans. J. M. Kennedy (Edinburgh and London, 1910), p. 126. There exist no works by Nietzsche in Unamuno's library, although it is possible that any he may have possessed have merely been lost.

This idea inevitably supports Nietzsche's rejection of Christianity and thus separates him from Unamuno, who does, nevertheless, use many of his concepts of the Superman in his own quest for personal plenitude.

Both Nietzsche and Unamuno see the individual ego as the basis for advancement, but in Nietzsche it is with a view toward supremacy while in Unamuno it is merely aimed at individual fulfillment and universal improvement. Both show an eagerness to achieve a type of immortality, but the religious question separates them so deeply that their means of achieving it differ greatly. Both of them see man as an essentially sick animal; but while for Nietzsche his sickness is due to the perversion of the natural impulses — mainly predatory — Unamuno sees it, rather, as an essential awareness of the great distance that remains to be traveled on the road to eternity and of the need to travel it if life is to have any meaning. It is hardly surprising, then, that Unamuno should scarcely acknowledge any debt to Nietzsche, since their differences are far more fundamental than their similarities, which are so general as to be scarcely indicative of any affinity. Nevertheless, as Gonzalo Sobejano points out, there are a great many points of contact that have yet to be explored.[24] For example, many stylistic similarities can be noted in "El sepulcro de Don Quijote," which link it to *Also sprach Zarathustra,* and if we were to accept Sobejano's belief in Unamuno's atheism, many other similarities could also be found.

Sidney Hook conceives of a certain type of hero as follows: "It is the hero as an event-making man who leaves the positive imprint of his personality upon history — an imprint that is still observable after he has disappeared from the scene." [25] This is a standard that will hold true for Carlyle, Nietzsche, and Unamuno; but upon looking beyond these limits one becomes aware of a scale of values and differences of purpose that will profoundly separate the first two from Unamuno. Nietzsche's Superman is to be part of a race and will be perpetuated in that way. Carlyle's hero has carved his name upon the rock of history and social change. Unamuno's hero will achieve

24. Sobejano, *Nietzsche en España,* pp. 293–97. See also Paul Ilie, *Unamuno: an Existential View of Self and Society* (Madison, Wisc., 1967), chap. 10.

25. Sidney Hook, *The Hero in History* (Boston, 1955), p. 157.

his immortality through personal effort transmitted from individual to individual, and also through Christian mysticism. Carlyle and Nietzsche, however, could see the hero alone as the epitome of life and its goal. Force and will become combined in an amoral man who will be history's motor and its supreme creation. What small rôle God (spoken of as "Providence" for the most part) may have had in the actions of Carlyle's hero has greatly diminished in Nietzsche; there is a brutality and blindness about the submission due his Superman that is much more ominous than the principles of the other thinkers who had an influence upon Unamuno's concept of the hero, Tolstoy and William James.

While there still remains a great deal of a bibliographical nature to be done regarding the relationship between Unamuno and Tolstoy, it is now clear that Unamuno owed a great deal more to the Russian novelist than merely the inspiration for the title of *Paz en la guerra*.[26] It is not yet known exactly when or how Unamuno first came into contact with Tolstoy's work, but it may well have been through the French translation of *War and Peace*, published in 1884,[27] and he makes his debt quite explicit in a letter to Federico Urales, in which he states candidly, "Tolstoy has been one of the souls that most profoundly stirred my own; his works have left a deep imprint on me." [28] To exactly which works he refers is unclear, but the affinity is by no means out of character; both men were cut in many ways from the same cloth, being by nature rebellious and romantic. Both were also deeply sensitive to the literary and philosophical currents that shook Europe in the last half of the nineteenth century, when Count Tolstoy wrote his most important works and Unamuno reached his manhood through his first novel, cast partly in the Tolstoyan mold, although their individual reactions to these currents were vastly different. Both were also affected, perhaps more

26. See Antonio Sánchez Barbudo, "Sobre la concepción de *Paz en la guerra*," *Estudios sobre Galdós, Unamuno y Machado* (Madrid, 1968), pp. 83–94; C. Marcilly, "Unamuno et Tolstoï: de *La Guerre et la Paix* à *Paz en la guerra*," *Bulletin Hispanique* 67 (1965): 274–313; H. Th. Oostendorp, "Los puntos de semejanza entre *La guerra y la paz* y *Paz en la guerra*," *Bulletin Hispanique* 69 (1967): 85–105.
27. Oostendorp, "Los puntos de semejanza," p. 90.
28. Quoted by Oostendorp, p. 87.

deeply than either realized, and again with differing results, by the work of Nietzsche.[29]

In their highly individualistic ways, both Unamuno and Tolstoy were deeply religious men, and all their work vibrates as they wrestle with the problem of faith, its possible substitutes, and its potential futility. Like Nietzsche, both saw through their own experiences the need man has for a support that will brace him against the violence of an all-consuming doubt — from which, however, neither Tolstoy nor Unamuno ever succeeded in freeing himself. Tolstoy searched for concrete solutions to the problems of life and hoped to find them in such things as history, scientific logic, and positivism.[30] The agony lay in the realization that empiricism could not satisfy man's higher yearnings. Like Unamuno, Tolstoy insisted on the need for egotism in life to give it conviction and meaning, and rejected the value, whether real or apparent, of selflessness. Unamuno separates himself from both Tolstoy and Nietzsche on the question of moral goals, since Tolstoy, like Nietzsche (whom he probably knew only at second hand)[31] saw that God was dead and aspired to fill the void with a striving for the Good, a sublimely moral good, or at least the emotional climate created by such a search. For Unamuno such an effort by itself was short-sighted and self-defeating. However, Tolstoy added to this a strong belief in fraternal love as a unifying force. In this he differed radically from Nietzsche but offered certain surface parallels with Unamuno, who was, however, far less concerned, even skeptical, about the usefulness of establishing any rigid moral code extending beyond the individual and his immediate human objective.[32]

In keeping with such a belief, Tolstoy's view of great men and their actions — as revealed in *War and Peace*, for example — is strongly motivated by a set of firm principles. As Lev Shestov points

29. It must, of course, be borne in mind that *War and Peace* was written in 1864–69, whereas *Thus Spake Zarathustra* was written between 1883 and 1885. See also Nietzsche, *The Will to Power*, trans. Walter Kaufmann (New York, 1967), pp. 51 (1887), 239 (1888), 528 (1887–1888); and Lev Shestov, *Dostoevsky, Tolstoy and Nietzsche* (Athens, Ohio, 1969).

30. See Isaiah Berlin, *The Hedgehog and the Fox* (New York, 1957), pp. 20 ff.

31. Shestov, *Dostoevsky, Tolstoy and Nietzsche*, p. 23.

32. Pierre says, "If there is a God and there is a future life, then there is truth and there is goodness; and the highest happiness of man consists in striving for their attainment." *War and Peace*, pt. 5, chap. 12.

out, "in it lives the consciousness that responsibility for human life is to be sought in the higher outside ourselves," [33] and for this reason above all, Tolstoy, like Carlyle, is repelled by Napoleon's self-confidence and arrogance. Whereas for Unamuno the question to be put would be whether such an attitude contributes to Napoleon's personally held objectives of self-expansion, for Tolstoy it is clear proof of a harmful delusion with damaging and far-reaching social repercussions. Isaiah Berlin observes: "What are great men? They are ordinary human beings, who are ignorant and vain enough to accept responsibility for the life of society, individuals who would rather take the blame for all the cruelties, injustices, disasters justified in their name, than recognize their own insignificance and impotence in the cosmic flow which pursues its course irrespective of their wills and ideals";[34] and Tolstoy says:

> In historical events great men — so called — are but the labels that serve to give a name to an event, and like labels, they have the least possible connection with the event itself.
> Every action of theirs, that seems to them an act of their own free-will, is in an historical sense not free at all, but in bondage to the whole course of previous history, and predestined from all eternity.[35]

The will as illusion. Tolstoy finds that even if true heroism were possible, it would have to be paid for in the coin of repression and stifling social structures created by the supposedly great man in his own image. This would be no less true of Tsar Alexander than of Napoleon, both of whom he regards with equal abhorrence. One of the basic premises of *War and Peace* is that great men are thrust into that rôle, not unwillingly, but as products of a mythology that bears no specific relationship to any external reality (generally, the situation of the people, conceived as one) and that such men are fraudulent.[36] For Tolstoy, the current of events is too strong to be in any way manipulated by individuals.

The laws of history are oppressively inviolable, according to Tol-

33. Shestov, p. 59.
34. Berlin, *The Hedgehog and the Fox*, p. 45.
35. *War and Peace*, pt. 9, chap. 1.
36. Cf. Berlin, p. 31. There is a contrast here with the attitude expressed by Carlyle in Lecture 3 of *On Heroes*, p. 79.

stoy, and individual man is merely an instrument of destiny, not its master. The higher his position in society, the greater his apparent power and the more ineffectual and benighted his efforts. Neither Alexander nor Napoleon succeeded in imposing his own will upon the flow of events, and Tolstoy even says that the ordinary soldier has greater real power than his leaders, whose arrogance supports an illusion — that of free will: "Consciously a man lives on his own account in freedom of the will but he serves as an unconscious instrument in bringing about the historical ends of humanity." [37] Later he says that, "they were all the involuntary tools of history and were working out a result concealed from themselves but comprehensible to us. Such is the invariable fate of all practical leaders, and the higher their place in the social hierarchy, the less free they are." [38] Such an attitude reflects the pessimism to which Nietzsche refers when speaking of Tolstoy; for one can contribute to progress only through self-sacrifice within a mass, such as that shown, says Tolstoy, by the Russian peasants, which brought about the defeat of Napoleon in 1812.

Regardless of the merits of this as political analysis, Tolstoy clearly felt that morality was the great strength of the people and was necessarily lacking in all who presumed to lead them. War serves to symbolize this disparity, since all the spiritual forces, both good and evil, meet in the circumstances of battle and become distilled to their essential elements: "How much more complex is the game of war, which must be played within certain limits of time, in which there is not one will controlling lifeless toys, in which the whole is the resultant of the innumerable *collisions* of diverse individual wills!" [39] Such collisions are fundamentally untrue and meaningless, since they represent only the arrogance of the supposed leader who, for Tolstoy, is he who holds the corrupting scepter of power. There is no distinction made between historical presence and corruption, and this becomes one of the historical laws that Tolstoy tries to enforce in his work.

This does not imply a narrow religious doctrine, however, and once again we find ourselves with another point of contact between

37. See *War and Peace,* pt. 9, chap. 1.
38. Ibid., pt. 10, chap. 1.
39. Ibid., chap. 7.

Unamuno and Tolstoy, who felt, as in the case of Anna Karenina,[40] that even wrongs, truly believed, can indicate a sincere and laudable effort at self-discovery. Whereas Unamuno relates this effort to the intentions with which the hero carries out his enterprise, in Tolstoy it extends itself into a realization that its logical extreme could imply, not only the arrogance of authority, but also a headlong pursuit of happiness for its own sake — a passion as debilitating as the conversion of good for its own sake into a substitute for a living belief.

Such discussions, for Tolstoy, merely underline the virtues of the common people, and *War and Peace* (as well as other later works) is the vindication of that class of society the very oppression of which controlled and conditioned them to an honesty of effort and intent that received no inspiration from the upper and leading classes, and owed even less to those who were entrusted with the people's destiny. For Tolstoy, then, the people are to be admired and, as is seen by his own example, emulated. There is implicit in them a certain naïveté — not unlike Unamuno's "faith of the collier" (*fe del carbonero*) — suggesting an unconsciousness bordering on blindness, which may indeed have been the fountainhead of their virtue but which could also be the very cause of their social restrictions.

Unamuno's idea of heroic effort, on the other hand, demands willed action within a context that is at once social and individual but never unconscious.[41] Tolstoy symbolizes the chasm between the great man and the people in the figure of Kutuzov, who is used to represent the passive hero (a contradiction in terms for Unamuno), stripped of all independence and merely fulfilling a mandate imposed from without. This is partly a device to dramatize further the effects of the war as manifested in the Russian populace at large, and partly an expression of the polarization Tolstoy sees between the aims of the leaders and the aspirations of the lower classes. Lukács summarizes it effectively:

At the heart of Tolstoy is the contradiction between the protagonists of history and the living forces of popular life. He shows

40. See Henry Gifford, *The Novel in Russia* (New York, 1964), p. 88.
41. Lukács also criticizes Tolstoy, for quite different reasons, namely, for not recognizing or understanding their conscious action; but whether this is accurate or merely an idealization of the other extreme is difficult to say. See *The Historical Novel* (Boston, 1962), p. 87.

that those who despite the great events in the forefront of history, go on living their normal, private and egoistic lives are really furthering the true (unconscious, unknown) development, while the consciously acting "heroes" of history are ludicrous and harmful puppets.[42]

Unamuno vigorously refutes the idea of development without knowledge and stresses that the heroes' consciousness actually prevents their being puppets. There is much in this with which one may take issue, and even Lukács remains less than totally convinced by Tolstoy's logic.[43]

The problem here, of course, is a direct result of the theory of "inner history" (*intra-historia*), the specific historical truth observed by both Tolstoy and Unamuno in almost identical terms.[44] Each recognized that historical cataclysms roll almost unnoticed over daily life; but for Tolstoy the gap between the two levels could be measured in terms of social position, whereas for Unamuno individual consciousness was only incidentally related to class standing. The active participation of the people in historical developments was all but nonexistent for Unamuno, and not always particularly useful in any event; but unlike Tolstoy (and Carlyle), his ideas of heroism were not predicated on historical figures raised against the backdrop of political or military accomplishment and illumined by repression and illusion, but simply on the ability of ordinary men to succeed in the tasks they had set for themselves, and despite the obstacles that might appear. Such a man, for Unamuno, would reveal no class limitations, and it is highly improbable that he would have shown Tolstoy's good-natured indulgence of a character like Nikolay Rostov, whose mediocrity, however disarming, is a product of his own self-image rather than of any destiny that overwhelmed him.

Henry Gifford has remarked, "Tolstoy's perpetual theme is resurrection, as it was later to be Pasternak's, and as more agonizingly it is Dostoevsky's";[45] but in such a context it is in no way a theme of Unamuno's, except within the very limited scope of the regeneration of Spain as envisioned by the Generation of 1898. He is much less

42. Ibid., p. 86. Cf. Berlin, p. 31.
43. Lukács, *The Historical Novel*, p. 87.
44. See *War and Peace*, Epilogue, pt. 1, p. 1 and *En torno al casticismo*.
45. Gifford, *The Novel in Russia*, p. 94.

interested in the possible political effects than is Tolstoy, and resurrection for the country is to be achieved only through individual self-fulfillment, whereas the universal resurrection of man is meaningless. Unamuno is therefore far less concerned about the repressive aspects of society than is Tolstoy, about whom it can be said that the world he "sees and depicts is to an increasing degree a world in which decent people can no longer find any opportunity for action." [46] For Unamuno, this in itself is a heroic challenge, whereas in Tolstoy we are confronted with the juggernaut of a misguided social hierarchy that destroys individual potential, expressed in terms of goodness. Unamuno will make it clear that the heroic man is he who creates the opportunities for action, and it is he who gives historical or intrahistorical events whatever implicit authority they have. Social reform is not effectuated by abstractions like "the people," but by an inner evolution of each member of that group, without which the body is paralyzed in its unconsciousness. Both concepts reveal great idealism: Tolstoy's lies in seeing such a group as the true directing force of history; Unamuno's lies in suspecting that being a member of such a mass could be a welcome respite from the demands of the heroic will.

A man of his time as Unamuno was could scarcely have failed also to be aware of the work of Dostoevsky, although the matter of how much he was influenced by him in any tangible way still remains to be determined. It seems, however, that whatever ideas he held about heroism owe nothing whatever to Dostoevsky, even though there are remarkable parallels due to the common bond of anguish.

Unamuno's fictional characters represent a different conception from those of Dostoevsky, whose basis is abnormality, irrationality, and passion. This last element in particular is fundamental, since Unamuno's characters never show anything like the heightened awareness and consequent nonrational involvement in a mode of action that we find in such characters as Raskolnikov, Ivan Karamazov, or Smerdyakov. To attempt to show parallels between the two writers, either as philosophers or novelists, would demonstrate nothing more than a common preoccupation with individual man's function within the social context of his existence and the problem of

46. Georg Lukács, "Tolstoy and the Development of Realism," *Studies in European Realism* (New York, 1964), p. 166. See also pp. 160–62.

exercising whatever liberty he may sense in a direction that justifies him. The use and failure of the Will to Power, for example, is delineated by both Dostoevsky and Unamuno in *Crime and Punishment* and "Nada menos que todo un hombre," [47] and it is the proximity to Nietzsche that should be studied as a common bond.

A thinker who did, however, contribute a great deal to Unamuno's concept of heroism was William James, who did not bring new grist to Unamuno's mill but, as he himself admitted, presented a new way of discussing old modes of thinking. He enunciated the principles of pragmatism with a lucidity that impressed his contemporaries, and Unamuno, always at the forefront of new currents, was deeply moved by James's arguments for a practical approach to truth and reality. Truth for James was that which has a progressive or useful effect: "Let me now say only this, that truth is *one species of good,* and not, as is usually supposed, a category distinct from good and co-ordinate with it. *The true is the name of whatever proves itself to be good in the way of belief, and good, too, for definite, assignable reasons.* . . . If there be any life that it is really better we should lead, and if there be any idea which, if believed in, would help us to lead that life, then it would be really *better for us* to believe in that idea, unless, indeed, belief in it incidentally clashed with other greater vital beliefs." [48] This leads directly to the importance of the individual as a free body and causes James to reject socialism, which insists, rather, on the preeminence of the state.

Although Unamuno considered himself through much of his life to be a socialist, heroism is for him, more than it was for James, the exceptional effort made by the individual to leave his mark upon society for the advancement of mankind away from its ontological crisis toward immortality. James, however, is much more rigid than Unamuno in his application of Darwinian principles to the develop-

---

47. See Manuel Durán, "Unamuno y 'El Gran Inquisidor,'" *Revista de la Universidad de México* 10, no. 7 (1955–56): 13–15.

48. William James, *Selected Papers in Philosophy* (London and New York, 1947), p. 215 (from *Pragmatism*). For a detailed study of Unamuno's interest in James, see Pelayo Hipólito Fernández, *Miguel de Unamuno y William James, un paralelo pragmático* (Salamanca, 1961). The following works by James are in Unamuno's library: *The Will to Believe* (New York, 1902), cat. no. 4286; *The Varieties of Religious Experience* (New York, 1902), cat. no. 4237; *Pragmatism* (New York, 1907), cat. no. 3826.

ment of society and in his belief that, in society, the fittest do indeed survive. He is certainly closer to Unamuno in the general structure of his beliefs than either Carlyle or Nietzsche and admits the belief in an afterlife that will represent the culmination of man's existence. This is a doctrine, however, based not upon empirical grounds but rather on the feeling that it is desirable that there be both a God and an afterlife. James does not find this difficult to justify, since he believes that emotion (Unamuno's *sentimiento*) must take precedence over reason, as the latter is too limited to be able to satisfy man's deepest cravings: "Our passional nature not only lawfully may, but must, decide an option between propositions, whenever it is a genuine option that cannot by nature be decided on intellectual grounds." [49]

Thus it is that, like Unamuno after him, James employs essentially the same argument as Pascal in his approach to religion and, consequently, the afterlife and the entire question of immortality. It is to man's advantage to act on the assumption that religion is valid, since he has nothing to lose and all of eternity and — for Unamuno, especially — immortality, to gain: "So proceeding, we see, first, that religion offers itself as a *momentous* option. We are supposed to gain, even now, by our belief, and to lose by our non-belief, a certain vital good. Secondly, religion is a *forced* option, so far as that good goes. We cannot escape the issue by remaining sceptical and waiting for more light, because, although we do avoid error in that way *if religion be untrue,* we lose the good, *if it be true,* just as certainly as if we positively chose to disbelieve." [50]

Belief for both of these men is a question of will: recall, for instance, Unamuno's declaration that "to believe is to want to believe." Moreover, like Carlyle and Nietzsche, James and Unamuno demand action and decision on the part of their readers who wish to fulfill themselves. James feels as Unamuno does, however, that heroism is not merely a question of breeding or circumstances but a potential that lies within most men. James refers to man's "reserve energies" and indicates that greatness is a question of the coordination of both external circumstances (historical, geographical, etc.) and individual impulses: "Now, I affirm that the relation of the visible

49. "The Will to Believe," in *Selected Papers,* p. 108.
50. Ibid., p. 120.

environment to the great man is in the main exactly what it is to the 'variation' in the Darwinian philosophy. It chiefly adopts or rejects, preserves or destroys, in short, *selects* him. And whenever it adopts and preserves the great man, it becomes modified by his influence in an entirely original and peculiar way. He acts as a ferment, and changes its constitution, just as the advent of a new zoological species changes the faunal and floral equilibrium of the region in which it appears." [51]

The references to Darwin notwithstanding, we must resist the temptation to relate this idea too closely to Nietzsche's Superman. James is not proposing the creation of a superior race, but the creation of a superior individual. For him, superior individuals have existed throughout history, and his conclusions are therefore a posteriori. Nevertheless, the great man is not the servant of society as he was for Spencer; rather, he is the result of Schopenhauer's exaltation of the will. Consequently, "Societies of men are just like individuals, in that both at any given moment offer ambiguous potentialities of development." [52] Like Unamuno, James sees heroism as being transmitted from individual to individual, whether the respective individuals be single men or entire societies. Here we are much closer to the intellectual socialism of Christ than to the aristocratic concept of Nietzsche.

Thus we see that Unamuno straddled two periods of great intellectual ferment and served as a bridge between them. Man of the twentieth century that he was, his roots were deeply imbedded in the traditions of the nineteenth century. The vocabulary was often new, but the problems to be faced were as old as the intellect itself.

51. "Great Men and Their Environment," in *Selected Papers,* p. 173.
52. Ibid., p. 174.

2. The Achievement of Heroism

Although any attempt to impose a system on Unamuno's highly organic philosophy may seem either arbitrary or patently simple-minded, there is an inner logic in his philosophical works that forms the basis for the artistic elaboration one finds in his poetry and fiction, where it is stripped of the more purely speculative aspects and is condensed into specific problems. The thoughts on heroism, however, are diffused through the entire body of his work and embrace all stages in his spiritual and intellectual development. It would seem most useful, then, to attempt first to perceive a general pattern and possible structure that will fairly reflect the progression from passive existence to heroic apotheosis, and then to examine the practical applications of these ideas in fictional contexts. That Unamuno ever considered the development of these ideas quite so strictly is unlikely, but the validity of the exercise lies in the revelation of both the real and the potential positions of individual man in society and the cosmos, and the means of his achieving that potential.

Ego and Consciousness

The ego is, in the simplest of terms, the material given us so we may each create a life that is identifiably ours, and it represents for Unamuno the very essence of the individual. Symbolically, much like Calderón's Segismundo, man begins in the formless darkness of his brute state, with neither direction nor aim:

> We wander without luck,
> without peace and without direction,

> lost in a world of shadows,
> with mangled feet,
> oozing blood,
> our courage shattered,
> and our heart asking for death.
>
> [Erramos sin ventura
> sin sosiego y sin norte,
> perdidos en un mundo de tinieblas,
> con los pies destrozados,
> manando sangre,
> desfallecido el pecho,
> y en él el corazón pidiendo muerte.] [1]

Life, not death, however, is the solution, for man must learn that the first effort is to question his role: "Hand in the shadow, I want . . . / What is it that I want? Tell me [Mano en la sombre, quiero . . . / ¿qué es lo que quiero, dime?]" [2] This awakening of the ego is the basis for our understanding of the exterior world because it serves as the touchstone that renders us capable of projecting ourselves toward other people, toward the potentialities of the world in general, toward our own fulfillment as individuals, and, ultimately, toward the infinite. Don Quixote was able to cry, "I know who I am!" and we as individuals must also learn to define our essence. The ego is the material for our extension. Man must create himself and be a monument to his own existence, since to be is concrete and a duty, for it means to be a totality, without losing one's identity. Unamuno declares: "More, more, and always more! I want to be myself, and yet without ceasing to be myself to be others as well, to pour myself into the totality of things visible and invisible, to extend myself to the illimitable of space and to prolong myself to the infinite of time. Not to be all and always is like not being; at least I want to be my entire

---

1. "Salmo I," vv. 135–41, O.C. 13: 285. Cf. Calderón, *La vida es sueño*, vv. 197–212: "and although since I was born / (if this is to be born) / I only discern / this rustic wilderness / where I live in wretchedness, / as a living skeleton, / as a dead soul; / . . . / I am a man among beasts / and a beast among men."
2. "Mano en la sombra," vv. 62–63, O.C. 14: 732.

self and to be so for ever and ever. And to be my entire self is to be everyone else. Either all or nothing!" [3]

We shall later see this final pronouncement of the absolute choice open to man changed at the portals of immortality, but this is the ideal goal: constant extension and expansion without diminishment or loss. If anything is taken away, if the ego becomes lost in the great All, the aim will be frustrated, for the individual must absorb all without in his turn being absorbed, and that is the tension and source of much of Unamuno's anguish: "I am the center of my universe, the center of the universe, and in my supreme anguish, I cry with Michelet: 'My ego, they are snatching my ego!' " [4] This despairing cry raises the problem of the individual in his own cosmos and within the universe as a whole. For Unamuno, there is scarcely a distinction to be made, since the ego is both the beginning and the end of all effort and of the universe at large. We live according to certain basic principles, but these are always based on our own personal and individualistic beliefs, as we have no other valid way of judging our actions.

This is not to say that mere egotistic individuality is enough, for man's responsibility is to take this raw material and, with it, to create a greater self: the personality. Paul Ilie makes this distinction in the following way: "Individuality alone is a brute state, unsocial and uncommitted. Personality is the humanizing quality that knits the individual into a social and cultural fabric, and causes him to act as a person." [5] As Pirandello and others discovered, man does not become real and complete except in relation to others, and it is his individuality projected onto "the other" that gives him his personality. He must believe in everything he does to achieve this goal, for the

3. *Del sentimiento trágico de la vida*, O.C. 16: 166. See Pedro Laín Entralgo, *La espera y la esperanza* (Madrid, 1962), p. 388: "*Radix vitae, spes:* such could be his motto"; and ibid., p. 387: "Hope, militant creative hope, hope capable of imposing itself upon our reason, as reality imposes itself upon it."
4. Ibid., p. 173. Cf. François Meyer, *La ontología de Miguel de Unamuno*, trans. Cesáreo Goicoechea (Madrid, 1962), pp. 25 ff., also p. 80: "the 'depths' of the person can only be the dimension of infinity, that is, a *bottomless* perspective, unfathomable, and, in this perspective, what is present is the *wish to be all*, in all its ambiguity."
5. Paul Ilie, *Unamuno*, p. 60.

foundation of heroism is faith in oneself. I alone am my own accurate measure: " 'I, I, I, always I!' some reader may say, 'and who are you?' Here I could answer him with Obermann, with the enormous man Obermann, 'For the Universe, nothing; for me, everything.' " [6] Until I have proven myself and set out to achieve my heroism, I create no waves except within myself. This implies a highly personal and subjective interpretation of man's existence, and indeed of the existence of all things: everything depends not on man as a species but, rather, on men as individual creatures. Man is himself the purpose of the cosmos, and both civilization and the universe direct themselves to each self.

It would be impossible to exaggerate the importance placed by Unamuno upon individual man. Often one is led to believe that he does this merely to make Miguel de Unamuno stand out more clearly, and this is doubtless true, for it is part of his own heroic effort; but Unamuno believes that he, like everyone else, has the duty to speak out personally. It is part of his influence and the contribution he can make to others. His opinions and ideas, however unpleasant or unrealistic they may seem, are valid, if believed, for the simple reason that Unamuno is unique, as are we all: "There is no other I in the world! Each one of us is unique and irreplaceable." [7] Each of us represents the totality of our past and the potentiality of our future, and this combination will never be duplicated. We can begin to reach out to our fulfillment only once this fact has been realized. Unamuno's apparent egocentrism is his way of affirming his own existence as a man and his deep confidence in his individual potential. It is a way of showing the path to those who would follow his example: "when a man affirms his ego, his personal consciousness, he affirms man, concrete and real man, he affirms true humanism — which is

6. *Del sentimiento trágico,* O.C. 16: 137. Unamuno's personal copy of James's *The Will to Believe* has a pencil mark beside the sentence, "To say then that the universe essentially is thought, is to say that I myself, potentially at least, am all" (p. 89). In *El Cristo de Velázquez,* the idea is reinforced when he speaks of Christ: "And here dreams and rests / his celestial head, in which the World / dwells uncreated, as upon a pillow / reclining on your breast, and at your touch / feels himself Man, who is the aim of All." pt. 3, xvii, vv. 2011–15, O.C. 13: 769.

7. *Vida de Don Quijote y Sancho,* ed. Bernardo G. de Candamo, in *Ensayos* (Madrid, 1964), 2: 340. Due to the inaccuracies that plague the *Obras completas,* all future references to this work will be to this edition.

not the humanism of the things of man — and in affirming man he affirms consciousness. For the only consciousness of which we are conscious is that of man." [8]

Therefore we may say that the ego is the consciousness of oneself, which immediately relates itself to the concept of immortality and which must continue to live, for it is an extension of the soul: "What we call soul is just a term used to denote individual consciousness in its entirety and continuity." [9] There appears, then, to be an equation of the ego, the consciousness, and the soul, but there is one fundamental difference: the soul is a passive element and alone is not enough to spur the individual on; consciousness is the soul in action, and must have immortality, even after it nears fulfillment. It is this consciousness that distinguishes man from beast; "consciousness is a sickness," [10] and is the source of the suffering that is unique to man and peoples. Each man's progression toward personality and heroism must start with the anguish of his consciousness, for this is what distinguishes him and gives rise to the feeling of futility and despair that will be the enemy, the void, the tragic feeling of life.[11]

Great emphasis is placed by Unamuno upon man's unique quality as a feeling creature and the importance of this to his ability to rise above himself to fulfillment. He says: "Perhaps what makes him different from other animals is feeling rather than reason." [12] This ability to feel, to sense, is a cognitive tool for man that makes him see the need to assure his immortality through self-affirmation, and makes the individual able to be the creator of an expanded consciousness and

8. *Del sentimiento trágico de la vida*, O.C. 16: 139. See also "What an abysmal wealth of strength / I feel in my breast!" "Salmo de la mañana" (1907), vv. 96–97, O.C. 14: 736. Laín Entralgo (*La espera y la esperanza*, p. 387) points out that "to the present indicative *sum* of the Cartesian conclusion he opposes an *ut sim*, a 'that I might be': *Cogito ut sim Michael de Unamuno*, he says."

9. *Del sentimiento trágico*, O.C. 16: 207. This idea was never abandoned: "For subsistence, assistance; / for consistence, resistance, / and for existence, insistence." *Cancionero* (Buenos Aires, 1954), Mar. 11, 1929, no. 854.

10. Ibid., p. 144. A similar idea appears in Nietzsche. See Sobejano, *Nietzsche en España*, pp. 306–07.

11. See Ilie, *Unamuno*, p. 35: "Pain replaces the physical distinctions that separate one human being from another, and substitutes psychological ones in their place." Also Meyer, *La ontología*, p. 39: "Pain and compassion constitute the immediate experience of self."

12. *Del sentimiento trágico*, O.C. 16: p. 129.

a dynamic soul, which is the activator of his committed personality: "Yes, one must make his soul. One is not born with it but, sometimes, one dies with it. Most are born, live, and die in total limbo." [13] The tragic feeling is a madness which, if he believes in immortality, impels the potential hero toward self-appraisal in the face of all obstacles. For this reason Don Quixote will emerge as the ultimate ego, the exemplary hero; his madness permits him to rely on his own beliefs and to build the existence that best suits him, for the sickness of his consciousness sets his reason aflame.

Unamuno accepts his challenge of self-creation willingly: "I am the idea of myself." [14] He recognizes the ego as movement, as constant progressive change, and his own ideas as the only ones valid for him; but he must actively offer them to others, who will have the opportunity to choose whatever part may seem valid for them, too, thereby creating an intimate human bond. Immediately after the crisis of March 1897, Unamuno wrote in his diary that he had decided that his own form of heroism would be to "make of the pen a weapon to fight for Christ," [15] and this would be his way of reaching others. The starting point for this movement of which the active ego consists, in constant development, is the phrase: "One owes oneself to one's name," [16] an idea that ultimately carries the implication of three lives: that of the flesh, by far the most imprecise as its immortality is perhaps achieved only through one's children; the life of the soul; and the life of one's name, that is, one's fame.[17] These last are essential for the development of the ego, and although it is by no means granted to all to succeed, man can strive to extend his individuality enough to give himself some degree of immortality; but while he lives, he will never be assured of this, since "your completed personality is at the

13. "El mejor público," O.C. 9: 814. The ever-present threat is, of course, the lack of self-awareness, as for example: "Beneath the wing of silence — grew in peace the poor thing / like a flower that folds — since it had sprung from the bud. / And thus at the foot of the mountain — it slept, without dreaming, its nights / until the last one arrived — beneath a copper moon. / And without knowing what is life — and without knowing that it did not know / gave up its calyx and crown — at the foot of the quiet mountain." *Cancionero*, no. 162 (1928).

14. *Del sentimiento trágico*, O.C. 16: 213.

15. *Diario íntimo*, ed. P. Félix García (Madrid, 1970), p. 102.

16. *Del sentimiento trágico*, O.C. 16: 183.

17. *Vida de Don Quijote*, p. 295.

end and not at the beginning of your life; only with death does it complete and perfect itself for you."[18] This adds to our feeling of despair and fear, but our work is to create ourselves day by day, always.

As Julián Marías points out,[19] there is a close relationship between this concept and Kant's *Critique of Practical Reason,* with which Unamuno was familiar. It is not for us to ask more than what the end will be, that is, where we are going, because this is our mission, and recognition of it gives us our purpose. All our efforts must be directed toward a critical self-appraisal and examination, a temporary end in itself that will lead us to a sincere understanding of our gifts and limitations. As Unamuno himself declares, "I have made myself into my own problem, question, and plans. How is this resolved? By making the plan into a trajectory . . . by fighting."[20] This is heroism, to fight on in one's aspirations regardless of the threat of failure, to convert the symbol into reality. The hero's faith is based on uncertainty, fear of extinction, the tragic feeling, and despair.

The Hero as Maximum Extension of the Ego

What, then, separates the hero from his fellow human beings? Unamuno says that the distance is small: "If the difference that exists between human individuals could be measured, taking the absolute worth of man as the unit of measurement, one would surely see that this difference would never exceed a tiny fraction."[21] Nevertheless,

18. "¡Adentro!", O.C. 3: 420. See also 33, *Rosario de sonetos líricos,* vv. 13–14: "It is necessary for the hero to succumb / in order to obtain the justice of death," O.C. 13: 540; and *Cancionero,* 12-XI-28, no. 549, v. 8: "death is truth." See also *La agonía del cristianismo,* O.C. 16: 464; "El fin de la vida" (1910): "And the aim of life is to make oneself a soul," *Rosario de sonetos líricos,* O.C. 13: 510. Cf. "Glosas al *Quijote,*" O.C. 5: 600: "To sacrifice oneself to fame instead of sacrificing fame to itself; here you have the intimate essence of Quixotism and the root of heroic endeavor."

19. Julián Marías, *Miguel de Unamuno,* trans. Frances M. López-Morillas (Cambridge, 1966), pp. 70–71.

20. "Continuación," *Cómo se hace una novela* (Buenos Aires, 1927), p. 152. Again, due to the inadequacies of the *Obras completas,* all references to this work are to the first and, as yet, only complete edition. See Allen Lacy, "Censorship and *Cómo se hace una novela,*" *Hispanic Review* 34 (1966): 317–25.

21. "La dignidad humana," O.C. 3: 240–41.

this fraction is crucial, for it distinguishes the hero from the frivolous, the sensualists, and those who are too logical. All of these are too concerned with immediate superficialities to be able to strive for eternity. The hero, on the other hand, knows who he is and, more important, who he wants to be, "and only he and God know it, and the rest of mankind scarcely know who they themselves are, because they do not really want to be anything, much less do they know who the hero is." [22] Unamuno says that the cry of "I know who I am!" is equivalent to "I know who I want to be!" [23] and this is the hero's recognition of his mission:

> "I do not know myself," you say, but look, be sure
> that man begins to know himself when he cries out
>
>> "I do not know myself," and weeps;
>> then before his eyes his open heart
>> uncovers the true pattern of his life;
>>> then comes his awakening.
>
> No, no one knows himself until the light
> of a kindred soul which comes from eternity
> touches him and lights his depths.

> ["Me desconozco" dices, mas mira, ten por cierto
> que a conocerse empieza el hombre cuando clama
>
>> "me desconozco" y llora;
>> entonces a sus ojos el corazón abierto
>> descubre de su vida la verdadera trama;
>>> entonces es su aurora.
>
> No, nadie se conoce hasta que no le toca
> la luz de un alma hermana que de lo eterno llega
> y el fondo le ilumina.] [24]

This is the strength that allows the hero to create the world according to his will, his insight. It is *voluntarismo,* and is the underlying impulse: "It is not intelligence, but will that makes the world for you, and the old scholastic aphorism of *nihil volitum quin praecognitum,* nothing is wanted without having first been known, should

22. *Vida de Don Quijote,* p. 110.
23. Ibid., p. 109.
24. "Veré por tí," vv. 1–9, O.C. 13: 419.

be corrected to *nihil cognitum quin praevolitum*, nothing is known without having first been wanted." [25] The will can do all, if the hero trusts in it sincerely, for with it he can mold external reality according to how he feels he must.[26] The potential lies within since: "We carry the world within ourselves; it is our dream, as is life; let us purify ourselves and we will purify it." It is necessary for us to externalize this internal world of ours in order to make it useful. Outside, it will be the reflection of our individuality and will give us the fuel for our heroism. As Unamuno points out, "Without inner life, there is no outer life," and the hero is he who is best able to create the outside world because he carries within him the most complete inner life. This is certainly true of Don Quixote, who "carries within himself a true world." [27]

There is a circular argument involved here. The hero, because he is a hero, knows who he is, and because he knows who he is, he is therefore a hero. It is a knowledge difficult to share, for his heroism lies largely in the fact that no one else will recognize it. He will often appear mad, and therein lies the relationship between Unamuno's concept of heroism and his idea of Quixotism. The two are similar, but heroism runs deeper and it will become evident that Quixotism is only an example of the larger concept. Heroism may not be assumed but must be truly believed, for when the hero cries out, "I know who I am!", there is no room for deception. He who truly believes in his own strength will bear all manner of adversity because he knows that he cannot be judged as other men, but rather by a special divine law.

---

25. *Vida de Don Quijote,* p. 181.

26. This is an idea common to both Nietzsche and James in their visions of heroism. Zarathustra says, for example, with heroic confidence: "Yes, something invulnerable, unburiable is within me, something that rends rock: it is called my WILL," Friedrich Nietzsche, *Thus Spoke Zarathustra* (Baltimore, 1961), p. 135; and Unamuno has put a series of red pencil marks beside the following passage in his copy of James's *The Will to Believe,* p. 56: "It is a fact of human nature, that men can live and die by the help of a sort of faith that goes without a single dogma or definition." See also Laín Entralgo, *La espera y la esperanza,* p. 411: "I am calling *activism* or *activist voluntariness* the constant use of the will in the task of achieving something, not so much for the absolute worth of what can be achieved as for the gratification of moving with effort and a fighting spirit toward it."

27. *Vida de Don Quijote,* pp. 293–94, 169, 148.

Man must not simply make life up as he goes along; rather, as we shall see, his duty is imposed upon him from without and his heroism lies in developing the greatest resources to fulfill the mission and in being able to know how to draw upon all of them. The events are not created by the hero but he must make decisions concerning them. It is up to him to accept the circumstances and bend or use them according to what his faith tells him, for "the heroic thing is to open oneself to the mercy of the events that overtake us, without trying to force them to come." [28] As Carlyle insisted, "it is the spiritual always that determines the material." [29] This represents the hero's opportunity to impose himself upon circumstances and use them to advantage; but he must do so immediately, for Unamuno feels strongly that the moment is now, always, and the place is here: "for the provisional is eternal, for here is the center of infinite space, the focus of infinity, and now is the center of time, the focus of eternity." [30]

The hero finds himself at the center of his world, as are all individuals, but he feels this more vividly and converts it into an impulse, and Unamuno advises the reader who would be heroic to follow the example of Don Quixote: "Follow the star. And do as the Knight: redress whatever wrong comes your way. Do now what must be done now and do here what must be done here." [31] There is no need to go in search of happiness or of wrongs to be righted, for they are everpresent, and the difficulty is not in the search, but rather in the recognition of them: "For some reason it was said that the greatest works are works of circumstance." [32] Don Quixote was thus able to become the child of his works. He accepted adventures as they came to him, and even before he had any victories upon which to reflect, he had

28. Ibid., p. 94. See also Meyer, La ontología, p. 94: "Man not only adapts himself to his setting, but adapts it to himself and thereby makes the earth his, first through force, then through intelligence." This seems, however, to differ from James's idea, also marked by Unamuno in his copy (Will to Believe, p. 205): "Invent some manner of realizing your own ideals which will also satisfy the alien demands, — that and that only is the path of peace!"

29. Carlyle, On Heroes, p. 155.

30. "Comentario," Cómo se hace una novela, pp. 45–46.

31. "El sepulcro de Don Quijote," Vida de Don Quijote, p. 76. See also "Comentario," Cómo se hace una novela, p. 45.

32. Vida de Don Quijote, p. 254. In the Diario íntimo, p. 59, he had already carried this a step further: "Worrying about tomorrow keeps us from thinking about eternity."

faith in himself, for he considered himself to be the child of the acts that he still hoped to perform. This is truly heroic faith, for it is faith in the unseen, the unproven. As Carlyle says, "At all times, a man who will *do* faithfully, needs to believe firmly." [33]

Don Quixote did not need to search because he had only to listen to the sounds of his own heart, his ego, to discover his mission. To the masses this may be madness, but Unamuno points out that it is only considered such because it is unique. If everyone were mad, madness would become sanity. Don Quixote sets the example: " 'He lost his wits.' He lost them for our sake; in order to leave us an eternal example of spiritual generosity. If he had kept his wits, would he have been so heroic?" [34] Unamuno's only regret is that the will to follow this path to heroism is given to so few, but this is inevitable, for heroism is relative too.

The fact that the hero may seem mad to his contemporaries means that his solutions to problems may often fail because of the abyss that separates his interpretation of a problem from that of his fellow men. This should not be cause for concern, says Unamuno, for, "Heroism lies in the vigor of his purpose and not in the precision of his knowledge." [35] The intention with which an action is performed is certainly of prime importance, since it is still a reflection of the hero's faith and "the error in which one believes is more respectable than the truth in which one does not believe." [36]

It will become evident that Unamuno does not deal with truth and fiction, or with right and wrong in any absolute sense, but rather with the subjective interpretation of external reality and its relationship to the inner man, the individual ego. It is not for us to decide

33. *On Heroes*, p. 118.
34. *Vida de Don Quijote*, p. 88.
35. Ibid., p. 150.
36. Ibid., p. 247. Cf. Carlos Blanco Aguinaga, "Unamuno, Don Quijote y España," *Cuadernos Americanos*, 11, no. 6 (1952): 205: "the important thing about Don Quixote is not the result of his actions, but the intention with which they were carried out; the important thing is the will to do, moved toward the ideal by the mechanism of the purity of his madness." In one of his poems "¡Sit pro ratione voluntas!" Unamuno sums it up as follows: "better than being disillusioned and dead / to live in the error that redeems us." *Rosario de sonetos líricos*, 99, vv. 7–8, O.C. 13: 610. See also the *Diario íntimo*, p. 172: "If one purifies one's intentions, the acts themselves will be pure."

what the hero should see in the world any more than it is for him to force his beliefs upon us. His is a task of education. He may suggest and even persuade, either through words or, preferably, through examples, but he must not be dogmatic. There is only one real truth. "This is the pure truth: the world is what it seems to be to each one of us, and wisdom lies in making it over according to our will, as we rave without reason, filled with faith in the absurd." [37]

Don Quixote does this and even succeeds in converting the tricks of "reasonable" men into the most profound truths. He is a seer, and until man learns how to ignore frauds and to profit by his visions, he cannot be heroic. Even if the visions may seem foolish, "the greatest fool is he who has never said or done anything foolish in his life," [38] for this is a sign of fear — fear of taking risks, fear of the ridiculous, fear of the apparential. It is only through appearing foolish that real progress can be made by the hero: "Only he who attempts the absurd is capable of conquering the impossible." [39]

Many times victory will seem impossible and the hero will wonder about the outcome. Unamuno stands firm in his belief that one must continue regardless. "I want to fight my fight, without worrying about victory." [40] After writing *Paz en la guerra* (1897), he decided that peace was not the answer, for it could give way to annihilation, and

37. *Vida de Don Quijote*, p. 166. The importance of dreams is described by Carlos París, *Unamuno: estructura de su mundo intelectual* (Barcelona, 1968), p. 37: "And given the possibility of an integrating solution of the total potential of man, it is possible only to dream, to exist creatively, to enliven our fragile, immediate life. Faced with the perennially present risk of constantly appearing problems, the creative imagination is a cry for help and a desperate attempt at consolidation." In the *Cancionero*, no. 492 (Nov. 13, 1928), Unamuno writes "The secret of the revived soul:/ to live dreams while dreaming life."
38. "El sepulcro de Don Quijote," *Vida*, p. 80.
39. *Vida de Don Quijote*, p. 197.
40. "Mi religión," O.C. 16: 119. It can be easily seen that, on many occasions, Unamuno sounded very much like Don Quixote. This is perhaps not surprising, since Don Quixote represented such a high degree of achievement. Moreover, throughout his life and especially during the years of his exile in Paris, Unamuno made a conscious effort to appear quixotic. Antonio Sánchez Barbudo points this out: "Unamuno played the part of Don Quixote, and he was well aware of it. He felt the pride of knowing himself to be unique, indomitable." *El misterio de la personalidad en Unamuno* (Buenos Aires, 1950), p. 216. See also Armando F. Zubizarreta, *Unamuno en su "nivola"* (Madrid, 1960), pp. 40–46.

that the only possible reply is to fight, although he admits, " 'I do not know what I conquer through my efforts,' I say along with Don Quixote," [41] but this is in itself heroic, for he says, addressing himself to Don Quixote, "your triumph was always one of daring and not of achieving success . . . your greatness lay in never recognizing your defeat." [42] Heroism is to dare, and is the result, not only of faith in oneself and in one's mission, but also of an impassioned enthusiasm, a burning desire to forge ahead, since: "Only passionate men carry out works that are truly lasting and fertile." [43] This is the enthusiasm that sets reason aflame and equips the hero to face ridicule and failure.

None of this obviates the need for the hero to think. On the contrary, Unamuno admits that Don Quixote "was a contemplative man, for only a contemplative man would undertake such a task as his." On the other hand, "He was not just a contemplative man, but went beyond dreaming to put his dreams into action." [44] This is an extension of the belief that without a visionary inner life there can be no great works, and also completes the picture of the hero as a rounded human being. Unamuno admits that he himself is part warrior as well as contemplator,[45] and there is no reason to suppose that he would settle for any less in a hero.

In the *Diario íntimo* he asserts: "Doing good works is not the same as being good. It is not enough to do good, one must be good. . . . It is better to be good, even though one may do evil some time, than

41. *Vida de Don Quijote*, p. 298. Despite the contrasting titles, two of Unamuno's poems cast light on the need for fighting and resignation. In "Resignación," vv. 5–8, O.C. 13: 465, he says, "Give daring as well as patience / to fight in the hard combat, / my sights set on the future boundary, / give active resignation, to my consciousness." In "Irresignación," vv. 1–9, *Rosario de sonetos líricos*, O.C. 13: 609, he exclaims: "No, I will not resign myself, for my lot / is to struggle with no hope of victory / and succumb in search of glory / from blows like those of Don Quixote. / As long as my stubborn longing is not exhausted / I will defend even the absurd, the illusory / belief which gives life, and will not make / the water wheel of sad knowledge work / at a slavish trot."

42. *Vida de Don Quijote*, p. 105.

43. "El sepulcro de Don Quijote," *Vida*, p. 80.

44. *Vida de Don Quijote*, pp. 87, 89. One of the reasons for the heroic figure of Mohammed lies, according to Carlyle, in the very character of the Arabs: "There is something most agile, active, and yet most meditative, enthusiastic in the Arab character" (*On Heroes*, p. 47).

45. "Conversación primera," O.C. 4: 550.

to be evil and do good, apparent good." [46] Heroes like Don Quixote
tend to be candid and childlike. These are positive attributes because
they show innate goodness and the capacity for innocent faith, two
of the roots of heroism. Alonso Quijano was called "the Good" even
before he was reborn as Don Quixote, but he was passively so. However, once his consciousness was put into action and he ventured
forth as Don Quixote, his positive qualities emerged. This goodness
causes the hero to be somewhat credulous, for he tends to believe
that all men are as sincere as he and that they, too, retain the innocence, candor, and goodness of childhood. Once again he sets, rather
than follows, the example.

The Progression from Consciousness to Heroism

Earlier we spoke of movement, the unending effort which for Unamuno is *voluntarismo*, the will to be. As Zarathustra says, "It is time
for man to fix his goal. It is time for man to plant the seed of his
highest hope." [47] The potential hero must make his goals clear. After
defining his duty, he must strive, fight, agonize, in order to fulfill it.
It is egocentrism, but for the common good, the good of civilization.
For Unamuno, his own duty is clear: "But the fact is that my work
— I was going to say my mission — is to shatter the faith of men
here, there, and everywhere — faith in affirmation, faith in negation,
and faith in abstention from faith — and this out of faith in faith
itself; it is to combat all those who are resigned, whether it be to
Catholicism, or rationalism, or agnosticism; the purpose is to make all
men live with anxiety and passionate desire." [48] Heroism must make
man uneasy and questioning; it must strip him of all complacency
and vacillation and reveal to him the ontological peril in which he
wanders. He must learn to *be* — individually, forcefully — and he
must be made to represent man's highest purpose. The very difficulty
of the task is its greatest immediate reward, as Unamuno himself has
discovered: "And the reader must not overlook the fact that I have
been operating on myself; that this work is a piece of self-surgery, and

46. *Diario íntimo,* pp. 167–68, see also p. 248. Cf. *Vida de Don Quijote,*
pp. 212 and 231.
47. Nietzsche, *Thus Spoke Zarathustra,* p. 46.
48. *Del sentimiento trágico,* O.C. 16: 444.

with no anaesthetic other than the work itself. The enjoyment of operating upon myself has ennobled the pain of being operated upon." [49]

Suffering and fulfillment are all but inseparable, but much of our suffering is caused not only by our own shortcomings but also by attempts to change our very essence as individuals. The hero may change completely over a period of time and within the framework of his own vision, but the changes must occur gradually so as not to interrupt his basic continuity or the unity of his action. These changes in themselves are relatively minor, for they do not alter the ultimate goal; it is too late for that. Even Don Quixote decides at one point to abandon the chivalrous life in order to take up the shepherd's crook, thinking thus to fulfill himself better, but as Unamuno points out, "He changes his path, but not the star that guides him." [50] He has kept his belief in the immortality of his actions as a justification for his works; otherwise the effort would be inconceivable: "But is it possible for us to work on something serious and lasting, forgetting the enormous mystery of the Universe and without trying to understand it? Is it possible to contemplate everything with a serene soul, as if with Lucretian piety, thinking that one day all this will no longer be reflected in any human consciousness?" [51] As in Pascal's wager, it is better to believe in immortality and hope than to believe in nothing and give up the fight. Even when we doubt, we exist to some extent.

We must not confuse this faith in eternity with a standard religious faith in salvation. For Unamuno, religion is no longer enough be-

49. Ibid., p. 442. Cf. *Teresa*, 88, vv. 6–10, O.C. 14: 414: "But I have been making and unmaking myself, / since that very day, / the day of the baptism / of common death, the day of the flame / which consumes my breast drop by drop."

50. *Vida de Don Quijote*, p. 328. See also the prologue to the *Cancionero*, O.C. 15: 33: "Yes, what we feel as the spirit of independence and call thus is the feeling of our identity; to be independent is to be identical, it is to be equal to oneself, it is to be oneself, it is to be a continuous person. And as infinitude is just continuity — that which is infinite is continuous, concrete — the continuous person is infinite and incommensurable. . . . I want to continue being myself so that all other Spaniards will continue being themselves and so that those who have stopped being themselves will be so again."

51. *Del sentimiento trágico*, O.C. 16: 230. Unamuno marked the following passage of James (*Will to Believe*, p. 83) in his copy: "Better face the enemy than the eternal Void!"

cause often it lulls the potentiality for heroism into that very complacency and satisfaction so dangerous to the ego: "This thirst for eternal life is quenched by many, the simple ones in particular, in the fountain of religious faith; but it is not given to all to drink from it." He prefers to substitute effort for religion because it is the true existence and affirmation of the ego: "And so, the old adage that *operari sequitur esse,* action follows being, should be modified to say that being is action, and only that which works, that which is active, exists, and only insofar as it works." [52] There are no limits to this striving, as it permits us to test and develop our capabilities. Contemplation and action complement each other, for Unamuno admits that "as you work you discover yourself." This was certainly true of Don Quixote, who discovered that "it is . . . action that makes truth." Nevertheless, all this effort is not advocated for its own sake; everything the hero does must have a purpose: "When man does not work in order to live and pass the time, he works to survive. He works for the sake of working, it is a game and not work." [53]

We are once more faced by the difference that separates the lesser man from the hero, who is in constant search of the very essence of life to justify his immortality.[54] He cannot avoid his responsibility, even momentarily, for he is distinctly a leader who must initiate action with confidence: "Someone has to do it. Why not I? is the cry of a serious servant of mankind who comes face to face with a serious danger." [55] This idea is very close to one marked by Unamuno in James's *The Varieties of Religious Experience* (p. 24), and quoted by him in "Almas de jóvenes" (O.C. 3: 734), with the comment, "Mad indeed are those who decide to be first; everyone wants someone else to precede him." In the *Rosario de sonetos líricos,* he says, "for I was born for something," [56] and this is the attitude of Don

52. Ibid., pp. 184, 274. He makes a similar exhortation to his readers in "¡Siémbrate!" vv. 7–8, *Rosario de sonetos líricos,* O.C. 13: 572: "To live is to work and the only thing that remains / is the work: put, then, your hand to the work."

53. "¡Adentro!" O.C. 3: 420; *Vida de Don Quijote,* p. 302; *Del sentimiento trágico,* O.C. 16: 182.

54. Ibid., p. 393. See also "En estas tardes pardas," vv. 50–54, *Rimas de dentro,* 14, O.C. 13: 873.

55. *Del sentimiento trágico,* O.C. 16: 413.

56. "A la esperanza," 2, v. 12, *Rosario de sonetos líricos,* 120, no. 2, O.C. 13: 633.

Quixote before the lion's cage. It is not a question of human charity, offered piously and without character as an individual effort, but rather of a duty to be fulfilled by a person gifted with the power of surpassing himself by means of a will that makes him capable of anything, since "rarely do we know of what we are capable until we get down to it, and often we surprise ourselves with something that we did not expect of ourselves." [57]

Continual surpassing of oneself creates new boundaries for the ego, but at the same time it also causes them to be pushed back: "And the evolution of organic beings is nothing but a struggle for the fulfillment of consciousness through suffering, a constant aspiring to be others without ceasing to be oneself, to break through one's limitations by limiting oneself." The desire to be all is even greater than the specific urge to be immortal, although by being all we feel that our chances of survival are proportionally greater. Doctor Montarco says: "It is not the instinct of preservation that moves us to work, but the instinct of invasion; we do not aim merely to continue as we are, but rather to be more, to be all." [58] Montarco speaks with some authority; for, as a true disciple of Quixotism, he was considered by his contemporaries to be mad.

Anguish

One of Unamuno's aims is to create a feeling of constructive imbalance in the minds of his readers so that they will suffer and try to remedy their failings. In "La locura del doctor Montarco," Atienza says, "One way or another we must use that unbalanced state without which the spiritual world would come to a complete halt, that is to say, would die." [59] Montarco sublimated the imbalance in his bizarre writings, while for Unamuno it becomes his task to use it to spur others on to follow him: "If, thanks to this agitation, someone else comes after who will do something lasting, my work will last in

57. "El individualismo español," O.C. 3: 618. See *Del sentimiento trágico,* O.C. 16: 405: "He who does not aspire to the impossible will scarcely do anything feasible that is worth the trouble."
58. Ibid., p. 269; "La locura del doctor Montarco," O.C. 3: 691.
59. Ibid., p. 696. Cf. "Mi libro," O.C. 8: 589: "On the day that life ceases to be a problem, it ceases to be life."

that." [60] Suffering spurs us on because it is the frightening knowledge of those inner lacks that can be our destruction. As Laín Entralgo points out, the burden of despair is converted by Unamuno into a basic impulse for heroic action, almost a sort of divine benefit: "Sentimental despair, thus converted into the mainspring of spiritual activity, came to be in Unamuno's existence — these stirring words are his — 'the basis of a vigorous life, of an effective action, of an ethics, of an aesthetics, of a religion, and even of a logic.' " [61] This is the distinguishing illness of mankind, the awareness of their own peril: "And all of us lack something; only some feel it and others do not. Or they pretend that they do not feel it, and then they are hypocrites." [62] Sincerity demands that the hero not evade the threat, but that he accept the grief and dedicate himself to still greater effort in an attempt to assuage it and to save himself and all he aspires to be.

Our consciousness makes us aware of our capabilities so that we may build upon them, but it is the awareness of how incomplete our knowledge is that gives us our most immediate experience of ourselves: "Depending on how you turn inward and penetrate more deeply into yourself, you will gradually discover your own emptiness, the fact that you are not all that you are, that you are not what you

60. "Mi religión," O.C. 16: 124.

61. Laín Entralgo, *La espera y la esperanza*, p. 384. The optimism that, somewhat paradoxically, underlies this despair is superbly expounded by Laín, who points out that "the problem of hope was the vital center of his existence as a man and of his work as a thinker and poet. In hope he saw the essence of human life; upon hope he sought to found his religion; with hopes he wanted to make of his spirit the best and most elevated possible." Ibid., p. 382.

62. *Del sentimiento trágico*, O.C. 16: p. 143. Cf. *Cancionero*, no. 529, vv. 7–8 (Dec. 2, 1928): "I only know that the swollen soul / lives not on water, but on thirst." The following statement of James (*Will to Believe*, p. 47) is marked in red in Unamuno's copy: "The sovereign source of melancholy is repletion. Need and strength are what excite and inspire us; our hour of triumph is what brings the void." The triumph of the will over despair is described by Laín as follows (op. cit., pp. 384–85): "the weight of despair, which acting on its own would sink the soul into immobility, is turned into flight by the vigorous and ceaseless effort of the will. The life of Unamuno was the result of a prodigious, feeling, agonizing, and creative act of the will." In his copy of *Oliver Cromwell's Letters and Speeches: With Elucidations,* Unamuno has marked the following passage that appears in Carlyle's introduction: "Our sorrow is the inverted image of our nobleness. The depth of our despair measures what capability, and height of claim we have to hope" (London: Chapman and Hall, n.d., vol. 1, p. 72).

would wish to be, that you are, in a word, just a nonentity." [63] This knowledge will open the hero to compassion. He is aware of the perils faced by every man and thus of his true relationship to external reality and to truth, for "The suffering of the spirit is the doorway to substantial truth. Suffer, so that you may believe and through believing you may live." [64] This anguished awareness of the distance that always remains to be traveled is another watershed for those who aspire to heroism, because it separates those who will allow themselves to become disheartened by their new awareness from those who will come to grips with it, as they did with their discovery of the threat of annihilation. New strength can come, since "only through suffering, through the passion never to die, does a human spirit take possession of itself." [65]

Suffering, then, is a quality of the will, and as such is a valid expression and proof of one's existence: "Pain is the substance of life and the root of personality, since one is a person only when suffering." In the hero it is a manifestation of the fear of annihilation, which makes him able to face failure and ridicule: "And fear itself reaches a point at which, if it does not kill its prey, it becomes intensified and, passing through suffering, converts itself into courage." Unlike the ordinary man, the hero does not hesitate, for his doubt is so strong, like that of all who truly believe, that he must act in order to save himself. Says Unamuno, "I believe . . . that many of the great heroes, perhaps the greatest, have been desperate men, and that out of desperation they carried out their feats." Despair, for Unamuno, is the same as absurd hope. In the face of despair, all hope seems mad, so the hero realizes that there is nothing to be lost in

63. *Del sentimiento trágico*, O.C. 16: 265. See also "Música," O.C. 13: 394–95 and "A mi buitre," O.C. 13: 592.
64. *Vida de Don Quijote*, p. 299. See especially the poem "Por dentro," O.C. 13: 325–27 and in particular vv. 138–39, 158–59 and 198–99, as well as vv. 41–47 of "Fatalidad" (1906), O.C. 14: 711, and *Nicodemo el fariseo*, O.C. 4: 28.
65. *Del sentimiento trágico*, O.C. 16: 339. Cf. *Cancionero*, no. 1006 (8-IV-29), vv. 9–16: "He who does not suffer does not feel, / he who does not feel does not live, / and when he does not live he does not conceive of / anything which can be faced / and make him into something out of nothing, / and he is lost in the depths / of not being, which is not even nothing, / All-Powerful Virgin.'

trying. As Atienza says, "are not these ravings the desperate leaps of the spirit as it tries to reach the other world?" [66]

Man must believe in God in order for God to exist, and the trick is to live, to be real and active, so that God has no choice but to believe in the hero as he rebels, like Augusto Pérez, against annihilation: "And if you believe in God, God believes in you, and by believing in you he creates you continuously. Because basically you are only the idea that God has of you; but a living idea, as if of a living and concrete God, as if of a God-Consciousness." [67] The hero, then, can achieve this immortality only by forcing himself, not only upon the mind of God, but also, as we shall see, upon the minds of others.

The Hero's Relationship with Others

Anguish is the knowledge and active awareness of the gaps that form one's being, and this tragic feeling is what pushes us toward fulfillment, implicit in which is the idea of the need for intercourse with other people. The ego cannot feed on its own substance: it must undergo the influences of others and exert its own influence on them. Only thus can the hero believe in his own value as a person, since "beyond what you are in society you are nothing." Without this interaction we would die, even in life, and the lesson of anguish is that it causes us to feel our own tragedy first and then compassion for others, as our perception of the existence and personality of others increases. It is, as Meyer says, the vital link: "compassion for oneself, so obviously different from self-love, is also the path that opens to us the ontological access to all other existing beings." [68] From this comes the interaction of egos.

All men must act as individuals but at the same time influence

66. *Del sentimiento trágico*, O.C. 16: 331; *Vida de Don Quijote*, p. 149; *Del sentimiento trágico*, p. 258. See also Julio García Morejón, *Unamuno y el Cancionero* (São Paulo, 1966), p. 110; "La locura del doctor Montarco," O.C. 3: 699. After all, this suffering is also, as we shall see, one of the elements heroes share: "I will suffer your pain,/ you will suffer mine;/ community in sorrow, my brother!" "La cruz" (1910), vv. 17–19, O.C. 14: 804.

67. *Del sentimiento trágico*, O.C. 16: 307.

68. Ibid.; Meyer, *La ontología*, pp. 39–40.

others, their philosophy being a paraphrase of Terence: "I am a man, no other man do I deem a stranger." [69] There is a community of egos, all of them in action and all of them alone but nonetheless forming the "holy and neverending crusade." [70] In order to influence others, it is necessary to know and love them. Since we naturally want the other to be like us, we must understand him first, for "he who does not live in others cannot live in himself, but must die." [71] Isolation is destructive, and society allows each person the opportunity of adopting the aspects of the other that are most useful to him because: "It is by trying to impose my ideas upon him that I receive his ideas. To love my neighbor is to want him to be like me, to be another I— that is to say, it is to want to be he; it is to want to erase the division between him and me, suppress the evil." [72] This is deceptively simple in tone, yet not entirely possible, as Unamuno himself recognizes. Interaction is a stimulus, much like individual effort, and must continue always if man is not to fall into complacency and spiritual laziness. The effort is not exclusively toward a sort of altruistic oneness with others; rather, it must be simultaneous with and beneficial to the development of the individual ego. Otherwise the hero joins the masses instead of profiting by contact with them and continuing his ascent.

The urge, then, is not toward true union but rather toward the predominance of the ego of the hero through its own merits, as well as through the enrichment it receives from others. This implies a sort of cynicism, for the hero wishes to profit from his knowledge of others, and his life has scarce validity if he cannot in turn exert an influence on them. Doctor Montarco points out the true issue: "The poor man who tries to impose himself on others is trying to save himself; he who tries to sink the names of others in oblivion wants to preserve his own name in the memory of mankind because he knows that

---

69. *Del sentimiento trágico,* O.C. 16: 127. Unamuno poeticizes this when he says: "I seek to wound myself by wounding you because I carry you / — my old, original man — in my innermost depths / and I strive to free my new man." "A los amigos trogloditas," vv. 47–49, O.C. 14: 681.

70. "El sepulcro de Don Quijote," *Vida,* p. 81.

71. "Mi libro," O.C. 8: 586.

72. *Del sentimiento trágico,* O.C. 16: 402. See also "En una ciudad extranjera," vv. 191–94, O.C. 13: 367.

posterity has a very fine sieve." [73] The difference between the hero
and those he dominates lies in his ability to save himself through his
will, while they can scarcely work with their basest characteristics.
This interaction, then, has as its starting point and ultimate aim the
individual, since the collective ego must not be a stagnant mixture
of complacencies, but a seething collection of man's greatest strengths
— of those who fulfilled their mission, retained their individuality,
and imposed themselves upon the eternal mind.

We know that the idea that the individual ego may be lost is ab-
horrent to Unamuno, who says, "for me, to become another, breaking
the unity and continuity of my life, is to cease to be who I am; that
is to say, it is simply to cease being. And that, no! Anything rather
than that!" Unity of being is the hero's overwhelming defense, for
with it he can most truly judge his effectiveness. Moreover, he is ac-
countable only to God. Thus, his individuality becomes an all but
absolute value, the fixed point from which he can move the earth:
"the more I belong to myself, the more I am myself, the more I belong to others; out of the fullness of myself I pour myself into my
brothers, and when I pour myself into them, they enter into me."
This community of action is, to a certain extent, individual fulfillment, since it is reflected in each hero's lasting influence, that is, in
what he leaves in others. The ego is worth nothing in the void and
to be effective it must be, not only the product of many influences
("My living I is an I that is really a We; my living, personal I lives
only in and through other I's"), but also the source of many influences, many of which will appear to be failures, for they will be rejected. Nevertheless, "You say that they do not understand you?
Well, let them study you or leave you alone; you do not have to
lower your soul to their level." [74] The masses, if they are to follow
the heroic example, must be prepared to labor also, for they cannot
blindly accept the hero's values without considering what good these
may have for them as individuals.

73. "La locura del doctor Montarco," O.C. 3: 691.
74. *Del sentimiento trágico de la vida,* O.C. 16: 137; 408; 301. This does
not, however, necessarily minimize the fear of annihilation as we see in
Rimas de dentro, 6: vv. 60–64, O.C. 13: 863: "How many I have been! /
And having been so many, / will I end up by being none? / Of this poor
Unamuno, / will only the name remain?" See also *Del sentimiento trágico,*
p. 303; "¡Adentro!", O.C. 3: 421

Speaking of his mission, Unamuno makes his philosophical objectives quite clear when he says: "Charity does not mean rocking and lulling our brothers to sleep in the inertia and drowsiness of matter, but rather to awaken them to the anxiety and torment of the spirit." In spite of its religious and purely contemplative dimensions, this is a forceful, almost warlike series of demands put upon the hero, who must knowingly disquiet and disappoint many who lived in happiness before. "One must stir up spirits and infuse them with powerful longings, even while knowing that they will never achieve what they long for." [75] Peace and happiness form no part of the goals, for the hero must reveal the misery and emptiness of the average man, dynamically and painfully. He will always have the feeling of crying in the wilderness, no matter how concrete and specific his human objectives may be. However, this is, once again, why it is necessary for him to be both slightly callous and prepared to appear ridiculous without fear. This is the torment of the mission and the price of eternity.

Therefore, it may be said that there is a constant flow between the ego of the hero, the influence of other egos, and finally the heroic ego made more complete by the new influences. The last never blends into the others, but it and they become richer from their mutual contact. Every ego, especially the heroic one, forms part of a continuity since it contributes to the immortality of that which went before, just as later egos will contribute to the immortality of present heroism. Once again the hero finds himself at the center of the space-time continuum, within which he acts as both receiver and source: "I carry within me everything that has passed before me, and I perpetuate it with myself, and perhaps it all goes into my germs and all my ancestors live undiminished in me, and will continue to live, along with me, in my descendants." [76] Here again we see more than one possibility for immortality: the spiritual, by means of fame and transmissible influences; and the physical, through children who can carry within them not only the blood but also the spirit of preceding individuals. Don Quixote, as we shall see, concentrates all his heroic energies on the first possibility, as do the saints.

75. *Del sentimiento trágico,* O.C. 16: 405; *Vida de Don Quijote,* p. 218.
76. *Del sentimiento trágico,* O.C. 16: 328–29.

Solitude and Fulfillment

We have seen how anguish leads the hero toward personal fulfillment through his compassion for others, but he must combine this
enrichment with some solitary purification, much like the saints. Solitude is as important for the hero as community, but neither one is
enough in itself. Ilie explains it as follows: "The barriers that exist
in the social situation are eliminated in solitude, and although this
might not be of immediate practical help, it can lead to mutual understanding." [77] Every man must confront himself alone and evaluate
his beliefs in order to see if they still serve. While it is true that there
exists the possibility of appearing ridiculous because of an uncommon
faith, "there is a more terrible ridicule and that is the ridicule that
man faces when he looks upon himself. It is my reason that laughs
at my faith and scorns it." [78] This is the threat of realistic logic and
the temporary flagging of faith. It is the continual conflict that each
man must resolve on his own terms. Ultimately, only solitude can
reveal the best solution.

Unamuno does state quite baldly that "life is solitude," and so also
is heroism, the ultimate expression of life, because after having dealt
with others the hero has formed his values and must be alone in his
uniqueness: "The more alone, the nearer to apparential immortality,
the immortality of the name, for names diminish each other." [79] Human memory is fleeting and the hero must learn to be able to isolate
himself in the popular eye. This is the immediate culmination of his
ego; yet fulfillment is not a clinical state, but something always unreachable which Unamuno discusses as an abstraction. It is more than
mere fame and is achieved in the independence of solitude, when the
hero's reality becomes concrete as the shadows dissipate. He reaches
true knowledge of himself in contrast to the faith and speculation
that were the bases of his heroic effort before. His uniqueness should

77. Ilie, *Unamuno*, p. 57.
78. *Del sentimiento trágico*, O.C. 16: 425.
79. "Soledad," v. 9, *Rosario de sonetos líricos*, 82, O.C. 13: 588; *Del
sentimiento trágico*, O.C. 16: 181–82. For this reason he urges his soul on:
"May all that you give be the germ / of something higher!" "Caña salvaje," vv.
17–18, *Rimas de dentro*, 1, O.C. 13: 849.

be clear, but his egotism is still valid because it is necessary; only now as an individual is he fully conscious of his place within the cosmos: "I am one, but all men are I's." [80] A more positive declaration of the distinctiveness of each ego — whether developed and fulfilled like that of the hero, or raw and unpolished like that of the masses — could scarcely be imagined.

God and Immortality

The fulfillment of the ego and the steps to heroism are based primarily on the feelings that, when approached sincerely, keep man from lying to himself. He confronts reality just as he feels it in the deepest reaches of his personality, and if he is sincere he cannot be wrong, for each man creates his own truth: "What I feel is a truth, as true at least as what I see, touch, hear, and have shown to me — I think even more true — and sincerity obliges me not to hide my feelings." [81] Thus can Unamuno explain the contradictions that exist in every ego, which he sees as sentimental, not rational. Feeling is life, and excessive rationalism is death because it is static, as exemplified in *Amor y pedagogía,* and we have already seen that the value of the ego lies in its dynamism.

Unamuno feels immortality; his faith and not his reason makes him believe in the possibility and acts as the impulse without which life would have no meaning. There is a passage in Unamuno's diary, written shortly after the crisis of 1897, in which he speaks of the tremendous difficulty of regaining his beliefs on rational grounds and finds that, like William James, he can accept God only through an act of the will and a leap of emotion: "With reason I sought a rational God, who kept vanishing because he was a pure idea, and thus I ended up with the Nothing God to which pantheism leads, and with pure phenomenism, the root of all my feeling of emptiness. And I did not feel the living God who dwells within us and who reveals

80. *Del sentimiento trágico,* O.C. 16: 251.
81. Ibid., p. 245. This clearly recalls the ideas of James, and Unamuno had marked the following passage in red (*Will to Believe,* p. 498): "so long as we deal with the cosmic and the general, we deal only with the symbols of reality, but *as soon as we deal with the private and the personal phenomena as such, we deal with realities in the completest sense of the term.*"

himself to us through acts of charity, and not through vain acts of vanity. Until he called my heart and thrust me into the agonies of death." [82] Based on his own experience, Unamuno demands acts of faith and an intuitive belief in God and immortality of all those who would be heroic.

This is a source of strength for heroism, but not, as Serrano Poncela points out, a means of discovering the innermost secrets of the cosmos: "It is necessary to believe and to desire earnestly, no matter how absurd it seems to us and regardless of whether we disagree with it, since in this belief and in this longing lies the only reason for living, not for understanding the universe." [83] This will sustain the hero on his journey to those secrets. Unamuno feels that perhaps heroism is possible without this belief, but it would be apparential, and he cannot see what would motivate such actions, if not faith, or at least hope in immortality: "A single individual can put up with life and live it well, and even heroically, without in any way believing either in the immortality of the soul or in God, but he is living the life of a spiritual parasite." [84] He sees God and immortality as the prizes won by heroes, for he admits the concept of James,[85] that God is the producer of immortality and that, like the saints, one reaches him only through suffering.

This would seem, then, to put Unamuno closer to the thought of Kierkegaard than to that of Nietzsche. The hero's saintly qualities are what make him believe in God: "May we not say that it is not believing in another life that makes one good, but rather that being good makes one believe in it?" If there is indeed no immortality, the efforts

82. *Diario íntimo*, pp. 12–13. God is, then, man's idea of him. See Laín, *La espera y la esperanza*, p. 391: "This Unamunian 'creating of God' consists in wanting to believe in God with such love, sincerity, and force that God, also through love, will manifest, open, and reveal himself in us."

83. Segundo Serrano Poncela, *El pensamiento de Unamuno* (Mexico, 1953), p. 155.

84. *Del sentimiento trágico*, O.C. 16: 154. Cf. "Salmo II," vv. 18–21, O.C. 13: 286: "Searching for truth goes thought,/ and it is not if it does not search for it;/ if at last it finds it,/ it stops and sleeps."

85. This passage by James, which was so often used by Unamuno, is marked by one horizontal and six vertical lines in his personal copy (*Will to Believe*, p. 524): "Religion, in fact, for the great majority of our own race *means* immortality, and nothing else. God is the producer of immortality; and whoever has doubts of immortality is written down as an atheist without further trial." Unamuno's own case is often proof of this.

not only of the hero, but of all of us will be lost and the ego will have no meaning because it will be an ephemeral thing lasting no more than a moment. The man who feels will be unable to accept such an idea because it would be the conquest of faith by mere reason, and the very basis of life becomes chaos. If the ego loses meaning, cosmic equilibrium is also lost, since the universe exists on behalf of man, and without him what justification for it is there? It is intolerable that individual efforts could be useless: "For my part, I cannot imagine the liberty of a heart or the tranquillity of a conscience that are not sure of their permanence after death." [86]

True religion, not the "collier's faith," is possible only when man's faith has reached this level of intuition in the development of his ego and can now serve for eternal hope, as indicated earlier: "religion is not the longing for self-annihilation, but for self-fulfillment, it is the longing for life and not for death." It is something that can have immediate value for the hero. When he succeeds in finding his place in the world, he can begin to look for his place in the universe and desire a union with God, particularly the anthropomorphic and personal God who represents the immortality and the projection toward infinity of individual man. When the hero has fulfilled himself, he must be united with God because he will have made himself essential to the universe, which has, of course, always been his purpose. Unamuno's advice is simple: "act in such a way that in your own judgment and in the judgment of others you may deserve eternity, act so that you may become irreplaceable, so that you do not deserve to die." [87] It is a sort of ontological blackmail: if the hero is sincere and believes both in himself and in what he has done, God will not be able to overlook him and it will no longer be possible for him to die.

The discovery of death made God necessary, and we believe in our

86. *Del sentimiento trágico,* O.C. 16: 371; 197.

87. Ibid., pp. 345; 387. Unamuno marked the following thought of Renan's, quoted by James in *The Will to Believe,* p. 170, n. 1: "This universe is a show that God puts on for himself. Let us serve the intentions of the great choregus by contributing to making the show as brilliant, as varied as possible." In the *Cancionero,* no. 103, he says, "it is the struggle with God that has to give us triumphal contemplation." See also "Vencido," vv. 35–41, O.C. 13: 393, and "¿Por qué me has abandonado?" vv. 1–4, *Rosario de sonetos líricos,* 113, O.C. 13: 624, which is appropriately preceded by a quotation from Senancour.

own death because we have witnessed the death of God made man. Nevertheless, the logic is not apparent, so we try to defeat it in an irrational way because we believe, and "believing is, in the first instance, wanting to believe." There is, for Unamuno, no more proof that God does not exist than there is that he does, and he never accepts Nietzsche's Man-God. It is a gamble: "Dance our dream on the edge / of the abyss in the hope / that it is to be a counterdance / in tune with the Lord's [Bailar nuestro sueño al borde / del abismo en la esperanza / de que ha de ser contradanza / con la del Señor acorde].[88] This is the only hope he has to justify his madness. We do not want to believe only in the immortality of the soul or in the immortality of some celestial essences we may contain, but also in the immortality of our entire being, and it is to that end that the hero's efforts are directed. The heroic vision of death is dynamic, as is his vision of life: "What we really long for after death is to go on living this life, this same mortal life, but without its ills, without tedium, and without death. . . . And what else is the meaning of that comical idea of *eternal recurrence* which sprang from the tragic depths of poor Nietzsche, hungering for concrete and temporal immortality?" [89] The influence is clear; yet it is by no means an eternity of peace and harmony but rather of effort and neverending hope. Man, in his immortality, awaits glory and, like Unamuno himself, must constantly strive for it: "And the soul, my soul at least, longs for something else; not absorption, not quietude, not peace, not extinction, but rather an eternal approaching without ever arriving, a ceaseless longing, an eternal hope which is eternally renewed but never wholly fulfilled." [90]

The heaven attained by Unamuno's heroes is the presence of God forever. The search for glory that is at the very root of heroism does not have as its aim mere fame — for it is acquired only after death — but the need to impose oneself upon the eternal memory. For Don

88. *Del sentimiento trágico,* O.C. 16: 241; *Cancionero,* no. 1665, vv. 5–8.
89. *Del sentimiento trágico,* p. 357. For Unamuno's vision of eternity, see Laín Entralgo, *La espera y la esperanza,* pp. 394–95.
90. Ibid., p. 381. Cf. "The hope of everlasting life thus becomes the basis, norm, and incitement of earthly life, and in turn this earthly life continuously prods the soul on toward eternal hope," Laín Entralgo, p. 396. However, at the time of the crisis of March 1897, Unamuno had hoped for less dynamism, and speculated: "Glory must be something like this: an immersion into eternal calm, and an outpouring of the spirit in eternal prayer" (*Diario íntimo,* p. 35).

Quixote, "the desire for glory was the source of his action," [91] because it meant that he would succeed in proving the enduring validity of his ideas and the continued justification of his existence. He contributed to life by serving as an example — which is, as we shall later see, what makes the hero historical rather than merely fictional ("to live historically is to survive, to make oneself eternal, to create values forever"). The fictional fades, while the genuinely historical lives on in men's minds for eternity because its values always apply. For this reason, the hope of glory and fame impel the hero just as they impelled Don Quixote: "The longing for renown and fame, the thirst for glory that moved our Don Quixote, was it not perhaps at bottom a fear of fading away, of disappearing, of ceasing to be?" [91] The aim of heroism is not merely self-enrichment but benefits for all men so that, if capable, they too may follow. If even one person is so inspired and gives the hero immortality, glory is achieved; the values for which the hero fought will perpetuate his memory.

Everything that is done fits within the concept of God as an unlimited and supreme extension of the ego. Man begins with his own ego and through his heroism joins the infinity that is God: "And that vast I into which each individual I wishes to put the universe, what is it but God?" However, God cannot absorb the heroic ego so that it loses its identity, but only accept it as an integral part of the infinite. This threat of absorption is really what the hero must combat with his personality, since "he who submerges himself in God is forgotten in God, / the eternity of God becomes a moment [quien en Dios se sumerge en Dios se olvida, / la eternidad de Dios se hace momento]" With all his strength he must resist and conquer this oblivion too, for this is part of the test set by God, who "in order to conquer us / wants us to attack him [para conquistarnos / quiere que le asaltemos]" The battle is part of the hero's plenitude, and anything that is held back will destroy his hopes: "If in order to spare your wick you extinguish the light, if in order to save your life you waste your idea, God will not remember you, for he will drown you in his oblivion as if it were supreme pardon. And there is no other Hell but this: the possibility that God may forget us and that we

91. *Vida de Don Quijote*, p. 87. See also *El Cristo de Velázquez*, I, xi, vv. 389-90
92. "Vida e historia," O.C. 5: 350; *Vida de Don Quijote*, p. 274.

may return to the unconsciousness from which we sprung." The
choice is absolute, and the hero's efforts must be so too: "Either God
or oblivion." There can be no rest during life and there will certainly
be none in eternity. The competition will continue, and some will be
more heroic in their immortality than others because they will penetrate more deeply. The hero can never know any rest, for even immortality will be tenuous and must be fought for in order to be retained. The threat of oblivion does not permit the truly heroic to
shrink from the task: "Give us your Paradise, Lord, but so that we
may preserve and work it, not so that we may sleep in it; give it to us
so that we may employ eternity to conquer step by step and eternally
the fathomless abysses of your infinite bosom." [93]

When one considers the amount of effort expended by Unamuno
upon the ways of achieving immortality, it is rather surprising how
little he had to say about exactly what it would be like, or what,
besides struggling, man would be doing there. Rather than hope for
an orthodox Christian heaven, he hopes for "eternal Purgatory, then,
rather than glory; eternal ascension." [94] Ascension toward what, he
does not really say. He does, though, draw a fine line between what
may be called apparential glory and the uniqueness that makes the
hero share the bosom of God. Apparential glory is merely the beginning. It is the fame that permits the hero to live eternally in the mind
of men, indispensable and vivid; whereas true glory is substantial, the
most cherished of rewards, the company of God and the privilege of
continuing one's heroism forever. All good men may eventually be
with God in one way or another, but many will be forgotten, both by
humanity and by God himself, while the heroes continue to live. For
this reason Unamuno urges his reader to heroism: "And may God
give you not peace, but Glory!" [95]

93. *Del sentimiento trágico*, p. 335; *Cancionero*, no. 157, vv. 15–16. See
also "La unión con Dios," *Rosario de sonetos líricos*, 121, O.C. 13: 634; "Vencido," vv. 55–56, O.C. 13: 393; *Vida de Don Quijote*, pp. 320; 265.

94. *Del sentimiento trágico*, O.C. 16: 381.

95. Ibid., p. 451. For a development of this entire problem see "Si vis
pacem, age bellum," O.C. 14: 880. Cf. Carlyle, *On Heroes*, p. 137: "Peace?
A brutal lethargy is peaceable, the noisome grave is peaceable. We hope for
a living peace, not a dead one!"

3. The Environment of Heroism

We have seen the general outline of abstract heroic development, but it is important to see how it manifests itself in specific human relationships. There is, in particular, a clear polarization between the hero and those who surround him as recipients of his achievements. Carlyle characterizes him as the fire that comes to set them aflame. Unamuno's abhorrence of pure ideas leads him repeatedly to insist on the need for concrete aims and benefits with a definite purpose, since theories are worthless unless applied directly to an individual. There is, therefore, an essential progression from humanity as an abstract aim to a specific beneficiary chosen as representative of those most likely to be receptive to the hero's ideals, and thus most likely to put them into action and give them and him enduring justification.

The human motivation of the hero, as set forth in this chapter, must be clearly distinguished from the characteristics he shows as a crusader for a cause, which we shall see in chapter 4, as one is a result of outward effects and the other determined by inner tensions. In order to see how and why the hero is differentiated from the larger body of mankind, we must know whom he chooses for his follower and understand why. Of course, the hero is above all an activist, and Unamuno states in *Del sentimiento trágico de la vida* that, "Man does not resign himself to being, as consciousness, alone in the universe, or to being one more objective phenomenon. He wishes to save his vital or passional subjectivity by making the whole universe alive, personal, and animated." [1] The hero is subjective — unique — always

1. O.C. 16: 274. This is to say that it is man's right to be, and one he should actively use. As Barry Luby writes, "In dealing with individualism, the Spanish philosopher upholds the Kantian idea of man as an individual who has,

and must impose the burden of subjectivity upon all men, for such is the nature of individuality.

It is not in the hero's personality to live in a vacuum with his ideals because his impassioned beliefs demand action. He needs an audience to whom he will direct himself, although those who are only indirectly brought into play may also profit by his example. He who is merely a meditator looks for harmony in his existence; but we know that the hero is also an *agonista*, a *luchador*, and anything that could lull him into peace or complacency (we are, of course, dealing now with the Unamuno of the period after *Paz en la guerra*) is repulsive and destructive. Like Christ, the hero comes to bring, not peace, but war. He is a complete human being, one in search of his fulfillment, and his existence can know no rest or annihilation will sweep over him. Unamuno and the hero live this tension. Unamuno's audience is the reader, and his duty, like that of the hero, is to make him live the same agony so that he too may avoid the ontological peril. We, then, are not only the audience for Unamuno's heroism, but from our midst will emerge his followers.

This emergence cannot be brought about by the mere expression of ideas, but by showing that heroism lies, not in theories, but in one's very existence as an individual. Like a troubadour, the hero must begin by making his presence felt: "I, a living appearance, am superior to my ideas, appearances of an appearance, shadows of a shadow." [2] Man is, as Tasso points out, the shadow of a dream, and so his ideas alone are purely apparential, nothing more than reflections, shadows of shadows. Ideas are dead and appeal only to reason, which can grasp only what is static. Life, which is movement and passion, appeals to the emotions, whereas reason must dehumanize ideals and convert them into generalities and debase them into abstractions so that they may be transmitted. Benardete states it as follows: "Reason seeks to establish paradigms, plans, systems, syllogisms; its essential function is to *de-individualize, depersonalize* things and men." [3] That

nonetheless, a part to play in the totality of the universe." *Unamuno a la luz del empirismo lógico contemporáneo* (New York, 1969), pp. 58–59. This rôle is the very essence of Unamuno's preoccupation.

2. "La ideocracia," O.C. 3: 220.

3. Mair J. Benardete, "Personalidad e individualidad en Unamuno," *Revista Hispánica Moderna* 1 (1934): 31.

is to say, reason converts feelings, essences, into a common form, strips them of their validity, their individual qualities, so that they may be used as bridges for communication between men; but heroism cannot be transmitted through commonplaces or abstractions, and one of Unamuno's most pressing concerns is the inability of men to communicate other than externally.

The hero is profoundly aware of his own existence as well as that of others, and he wants all men to feel each other's existence in the deepest possible way: "since we are conscious we feel ourselves existing, which is quite another thing from knowing that we exist, and we want to feel the existence of everything else; we want each of all other individual things also to be an I." Consciousness, the root of the ego in motion, is the criterion for individuality. Other men are distant, but we can touch them through our feelings and through our will because our limitations, although not identical, are similar. Ideas may have a certain descriptive function, but Unamuno states: "People interest me more than their doctrines, and the latter only insofar as they reveal to me the former." There is, however, a progression we shall try to trace, for as he points out in an article in 1923, published in French, man needs and demands heroes who will help and inspire him and lead him to a final goal: "For man feels the need to adore man, that is, to adore himself, projected outside himself. . . . Man feels the need to be commanded by man, and this feeling of primitive, mystic dependence which, according to Schleiermacher, produced religion, is exactly the feeling that has been given to us by the perception of divinity." [4]

The echoes of Carlyle can be heard again, and we are close once more to the Nietzschean Man-God as well, but only as an intermediate step that carries us back to the distinctly religious basis of Unamuno's preoccupation. The aim must be human, whether man or woman, but the ultimate good is, as always, God:

> And thus it is always in all great work among men, and the truth is that such work, if it is truly to be great, has to be done in

4. *Del sentimiento trágico*, O.C. 16: 274; "La ideocracia," O.C. 3: 220; "L'Avenir de l'Europe," *Revue de Genève*, no. 31 (January 1923), p. 19. Carlyle agrees, but in much stronger terms: "We all love great men; love, venerate and bow down submissive before great men: nay can we honestly bow down to anything else?" *On Heroes*, p. 15.

honor of man — of man or woman, and better of woman than of man. The goal of man is Humanity, Humanity personalized, made individual, and when he takes Nature as his goal, he must humanize it first. God is Humanity's ideal, man projected into infinity and made eternal there. And thus it must be.[5]

We shall investigate each of these aims in turn, for Unamuno speaks at considerable length about all of them.

The Hero and Humanity

This polarization of hero-humanity is part of the essential structure of society itself, and its origin lies within the individual's instinct to perpetuate himself through his effect on others. This is a fundamental tension based on the efforts of the individual to rise above himself and the masses. Unamuno is not concerned with the mere self-seeker but rather with the man who is striving to contribute. He is polarizing his actions through his attempts to help others go forward with him as he progresses. Unlike Tolstoy, Unamuno feels that the advances made by society are not caused by those who rest but by the heroes and their followers.

Everything begins with the ego and the efforts of the will, but Unamuno clarifies this further: "For each of us the center is in himself. But we cannot act if we do not polarize it; we cannot live if we are not uncentered. And how will we be uncentered except by reaching for another being like ourselves?"[6] An effective polarization makes the hero one person whose existence we cannot doubt. He imposes himself upon the memories of others, as he simultaneously separates himself from them and urges them to move toward him with love and compassion, which are always one for Unamuno in the heroic context. This is something that also links the hero with the saint; for through this love he may be of benefit to others, since

5. *Vida de Don Quijote*, p. 178.
6. Ibid. Unamuno's insistence on a necessary polarization between individuals can be seen in the *Diario íntimo*, pp. 185–86: "It is a sad thing that each man should sacrifice himself to humanity, that we should all sacrifice ourselves to it! We all sacrifice ourselves to humanity and when it becomes an abstraction of all of us who have sacrificed ourselves, what is this humanity? That is certainly pure idolatry, and of the worst kind."

"he who not only shines, but casts light on others while shining, shines by casting light on himself." [7] Self-enrichment rises from the fulfillment of others, and it is from this awareness of being a paradigm for mankind that the hero derives much of his understanding of his mission, and thus of his own individuality.

The hero represents to his audience an entire concept and, as such, becomes a symbol for all who pay attention to his vision: "Well, then, a man, a real man, whether he wants to be or wants not to be, is a symbol, and a symbol can become a man. And even a concept. A concept can become a person." [8] A man, with his consciousness, sets his individuality in motion and becomes heroic. As a hero, he sets an example for his audience, and from the example of his life derive concepts that live on and give him immortality. He has revealed to his followers their own potential. He is exceptional, but not detached from the masses, whose maximum capabilities he represents: "The hero is nothing more than the collective soul made individual, one who, precisely because he feels most in unison with the people, feels in a most personal manner; prototype and end result, he is also the spiritual node of the people." [9]

The hero must not lose contact with the people; his invincibility lies in his ability to raise them along with him. They reinforce him, not because he lacks faith, but because "faith needs something material upon which to work." He must see himself reflected in humanity, for although he does not live his life according to ideas, the principles become manifest through his example. This was the supreme contribution of Don Quixote: " 'And what has Don Quixote left?' you will say. And I will say to you that he left himself and that a man, a living and eternal man, is worth as much as all theories and all philosophies." [10] His very existence, rather than any specific doctrine, makes his example continue to live to such an extent that he can still attract an audience, and perhaps even followers, after his life is over. This is Don Quixote's immortality; his fame does not rest on the ab-

7. "Continuación," *Cómo se hace una novela*, p. 158. Notice the similarity to Carlyle's comment: "I said, the Great Man was always as lightning out of Heaven; the rest of men waited for him like fuel, and then they would flame." *On Heroes*, p. 77.
8. "Prólogo," *Tres novelas ejemplares*, O.C. 9: 419.
9. "El caballero de la triste figura," O.C. 3: 171.
10. *Del sentimiento trágico*, O.C. 16: 314; 444.

stractions he leaves behind, but rather on a more tangible memory. Therefore, let the people remember the totality of the hero's life and from that draw the ideas they choose: "The immortality of the soul is something spiritual, something social. He who makes a soul for himself, he who leaves a work, lives in it and through it in his fellow men, in humanity, as long as humanity may live. This is living in history." [11] The hero will live as long as his life is worthy of being remembered.

Man cannot rely on his ideas, for they have the power to live on their own and so are unfaithful to their creator; but life itself is unique and cannot be separated from the individual who formed it and gave it everlasting validity. Unamuno himself was deeply affected by the question of gaining and influencing an audience that would justify his existence, and of course he tried to do this principally through his books. In a letter to Jiménez Ilundain, written in 1899, he said: "it pleases me that my voice is listened to attentively by a greater number of people, because thus can I pour my spirit into more spirits and join my voice, 'a poor thing, but mine own,' with the universal chorus." [12] As for any man with heroism in his soul, the larger his audience, the greater his chances for success and perpetuation.

The Hero Misunderstood: Curates and Barbers

Polarization is not easy, for the hero is neither universally acclaimed nor immediately recognized for his outstanding qualities. Emerson's dictum, "To be great is to be misunderstod," seems to have been taken very seriously by Unamuno, who agrees that the hero will inevitably come across those who are incapable of understanding his excellence because their minds cannot or dare not share the fire that moves him, and who thereby lock themselves in the oblivion of their complacency.

The hero lives in a substantial world of his own creation (Unamuno borrows the vocabulary of Kant, calling it the "noumenal world"), while so-called reasonable men live only in the apparential —"phenomenal"— world. The two attitudes are irreconcilable, and

11. *La agonía del cristianismo*, O.C. 16: 478.
12. Quoted by Emilio Salcedo, *Vida de don Miguel* (Salamanca, 1964), p. 101. See also the poem "Id con Dios," O.C. 13: 198.

until reasonable men can penetrate to the deeper essences of life, the hero must leave them where he finds them. He has presented them with new forces that their placidness keeps them from judging. They suffer, perhaps incurably, from "mental sloth, the inability to judge except in accordance with precedents." [13] They are those who live a negative existence — their destructive laughter and bitter ridicule attest to it — for they represent "not wanting to be," the total lack of will, without even the strength of the heroes of *noluntad* (the will-not): the suicides. Unamuno's scorn for them is blistering:

> This is the common man,
> the one with common sense,
> the one who always agrees,
> the one carried along by the current,
> let him be dragged in the shallow stream,
> the man of the happy medium,
> without surprises; what can you do?
> Just a sane man.
> He is the envious man,
> the man of the Holy Brotherhood,
> who serves His Majesty,
> as a pawn in the fight.
>
> [Este es el hombre corriente,
> el del sentido común,
> el del conforme y según,
> a quien lleva la corriente
> que se arrastre en lecho llano,
> hombre del término medio
> sin esquinas; ¿qué remedio?
> nada más que un hombre sano.
> Es el hombre de la envidia,
> el de la Santa Hermandad,
> que sirve a Su Majestad
> como peón de la lidia.] [14]

13. "Prólogo," *Tres novelas ejemplares,* O.C. 9: 413.
14. *Cancionero,* no. 1566, Oct. 30, 1930. Carlyle also emphasizes this visionary quality of the hero: "A Hero, as I repeat, has this first distinction, which indeed we may call first and last, the Alpha and Omega of his whole Heroism, That he looks through the shows of things into *things.*" *On Heroes,* p. 55.

These men can be taught nothing, for their lack of will keeps them from moving in either direction and the hero cannot debase his ideals in order to convince them. The initiative was theirs to take.

They, however, are not the worst. There are always the close friends and family who know the hero so well that they cannot see his hero-ism. They love him selfishly without trying to understand him. It was for this reason that Don Quixote was so vilified by his niece and housekeeper. One may love a person so well that one creates an erro-neous image of him. Don Quixote's niece knew her uncle without looking at him as he saw himself or as he might have been. The actions that were inconsistent with her concept of him were, for her, only sources of ridicule and disgrace, since even in these she saw only what she chose to see. This fact should not deter the hero either, though, for Christ himself recognized the problem (Mark 3: 20), as do the saints: "To no one does the hero, the saint, the redeemer, seem as mad as to his own family, his parents, and brothers." The hero must simply love these people in return and let them love him in their ignorance; he cannot help them any more than the saint can save them if they do not want it. They are too close to see the obvious, and this is what forces the hero to be alone at all times: "The hero ends up by being unable to have friends, by being forced to be alone." [15]

Those who will be close to the hero will be more than friends: they will believe in him. The relationship is instinctive but not merely sentimental. Yet this is part of the agony of the hero — to find himself always out of step with the masses, and no matter how hard he tries to help those who refuse to believe, to see the abyss between them grow larger and develop into loneliness: "Solitude! Solitude is the marrow of our existence, and with this business of congregating and flocking together we only deepen it." [16] All efforts to go against the

15. *Vida de Don Quijote*, p. 170. Like Don Quixote, Unamuno tries to ignore public scorn: "Thank God I don't hear everything that they could say about me. And together with the insults of some is the joy of others, especially of those who really love me." *Diario íntimo*, p. 104. In volume 3 of Carlyle's *The French Revolution: a History* (London, 1907), p. 153, Unamuno has marked this idea in red: "No man can explain himself, can get himself explained; men see not one another, but distorted phantasms which they call one another; which they hate and go to battle with: for all battle is well said to be misunderstanding."

16. "Comentario," *Cómo se hace una novela*, p. 39.

will of the masses seem futile, and even Unamuno was haunted by
doubts when he found himself constantly misunderstood, as expressed
in a letter to Federico de Onís, dated 4 December 1907: "Have I set
a bad example? . . . I am in a period of remorse. With pain I am
beginning to see that, with the exception of a few — you are one of
them — most people have deliberately misinterpreted everything I
have preached and are discrediting me." [17]

This is, of course, as it should be; it is what sets the hero and his
faithful apart from the mediocre masses and makes them heroic. The
curates and barbers will always laugh at both the hero and his audience — Don Quixote and Sancho — for heroism is only a source of
amusement for them. Their embarrassed laughter reveals their desire
to goad the hero on to even more of such humorous deeds to create
further entertainment for them. Thus they exalt themselves by making others appear petty and ridiculous. Nevertheless, "more foolish
are the fools / who do not know their parts." Their self-aggrandize-
ment, contrary to that of the hero, is solely at the expense of others.
Here Unamuno and Nietzsche come surprisingly close, for both feel
that decay from the masses can infect the hero and reduce him to
nothing. Zarathustra says: "Yes, my friend, you are a bad conscience
to your neighbours: for they are unworthy of you. Thus they hate
you and would dearly like to suck your blood." Unamuno's hero is
also in peril from those he would save. Nevertheless, just as he must
not debase his ideals to satisfy the ignorant, he must not act to delight
the fools: "Therefore, never do anything heroic or say anything subtle
or new to please those who will take your words and deeds as mere
ingenuity." [18]

The hero must choose his followers just as closely as God chose
the hero. Everyone has the potential to be either hero or follower,
but only some have the will and the courage to accept the challenge.
"He who does not see his star in daylight, / nor feels the burning heat

17. Quoted by Salcedo, *Vida de don Miguel,* p. 143. Carlyle notes that
Mohammed faced the same problem: "He spoke of his Doctrine to this man
and that; but the most treated it with ridicule, with indifference." *On Heroes,*
p. 58.
18. *Teresa,* no. 25, vv. 19–20, O.C. 14: 328; Nietzsche, *Thus Spoke Zarathustra,* p. 80; *Vida de Don Quijote,* p. 171. See also the poem "Por dentro,"
vv. 132–37, O.C. 13: 325.

of its soft light / in his breast, cannot be a guide; / let him stay at home [Quien su estrella no ve si se hace día, / ni de su dulce luz siente la brasa / dentro el pecho, no puede ese ser guía, / quédese en casa.]" There must be no hypocrisy or sham on the part of the hero, and Sánchez Barbudo sees here a revealing facet of Unamuno's own inner conflicts: "Unamuno must have thought, even when he was very young, that there was an abyss between what he really was, inwardly, and the Unamuno that everyone else saw." He attributes to this fact much of the hypocrisy of which he accuses Unamuno, but it seems that the identity crisis was due more to an inability to reconcile this duality easily than to a conscious cultivation of it for its own sake. The idea is clarified in the prologue to *Tres novelas ejemplares,* in which, developing an idea of Oliver Wendell Holmes's, he theorizes that there are in fact four "persons" in each individual: the person we think we are, the person others think we are, the person we would like to be, and the person we really are. The hero tries to make the progression from what he thinks he is to what he would like to be, for this is his salvation: "We will be saved or lost on the basis of what we wanted to be, not on the basis of what we have been. God will reward or punish each one so that throughout eternity he may be what he wanted to be." [19] For the hero, this is the goal.

It is once more a question of the intentions behind the action rather than the concrete results of it, but the hero is more deeply aware of the various persons that make up his ontological self, and his life is centered around this tension. It would seem, however, that the person others believe him to be could be further subdivided, since we now know that the follower, the masses, and the close friends and relatives all may have their own concepts of him. The mystery of the personality is undeniably greater in the hero than in other men. Unamuno feels, though, that when the time comes, they will be forced to admit their error and he will still come to their aid. This is part of the tragedy: "It is all very well to mock the madman, but then, when we need him, we have to run to him. Unfortunate is the hero who places his heroism at the service of every comer and thus cheapens

---

19. "La huella de sangre de fuego," vv. 61–64, O.C. 13: 415; Sánchez Barbudo, *El misterio de la personalidad,* p. 204; "Prólogo," *Tres novelas ejemplares,* O.C. 9: 416.

it." [20] It may seem unjust, but his duty is largely charitable and he must help all those who need him. Those who appreciate his worth and follow him may be almost as heroic as he, but those who laugh at him may still benefit, although they can never be heroes.[21] Unamuno considers Don Quixote's greatest adventure to be that of the "basin-helmet" (*baciyelmo*) (pt. 1, chap. 45) when he succeeds in convincing, not only Sancho, his follower, but also those who make light of his ideals. As Unamuno points out in the *Diario íntimo* (p. 58), truth is a constant and will always prevail: "Present your feelings with sincerity and simplicity and allow truth to work by itself on the mind of your brother; let truth win him over and you need not subdue him. The truth that you may put forward is not yours; it is above you and is sufficient unto itself."

The mission is one of discernment, because the hero must decide what is best for those who come to him and do as his heart tells him, regardless of what may be asked of him. The goatherds certainly felt no need for a discourse on the Golden Age (pt. 1, chap. 11), but Don Quixote gave it to them anyway, because through this he could create a spiritual bond. Without understanding either his words or his ideas, their innocence and that of the hero did communicate, and they discovered that, in their very essence, they were of one blood. Don Quixote understood better than they themselves what they needed, and we shall see this idea expanded later: "It is indeed an adventure, and one of the most heroic. . . . One must have robust faith in the spirit in order to speak in such a way to those of coarse wit, convinced that they will understand us without understanding, and that the seeds will settle in the furrows of their souls without their noticing it." [22] They responded in kind with their songs, and after having confronted the possibility of ridicule once more, the hero emerges

20. *Vida de Don Quijote*, p. 193.

21. This idea also appears in Carlyle's concept of the hero, when he states, "We cannot look, however imperfectly, upon a great man, without gaining something by him" (*On Heroes*, p. 1). Nonetheless, the call made to the disciple will contain no promises of ease: "Difficulty, abnegation, martyrdom, death are the *allurements* that act on the heart of man" (ibid., p. 70). Unamuno certainly recognized this in the hero, but was probably more practical about the inducements needed to attract followers.

22. *Vida de Don Quijote*, p. 125.

unscathed and victorious, having conquered more followers by instilling them with a new feeling. However, the hero may not always
be so well received, as occurred in the case of Andresillo, who repaid
Don Quixote with vicious ingratitude. Don Quixote's action was
nonetheless heroic; for although his efforts to free the boy failed, his
motives were noble, and had the boy possessed the clarity of perception to understand Don Quixote's efforts, he, like the goatherds,
would have responded in kind.

The hero fulfills a definite need for he is specifically chosen for
his mission and at the same time discerns the course his actions must
take. It is not possible for the hero to change mankind completely
at one stroke: that would mean breaking the continuity, a possibility
we have already seen is unacceptable. There is, then, a certain inevitability surrounding the hero, which does not seem to preoccupy
Unamuno unduly. His actions must follow a certain pattern and all
progress must be made one step at a time. This step may be small or
large, depending upon the capabilities of the individual and the aims
of his mission. Even the small can be, in their way, heroic.

The hero lives in a particular environment and is therefore suscep-
tible to its needs. On several occasions Unamuno mentions the need
for limiting one's heroism to a fairly restricted area. He points out
that Don Quixote's defeat came only when he ventured beyond his
territory of La Mancha; and Unamuno himself, torn out of his context and thrust into exile in Paris, did less writing and found himself
relatively stagnant there.[23] The environment is not, then, a product
of an individual's heroism, although it will certainly be affected and
changed by it, whereas we have seen that the hero is definitely a
product of the tension between outside forces and inner motivation.
It is this particular tension that makes him unique and gives him
momentum:

> In each age, it is said, the hero who is needed appears. Of course.
> Just as in each age the hero breathes the great ideas of the mo-
> ment, the only ones that are necessary in his time, and he is
> soaked in these ideas and needs. And every hero other than the

23. See the sonnets of *De Fuerteventura a París*, especially number 102,
as well as "Razón y fe," "¡Adiós, España!" and "Polémica" of the *Rosario de
sonetos líricos*, O.C. 14: 597 and O.C. 13: 560, 616, 634.

one needed must end in wretchedness or scorn, in the galleys or the madhouse, perhaps even on the scaffold.[24]

Unamuno does not explain, however, how one could be heroic without fulfilling a need of one's time. Christ died in mockery on the cross and Don Quixote faced scorn until the moment of renunciation. Love toward his fellow men and faith in himself are the hero's criteria. He may administer blows, but they come from his spirit with sincere concern; he may be scorned always, but even this is a sign of a certain measure of success, for it means that he has not acted in a void. His ideals have had at least some effect, and have not been merely ignored: "Yes, my poor Don Quixote, yes; we would rather be laughed at than ignored." [25] He was formed largely by this environment, but in his fulfillment he can in his turn alter it; this is the value of the polarization.

The Specific Human Objective: Sancho

The hero confronts all humanity in his desire to find a follower. Unamuno said that he would be satisfied if only one person followed him on the strength of his philosophy, and Don Quixote achieves this in Sancho. On his first sally he faces the world at large and meets with ridicule, rebuffs, and the problem of material things without the satisfaction of seeing his ideals conquer any spirits — or even of having the opportunity to express his deeper ideals to a sympathetic audience. He therefore persuades Sancho to accompany him, and although he will always be confronted by ridicule and scorn, he can now have hope in his squire, for he led him from his home by firing him with ambition rather than greed and planting within him the desire for glory. Sancho wants to follow and all his actions will be based on his own volition.[26] He believes in Don Quixote's motives and

24. "El caballero de la triste figura," O.C. 3: 373. The hero as product and function of his race was also treated in the poem "Un patriota," O.C. 13: 566. The idea is clear also in both Carlyle and James, but probably less so in Nietzsche.

25. *Vida de Don Quijote*, p. 192. See also Unamuno's own commitment to this in the note to sonnet 58, *De Fuerteventura a París*, O.C. 14: 538.

26. He is like the followers sought by Zarathustra, except that he needs the hero to clarify his own mind. Cf. "But I need living companions who follow me because they want to follow themselves — and who want to go where I go." Nietzsche, *Thus Spoke Zarathustra*, p. 51.

goals and accepts them as his own. He accepts the challenge, not because he is more stupid than the others to whom the opportunity presents itself, but rather because his heart, like that of the hero, still retains much childlike innocence, which makes him open to the faith of heroism.

Don Quixote's life is a series of creations. The knight himself springs fully armed from the head of Alonso Quijano the Good, and then, after looking upon his world and seeing that it can be good, he creates a man — Sancho — to live in it with him and eventually to carry on his work. Don Quixote, like God, needs someone to believe in him, so Sancho becomes his sounding board and the link between him and the greater body of mankind. In him Don Quixote sees all humanity, and through him he loves and feels compassion for all his fellow men. Unamuno believes that it is impossible to love all humanity as an abstraction and that the concept must be made concrete to be meaningful. For Don Quixote to love man, he had to be able to fix his affection upon one person: "A love that does not settle on an individual is not true love." [27] To be useful, his efforts must be concentrated so that they do not become weakened in a generalized mass anonymity. Individuality must be passed on to another individual to have its full value, and the pride of seeing his essence reflected in another adds to his glory, for he is instilling him with the heroic ideals — especially heroic faith.

As the hero climbs upward and increases in heroism, so does the follower, illuminating his master's convictions:

> As far as Sancho himself is concerned, let us begin by admiring his faith, the faith that leads him toward eternal fame along the path of believing what he has not seen, a possibility of which he had not even dreamed previously, and lends splendor to his entire life. For all eternity he can say: 'I am Sancho Panza, the squire of Don Quixote.' And this is and will be his glory for ever and ever.[28]

He knows who he is. He benefits from his master's glory, and as the ripples spread, the validity of Don Quixote's faith is reinforced, for

27. *Vida de Don Quijote*, p. 112.
28. Ibid. Carlyle feels that the hero must inspire faith in his followers: "Faith is loyalty to some inspired Teacher, some spiritual Hero." *On Heroes*, p. 12.

we see that it can be effective for others as well. His fame, his apparential glory spreads too, bringing him closer to immortality. Sancho stands out as the one man who would follow the hero and make
his beliefs his own. The hero is reflected in him, and he achieves
glory because of his willingness to believe.

This interaction should not be oversimplified, however, for Sancho
does not blindly accept either Don Quixote or his beliefs. His heroism
will not be a result of his naïveté but rather of his tolerance: he is
prepared to be convinced because to believe for him, as for the hero,
is the will to believe. He would be no less heroic were he ultimately
forced to reject the hero's ideals as unsuitable for him, as long as he
followed his faith in himself and listened to his own heart. Sancho
believes (but not through reason) that he should follow Don Quixote,
and although his faith wavers even more than that of his master, he
remains true.

Sancho starts out with an instinctive feeling that what he is about
to do is right; but it would have broken his continuity to accept everything immediately and without question, for he is fundamentally a
positivist. He demands concrete solutions to the problems at hand, and
these are not always to be had in the world of heroism. Unamuno attacks him first with a cry of despair: "Concrete solutions! Oh, practical
Sancho, positivist Sancho, materialist Sancho! When will you listen
and hear the silent music of the spiritual spheres?" [29] He wants to
hear, and his willingness to listen will permit his master to teach him.
Sancho differs from Don Quixote in that he had to be created from
without and his mission had to be shown to him, but later he reveals
himself to be capable of equally great heroism. His impetus does not
come completely from within, but from his master, just as his master's
comes from God: Unamuno says that he lives through and because
of his master. He is Don Quixote's creation, and if God can stop
dreaming man, Don Quixote can also stop dreaming Sancho.

Don Quixote constantly renovates the squire's faith so that he may
continue to follow. In a sense, Sancho becomes more and more
dependent on his master for he has eaten of the tree of madness and
cannot return to his previous complacency, from which Don Quixote
tore him. The more Don Quixote reveals to him, the more he must

29. *Vida de Don Quijote*, p. 128.

follow, for the hero's actions seem progressively less mad and the
follower himself sees ever greater opportunities that must be seized:
"And you, faithful Sancho, believe in a madman and in his madness,
and if you are left alone with your previous sanity, who will free you
of the fear that will descend on you when you find yourself alone
with it, now that you have tasted quixotic madness? That is why you
ask your lord and master not to leave you." [30] The gap between the
possible and the merely plausible becomes continually narrower.

Sancho's faith is never quite as secure as that of Don Quixote, but
he must overcome even greater obstacles than his master, if such is
possible. It is one thing for a man to believe in himself, in the face of
all reason, but is it not even more surprising that a supposedly reasonable man should be prepared to believe in him too? This is the source
of Sancho's heroism: "The man who believes in the hero is no less
heroic than the hero who believes in himself." Sancho is heroic because he reveals even more Quixotism than his master by accepting
and believing in another man's madness. His leap of faith is greater
than Don Quixote's and, in its own way, his reason is aflame just as
much as the hero's: "a sane man following a madman shows greater
evidence of Quixotism than does a madman pursuing his own follies."
Sancho must also work constantly to maintain his faith, but he always
succeeds, and Unamuno underlines the efforts he must make. The
trials of a follower are no less arduous than those of the hero: "Your
career was one of inner conflict, between your rude common sense,
spurred on by greed, and your noble aspiration toward the ideal, lured
by Dulcinea and your master! . . . From enchantment to enchantment you reached the heights of redeeming faith." [31]

Unamuno is making an essential point here, for the hero is a sort
of monomaniac, as he sees only his internal reality projected outward.
The choice for him is limited because he has conquered mere reason
and is no longer disturbed by it, as his followers may be. Sancho, on
the other hand, began with an ability to see nothing but external
reality and to live with it, since he had virtually no internal reality of
his own. He must therefore conquer his reason — accept, believe in,
and make his own the inner world of another man — and this, too,

requires *voluntarismo,* as "faith is something that is conquered inch by inch and blow by blow." He does not initially have the ability to distinguish his own mission as the true hero does, but in order to follow and carry on, he must discern the value underlying his master's madness and overcome obstacles far too steep for ordinary men. Once this has been done, he will be rewarded because the hero is generous and, "don't you feel that it is better for your fame and your eternal salvation to follow a generous madman rather than a mean sane man?" [32] Again it is a question of purity of intent, and the follower is moved by the same impulse as the hero: the concept of instinct as opposed to intelligence. The difference, of course, is that Sancho sees everything through his master and through his faith in his vision.

Unamuno brings out, in the *Vida de Don Quijote y Sancho* in 1905, an idea similar to that developed by Salvador de Madariaga in his *Guía del lector del Quijote* in 1926 — that of quixotification and sanchification. Sancho's glory lies in the fact that, through his instinctive faith in his master, he ultimately becomes quixotized and thus carries on the ideals. He, too, comes to suffer from the same madness, as even Don Quixote himself realizes (pt. 1, chap. 25). Unamuno sees, however, that Sancho reaches nearly the same heights of heroism because he approaches his master with a pure heart and an open mind. Appreciation is, then, no less admirable than the act of creation. Unamuno explains to Sancho: "You are a hero like him, as much a hero as he. And the truth, Sancho, is that heroism is catching when we approach the hero with a pure heart. To admire and love the hero with disinterest and without malice is already to participate in his heroism; just as he who knows how to enjoy the work of a poet is, in his turn, a poet for knowing how to enjoy it." This is the reason that priests, barbers, nieces, and housekeepers were left by the side of the road. Sancho realizes, while governor of his "island," that he needs his master and, at the same time, becomes more acutely aware of his own limits. He has aspired to be a governor but, entitled to alter his course, he sees that his mission is to be at Don Quixote's side, so he abandons his position in order to return to him. He is not heroic enough to sustain himself from his own inner world alone, for he

32. Ibid., pp. 140, 261.

still lacks polarization. He has profited from his experience and has thus reaffirmed his individuality. By making this serious decision in the depths of his heart, he has once more put his ego into action: "I said that only the hero can say 'I know who I am,' and now I add that whoever can say 'I know who I am' is a hero, no matter how humble and obscure his life may appear to us. And Sancho, when he left the island, knew who he was." [33]

He is heroic who makes decisions according to the dictates of his faith, and Sancho abandons the island because he has seen the degree to which he is dependent upon Don Quixote. He chooses to continue this relationship and to benefit from his master's superior will, rather than strike out on his own. This, however, does not reveal any loss of heroism, for Sancho does not make the decision blindly. He had followed Don Quixote because he instinctively felt that he should; he became governor because he felt that he was capable of it and he wanted to assert his individuality; yet he leaves the island because he wants to do so, realizing that he can contribute more at the side of his master. All these actions are exercises of the will in a growing progression, as Sancho rebels against the past and demonstrates his concept of his own ego. He suffers no loss of identity at any time, because he acts in order to expand his own consciousness and fulfill his own visions: "But, upon further reflection, it is not altogether wrong for Sancho to rebel like this, for if he had never rebelled he would not be a man, a real, entire, and true man." [34] His errors are honest and clarify his sense of purpose. He differs from Don Quixote because his mission is derivative, but it is not, for that, intrinsically less heroic.

We see, then, that there are really two types of heroism: that of the man who has faith in himself and that of the one who would probably never reach any sort of fulfillment if the first type of hero did not inspire him to believe in himself. Don Quixote wrenches Sancho from the bog of mediocrity, makes him more of an individual, impresses him upon the mind of mankind, and makes him worthy of his immortality.

33. Ibid., pp. 283, 281–82.
34. Ibid., p. 305. Carlyle would see it in somewhat the same light: "*is* it not, indeed, the awakening for them from no-being into being, from death into life?" *On Heroes*, p. 21.

The Importance of the Follower: The Need for Sancho

The hero lives as a function of his followers who, in the broadest sense, can be considered to be any who are voluntarily influenced by the hero's decisive actions. Unamuno feels that there can be no heroism without masses although there can, he claims, be masses without heroes. This means that the hero is dispensable, but not that life without heroes is desirable. His task, we have seen, is the noble one of uplifting men's individual spirits and pushing them toward full understanding of themselves. Without heroes, man would exist, certainly, but his existence would be poorer. Life without masses, though, is inconceivable, for a world made up of heroes would lack incentive and motivation. Heroism is relative to that which surrounds it and (overlooking the obvious fact that heroes would cease to be heroic if they were the only people alive), without masses upon which to exert his influence and move by his example the hero's existence would be entirely superfluous. The individual salvation of the hero is not the ultimate aim of the exercise, and indeed would be impossible as Unamuno conceives of it.

Unamuno sets up a curious interdependence between the hero and his environment. By no means does he see the distinction that separates them as clear, for we have seen that Sancho can attain heights nearly as lofty as those scaled by Don Quixote. Nor does he see the relationship as a question of a master who tolerates his servant's presence and stoops to scatter the crumbs of genius. Rather, the situation is the reverse, for Sancho appears to be more necessary to his master than his master is to him, simply because the hero's objectives lie without, in mankind, and he must constantly see the justness of his actions confirmed in some external human objective.

Sancho, taken as representative of the masses, needs no justification at all. Without Don Quixote, he would still be able to return home as before, although never would he be able to regain his complacency. His life would continue with few questions and, while it is true that the hero taught him how to rise above himself, we have seen in what way these teachings are similar to the fruit of the tree of knowledge, for once his eyes have been opened, there is no turning back for Sancho. His very existence was not threatened before he met Don

Quixote, while Don Quixote's life will become totally meaningless and he will be faced with the possibility of sinking into the mire of historical oblivion if his efforts do not bear at least one slightly withered fruit. Throughout Cervantes's novel, Don Quixote's faith is reinforced by the devotion of his squire, and so it must be in life. He does not, however, rely upon his followers at any time in the direct fulfillment of his mission. All his efforts are his own and come, like his motivation, from within. Unamuno even goes so far as to say: "A zealous man is more often hindered than helped by the defense of his followers." [35] Sancho gives him the strength of character to continue, but he cannot directly aid him in his efforts. The relationship is highly intimate and the support given to the hero by his follower is not public. It forms part of the spiritual diet that gives him strength, but it is not part of heroism itself.

There is not, however, any real "sanchification" of the hero in the strictest sense of the word, for that would represent the debasement so repellent to Unamuno. He becomes like Sancho only in the balanced use of reason to strengthen his faith and preserve him from complete blindness in his actions. Don Quixote needs Sancho, not to emulate him, but merely for the encouragement and social perspective he can offer. Thus he often needs him as his guide through the torments of the physical, apparential world, so that they may both ultimately reach glory: "He who considers himself to be the leader is often the one being led, and the faith of the hero feeds on the faith he manages to inspire in his followers. Sancho was Humanity for Don Quixote, and Sancho, weakened and often burning up with his own faith, nourished the faith of his lord and master. We usually must be believed so that we may believe in ourselves." [36] He is creating Sancho in his own image; and so again we begin to see the parallel between Unamuno's concept of the hero and his vision of God.

The Objective Idealized: Dulcinea

The highest human objective, according to Unamuno, is an idealized womankind, and in the figure of Dulcinea he sees the incarna-

---

35. *Vida de Don Quijote*, p. 117.
36. Ibid., p. 210.

tion of the heroic achievement. There can be no doubt but that this is largely a romantic approach; yet it is nonetheless valid because he feels that this devotion to the service of woman brings out the best virtues in the hero. For the saint, this objective is converted, of course, into a more religious concept such as the Virgin, but for both types of hero it is a pure and highly intellectualized courtly love. This is consistent with Unamuno's personal life; he lived devoted to Concha and, after her death in 1934, he confided to Maurice Legendre, during the homage offered to him by the city of Salamanca: "This doesn't matter any more; nothing matters any more since she died." [37] He had dedicated himself to his "gentle habit" (*dulce costumbre*), and his concept of polarization was very concrete.

A woman is conquered by the hero through ideals and, as always, through his example — not through reason and logic. There is an egocentrism here, since his dedication will ultimately enhance his own reality, and Abellán points out: "In short, his thinking about love ends in the same personalism that we observed in his quixotism. But here this personalism becomes, or tries to become, transcendent; its aim is God — but God understood as a projection of consciousness, of the ego." [38] Through woman, the hero can aspire to surpass mere fame and move toward immortality with God, and this is exemplified in Don Quixote's relationship with his vision of Dulcinea — a vision born out of frustration — and in Unamuno's own work, *Teresa*, where Rafael declares to his beloved, "You are the only unfailing proof/ of my immortality." [39] Both Rafael and Don Quixote dedicate themselves to their Dulcineas in order to justify the nobility of their aspirations. The lady is always a creation of the hero because she represents for him the summa of all goodness and also because, through his heroism, he can give her immortality. Serrano Poncela interprets the need as follows: "act in every moment as if Dulcinea — Fame — had her eyes fixed upon you. Which means for Unamuno the need to have constantly a hypercritical stimulus that weighs all

37. Quoted by Salcedo, *Vida de don Miguel*, p. 375. The extent to which he was devoted to Concha in this sense can be felt in such poems as no. 26 of *De Fuerteventura a París*, and no. 1697 of the *Cancionero*, Aug. 29, 1934.
38. José Luis Abellán, *Miguel de Unamuno a la luz de la psicología* (Madrid, 1964), p. 120.
39. *Teresa*, p. 49, vv. 19–20, O.C. 14: 357.

actions." [40] Thus Dulcinea represents the melding of two concepts: the abstraction of fame and the possibility of true immortality through human polarization. The follower, Sancho, gains immortality through his efforts with his master; the lady is immortal because she offers the hero the immediate inspiration for his deeds. She need do nothing more, for such inspiration is proof enough of her outstanding qualities.

It seems appropriate to note that Unamuno shows an almost monumental unconcern for heroism on the part of the beloved, or, for that matter, on the part of any woman. Indeed, Teresa herself says to Rafael, "Man has to live his own life; / you have much to do . . . / Us? Ah! Life is only a copy/ in woman [El hombre ha de vivir su vida propia; / tenéis mucho que hacer . . . / ¿nosotras? ¡ay! la vida es sólo copia / en la mujer.]" In our discussion of the fictional works this idea will become clearer, as we see that woman needs no such efforts in order to ensure her immortality because she has the power to give birth, and Unamuno sees no particular reason for greater extension of her ego. In his works, woman is a symbol for many things, as he admits quite candidly: "each woman of flesh and blood and bone, as was my Rafael's Teresa, is a symbol — that is, a summary, and a myth and a legend, especially for her lover. Because to love is to symbolize, to summarize, and to mythicize, to create legends." Thus, she does not need to be endowed with any significant intellectual capacity or even to have any real individuality, except as a function of the hero's will. Her personality is apparent only to the hero because he creates her as a complement to his actions. Rafael declares of Teresa: "She is and I am in her and through her; she creates me so that I may create her and, thus having created her, believe in her, as she believes in me." [41] Creation and re-creation between man and God, author and character, hero and masses, and man and woman represent the essential texture of life.

Nevertheless, whatever she may have been in external reality, Dulcinea inspired Don Quixote to such a degree that mankind can never forget her, at least as she appears in the mind of her devoted knight. His valor in battle, says Unamuno, is a sublimation of his

40. Serrano Poncela, *El pensamiento de Unamuno,* p. 262.
41. *Teresa,* p. 55, vv. 13–16, O.C. 14: 369; ibid., "Presentación," pp. 279; 291.

desire to conquer his timidity before his lady, and he even suggests that this is true of all heroes: "I know how timidity is mistress of the heroes' hearts." [42]

There is an even deeper effect, however. The very concept of love itself urges the hero on, as he thrusts his presence upon the awareness of his lady, "because in order to become immortal one must love and one must die." [43] In the case of Don Quixote love is even one of the sources of his madness and one of the most fundamental and noblest impulses in the hero's motivation, even though he himself is not aware of it. It is possible, too, that as Blanco Aguinaga points out, woman represents for Unamuno the calm to which he can return after the agonizing battles of life: "But woman is not just the center and support of the unconscious peace that settles on life in the home; she is also a refuge in herself, a *lap* in whose warm depths man loses himself from history, returning to 'the blessed age in which he was just a son.' " [44] Unamuno explains this in considerable detail, and we shall see that it is to be one of the cornerstones for his characterizations in the novels:

> Here [pt. 1, chaps. 12–13] you see how all heroism springs from love for woman. . . . The longing for immortality is rooted in love for a woman, for it is here that the instinct for self-perpetuation triumphs over the instinct for mere self-preservation, substance thus triumphing over appearance. The longing for immortality leads us to love woman, and thus it was that Don Quixote found in Dulcinea both woman and glory, and since he could not perpetuate himself through her in a child of the flesh, he sought to make himself eternal through her in spiritual deeds . . . he engendered spiritual children in Dulcinea.[45]

42. *Vida de Don Quijote,* p. 136.

43. "Presentación," *Teresa,* p. 283. Although he did not have to die for her, Mohammed found his Dulcinea in the widow Kadijah who, being married, truly fulfilled the requirements of the courtly love convention; and, of course, Dante had his Beatrice. See Carlyle, *On Heroes,* pp. 53, 87.

44. Carlos Blanco Aguinaga, *El Unamuno contemplativo* (Mexico, 1959), p. 121.

45. *Vida de Don Quijote,* p. 133. See also the *Diario íntimo,* p. 112: "Virginity is the specifically Christian virtue (Harnack, II.10.5)." We are here faced with the question of the true place of eros in the heroic will. Plato says in *The Symposium:* "Those whose bodies alone are pregnant with

Woman is, above all else, a source of limited physical immortality, through her ability to bear children; but for the hero the great aim must be endless spiritual, as well as physical, immortality, and Dulcinea inspires Don Quixote's greatest conquests. The memory of himself which he will thus create is their spiritual child and a most noble and pure creation.

Unamuno at times considers heroism a substitute for having children, or at least a sublimation of that desire, which he believed to be universal. The timidity of the hero steers him away from carnal desires and he turns this urge into heroism. This is true of both Don Quixote and Rafael, about whom it is said: "His hunger was to learn and at the same time to produce. And not exactly for glory. Since he had not been able to have with Teresa children of flesh and blood and bone, he wanted to have children of the spirit, he wanted to immortalize himself, or rather immortalize his fleeting beloved; he wanted to make into marble what had been a cloud." [46] It is just as implicit in the actions of Don Quixote: "And since you did not succeed in overcoming yourself so as to give up your life by losing it in love, you longed to perpetuate yourself in the memory of mankind. Observe, my Knight, that the longing for immortality is but the flowering of the desire for lineage." [47]

It seems that in writing about Don Quixote Unamuno assumed

---

this principle of immortality are attracted by women, seeking through the production of children what they imagine to be happiness and immortality and an enduring remembrance; but those whose souls are far more pregnant than their bodies, conceive and produce that which is more suitable to the soul" (*Five Dialogues of Plato* [London, n.d.], p. 57). A provocative and highly relevant discussion of this very point is to be found in Rollo May, *Love and Will* (New York, 1969), pp. 77–81.

46. "Presentación," *Teresa*, p. 268.

47. Ibid., p. 137. Further discussion of this problem may be found in Armando Lázaro Ros, "Unamuno, filósofo existencialista," in Marjorie Grene, *El sentimiento trágico de la existencia* (Madrid, 1952), esp. pp. 270–74. See also the interpretation of Sigmund Freud, *An Introduction to Psychoanalysis* (New York, 1966): "We therefore have to conclude that the sexual impulse excitations are exceptionally 'plastic,' if I may use the word. One of them can step in place of another; if satisfaction of one is denied in reality, satisfaction of another can offer full recompense. . . . We call this process SUBLIMATION, by which we subscribe to the general standard which estimates social aims above sexual (ultimately selfish) aims" (p. 354). Thus it is that, had Aldonza responded to Alonso Quijano's love, he would perhaps never have become Don Quixote, nor she Dulcinea.

that many of the characteristics he noted in him were universally applicable, but remaining true to his dictum of ideas following life, he appears to have modified and clarified his concept of heroism as he further developed his philosophy at large and saw better how this concept could be reconciled with his broader notions. Thus we must approach with reservations anything said in the *Vida de Don Quijote y Sancho* that seems to be out of keeping with his later writings. The need for physical love was never denied, but it never again was advanced as being the true motive for heroism. The two were seen as different paths, with heroism being the more restricted.

In many aspects of heroism there is an interchange between elements which makes them interdependent. This is true especially of the hero and his followers, but also of the hero and his environment. It is this very tension between apparently contradictory values that gives Unamuno's philosophy its unity, and it reappears in the relationship between the hero and his beloved. We have seen that she is an image he has created and made part of his inner world so that he may project her outward, but we also know that this is what gives her her immortality. "To carry out my conquest I gave myself my kingdom, a city of God; / Not I, Teresa, the sight of you gave it to me; / We made the world between the two of us [Para llevar a cabo mi conquista / me di mi reino, una ciudad de Dios; / no yo, Teresa, me la dio tu vista; / nos hicimos el mundo entre los dos]." [48] The hero derives so much of his life from her that she — the image — acquires a validity of her own. Speaking of Don Quixote and Dulcinea (now separated from Aldonza, the shadow of external reality), Unamuno says: "He had created her, it is true, he had created her in pure faith, he had created her with the fire of his passion; but once she was created, she was herself, and he received his life from her. I forge my truth with my faith and against all others, but once it is forged, my truth has its own worth and will stand alone and will survive me, and I will live through it." [49]

This is, of course, the hero's reason for being. Dulcinea is, for Don Quixote, glory incarnate, his purpose from the very outset. For this reason all discussions about the existence of Aldonza Lorenzo as op-

48. *Teresa*, p. 58, vv. 17–20, O.C. 14: 374.
49. *Vida de Don Quijote*, p. 318.

posed to Don Quixote's vision of Dulcinea are of little importance. Dulcinea was his own creation: his vision and his goal. His was not a love designed to conquer her physically, but to permit him to lay his accomplishments at her feet. He did not ask that his love be returned, for this could, in fact, weaken his sacrifice. Unamuno says that Don Quixote's immortality emanating from the vision of Dulcinea is entirely due to his devotion, which desired no other prize than the glory that would come from having served an ideal nobly. She may, indeed, never even be aware of the inspiration that she offers, but that diminishes nothing, since she is nonetheless real for the hero: "I believe that there are Aldonza Lorenzos in the world who launch Alonso Quixanos upon the most unheard-of deeds, and who then die tranquilly and with a peaceful conscience, without having sensed the maternity that was theirs in such heroic exploits." [50] From the rudest materials spring both the hero and the inspiration, and this is the achievement of his will: to transform both himself and his inspiration into transcendental and imperishable good.

The Hero's Success

The hero is rejected by society and disdained by his beloved; he is ridiculed by the ignorant and at times viewed with suspicion even by his followers. He may be so outstanding that his madness seems absurd, yet through all this he can achieve immortality and glory because of his faith in himself and the inner world in which he sees his potentiality. To profit by the example that he offers us, we must, says Unamuno, do as Sancho does: "we must be ready to receive from his hand whatever he gives us, just so long as it relieves our needs." [51] Often our needs will not be what we think they are, and the hero's decision will reveal more wisdom than we could hope for.

Heroism is a difficult concept even for Unamuno. It is, like all things of consequence, a feeling, and to try to define it, as we have seen, forces us to run the risk of losing it entirely. It is a sort of mysticism, as we shall discover in the next chapter, and the parallels between the hero and the saint and between the hero and God become

50. Ibid., p. 138.
51. Ibid., p. 288.

ever more important in Unamuno's thinking, as he senses in himself an almost religious admiration for Don Quixote. Addressing himself to Sancho, he says: "What happens between you and your master, though on a finite and relative scale, is what happens between your master, you, me, and all mortals, and God, on an infinite and absolute scale: the more we sense the infinite distance that separates us from him, the closer we are to him, and the less we succeed in defining and picturing him, the better we know and love him." [52]

It is always a question of understanding and feeling the very essence of man. The inability to define the hero means that we are less dependent upon ideas and generalities and are closer to understanding the personality that permits us truly to know him. His madness is infectious, and the more confident we feel about him, the more closely we approach heroism ourselves, until ultimately the concept of madness will wither away altogether and leave heroism clearly in our minds: "And we have agreed that any madness ceases to be so as soon as it is the madness of an entire people, even perhaps of the whole human race." [53] For Don Quixote, immediate success lies in Sancho, who will perpetuate his master's ideals on earth. In actual fact, however, Don Quixote left a trail of heroism wherever he went, for even those who laughed at him accepted his existence to a certain degree. Whenever people pay attention, the hero is succeeding: "With laughter you carry them along behind you, admiring you and loving you." [54]

52. Ibid., pp. 285–86.
53. "El sepulcro de Don Quijote," *Vida,* p. 75. The warning in the *Cancionero* (no. 1536, 26-VIII-30) is clear: "And he is nothing more than crazy / who does not know himself to be comical."
54. *Vida de Don Quijote,* p. 175. The hero can always take courage from Carlyle's assertion that "No great man lives in vain." *On Heroes,* p. 29.

4. The Religion of Heroism: The Hero as Saint and Crusader

We have seen the principal motives for the hero's taking his place as a leader. Unamuno says that saints are moved by this same concern for the salvation of their fellow men, although the two ideals take different courses and, really, the intentions themselves are often dissimilar. Nevertheless, the parallels are striking because both types are visionaries. The hero has a clear concept of his duty as it corresponds to his place in history and he can therefore use his faith in himself and this duty to help his fellow men, even when they do not see their own needs as clearly as he does. The saint is not as concerned about the danger of oblivion but, like the hero, he is devoted to the elevation of man to reach God.

On the surface, then, both wish to devote themselves to the betterment of man so that he may become immortal, but we must beware, for the similarities are problematic and circumstantial, as we can see in Carlyle and Nietzsche, and Unamuno recognizes this danger, using the analogy specifically for its surface value. It supports his development of heroism (and it must be remembered that he was much more preoccupied with creating heroes than saints, who represented ideals about which he had far greater doubts) and serves as one step toward removing the theories from the realm of mere abstractions and giving them another concrete form in a slightly more dramatic context. Speaking of saintliness, Unamuno asks, "What is all this but divine or religious knight-errantry? And in the end, what were they all looking for, heroes and saints, but the possibility of surviving? The former in the memories of men, the latter in the bosom of God." [1] Saints are in many ways heroic, but their only hope for immortality is with God, and their concept of eternity is much more placid than that of Unamuno. So although he could not admire them as much as he could Don Quixote, who came to fill some of the gaps in his personal religious beliefs, he could at least admire their single-mindedness of purpose and, as in all things, take from their actions that which best suited him. The important distinction is that whereas saints consider God to be an absolute goal, the hero, in Unamuno's concept, views him as a good, less for what he may be in any concrete way, than for what he represents: the source and proof of all immortality. The hero is making an assault upon God in the hope that by making himself unforgettable (always in a positive sense) to mankind, he will have to be accepted as immortal by God too. Unamuno's hero builds his hope on both possibilities and uses human memory as his vehicle, while saints dedicate themselves to God alone as their ultimate objective.

As long as Unamuno has any doubts as to the existence of God, so must his heroes, and thus it is impossible for them to rely blindly on him. If "to believe is to want to believe," a supreme exercise of the will throughout a lifetime of striving, effort, and suffering can perhaps make God exist and thus give the hero his hope for salvation. For both saint and hero, then, success is largely, if not entirely, the triumph of volition over personal — human — limitations. The success of the hero, though, also depends upon his individual qualities to a far greater extent than does the success of the saint, whose actions necessarily lead him to a sort of divine mold: "The hero, formless, enormous, / we might say abnormal; / the saint always agreeable; / this is all that is true to form [El héroe informe, enorme, / vale decir anormal; / el santo siempre conforme; / es lo único formal]." [2]

The saint tries to gain immortality for himself and mankind by conforming to the will of God as he sees it in such a way that his very submissiveness may make him pleasing. The hero takes an opposite course: his uniqueness must, we have seen, make him

1. *Vida de Don Quijote,* p. 221.
2. *Cancionero,* no. 1042, Apr. 22, 1929.

indispensable. He alone can fulfill the need that he has spent his life creating, and he alone can gain immortality by actively opposing or rebelling against God. The saint gives what he can; the hero gives all he is — that is, all he may be: " 'I give what I am,' says the hero. 'I give myself,' says the saint." [3] The saint works for human betterment through direct improvement of and aid to those with whom he comes into contact. The hero works for betterment through self-improvement and the subsequent example of his own refusal to annihilate his ego.

Purity of intent is stressed time and again throughout Unamuno's writings, and the hero accepts other men on this basis: " 'I will help you in everything,' is what Don Quixote says to every man who is plain and free of ulterior motives." [4] This is also the criterion for religious salvation, as Unamuno shows in examples drawn, not only from the lives of saints, but also from the life of Christ himself. Saintliness, like heroism, is an exercise involving effort and action as well as contemplation and instinctive penetration, and neither element can be separated from its complementary aspect, for just as instinct requires the support of intelligence, action must be backed by reflection: "And it is pointless to ask whether mysticism is action or reflection, because it is active reflection and reflective action." [5] For this reason, Unamuno's admiration falls, not upon the stylites, but rather upon those saints whose beliefs — or more specifically, whose faith — led them to heroic actions, such as Saint Ignatius, creator of a militant order, or Saint Theresa, "divine Quixotess," [6] reformer of an order. He rejects accidental sainthood or heroism as absurd and feels that man can achieve either of these states only through fervent militancy: "He who is called an unconscious saint is nothing more than an imbecile, and he who is called an unconscious hero is a beast, and nothing more than a beast." [7] The

3. "¡Adentro!" O.C. 3: 427.
4. *Vida de Don Quijote*, p. 245. The same is said about God: "God does not discriminate among persons. He responds to all who seek him with their hearts and with righteous intentions." *Diario íntimo*, pp. 336–37.
5. *La agonía del cristianismo*, O.C. 16: 517.
6. "Irrequietum cor," vv. 5–6, *Rosario de sonetos líricos*, 118, O.C. 13: 629.
7. "La santidad inconciente," O.C. 9: 836. Evidently, however, the true saint is as difficult to recognize as the true hero: "If I knew a saint, I would surrender myself to him. And by what would I recognize a saint?" *Diario íntimo*, p. 268.

first duty of an agonizing man is to work in maximum consciousness.

These activists, like Don Quixote, do good partly for its own sake, but they also have other motivations that reveal their heroic qualities: "the saint is he who does good, not for the sake of it, but for God, to be made eternal." [8] This gives their efforts the necessary concrete goals to keep them from becoming mere abstractions. Sainthood is knight-errantry, but just as all knights-errant are not heroes, neither are all saints. It therefore becomes more apparent that heroism is not automatically accorded anyone, that it must be fought for and won, no matter what a man's mission.

Even sainthood requires an effort to conquer oblivion by creating a substantial existence that will justify immortality and prove the validity of the saintly man's doctrines: "Every heroic or saintly life was a hunt after glory, either temporal or eternal, earthly or heavenly. Do not believe those who tell you that they search for good for its own sake, with no hope of reward; if that were true, their souls would be like weightless bodies, purely apparential." [9] A saint can be forgotten just as easily as an ordinary man, and especially if he lives unto himself in pure contemplation. Heroism in sainthood is still a projection of the peculiar inner world of the individual onto his historical circumstances through the effort of his will. Mere conquest of the self for the benefit of the self is not enough, for it may wither unseen. Heroism lies not in being able to grow the fruit, but in knowing how to cultivate it so that it may propagate. Unamuno cannot accept the possibility that any effort, however small, can be made without some hope of perpetuation, rooted in a sincere love (or compassion) for one's fellow men and a dynamic desire for the continuance into eternity of one's beliefs. The good works of the heroic saint are reflected in mankind, improved by his faith and example. Not only is sainthood a sort of knight-errantry, but heroism is a sort of religion, since "this cult, not of death, but of immortality, is what starts and preserves religions." [10]

8. *Del sentimiento trágico,* O.C. 16: 416.

9. *Vida de Don Quijote,* p. 94.

10. *Del sentimiento trágico,* O.C. 16: 153. Carlyle supports such an idea when he asserts that "the thing a man does practically lay to heart, and know for certain, concerning his vital relations to this mysterious Universe, and his duty and destiny there, that is in all cases the primary thing for him, and creatively determines all the rest. That is his *religion.*" *On Heroes,* pp. 2–3. Clearly this could embrace saints and heroes.

Unamuno discovers appropriate symbolism when Don Quixote comes across the four religious images: it is a crossing of the two paths (pt. 2, chap. 58). Here the discussion becomes less a contrast of two ideals than a comparison of two types of saint, the celestial and the earthly. Unamuno insists throughout that it is no coincidence that many references to the closeness of sainthood and knighthood are made in Cervantes's novel. Indeed, we shall see that this is used as part of the case for the canonization of Don Quixote and his holy madness:

> The poor and ingenious gentleman did not seek either passing profit or bodily comfort, but rather eternal name and fame, placing his name above himself. He surrendered to his own idea, that of an eternal Don Quixote and the remembrance of him that might remain. "Whosoever loses his soul shall gain it," says Jesus; that is to say that he will gain his lost soul and not something else. Alonso Quijano lost his powers of judgment so he might find them in Don Quixote; a glorified judgment.[11]

Until now we have considered mainly the question of the earthly effects of heroism and their ultimate outcome upon the hero's immortality. This would seem at least to indicate that immortality is only coincidentally religious in nature. Throughout Unamuno's writings, though, it is clear that religion is anything in which faith triumphs: in other words, whenever man believes in the unseen, the unproven, the intuitive, or the instinctive. Heroism, like sainthood, *is* religion, and Don Quixote leads a no less godly life than Saint Ignatius merely because he chooses to reach the first cause through a closer association with worldly values. His faith and his intentions are no less sincere or grandiose, but he can reach a belief in God only through faith in himself. A prima facie case could be made for the hero as one with less grace, but this is not really relevant to Unamuno's theories. The hero's beliefs must simply take another direction because his mission is so different from that of the saint. He must appeal to another segment of humanity in order to bring out a different contribution from them. There is no room for a world of terrestrial heroes, but neither is there room for a world of saints. We are dealing with two quite distinct groups

11. *Vida de Don Quijote,* p. 89.

whose influence upon the masses is similarly inspired and similarly motivated, but no equation can be made between them.

Suffering and Purification

We know that the hero achieves his complete individuality partially because of his suffering, which is caused both by his fear for his own immortality and by his compassion for others. A greater capacity for suffering spurs the hero on to greater deeds than his fellow men, and Unamuno also adds that this even makes him more godly: "Man is the more man, that is, the more divine, the greater his capacity for suffering, or rather, for anguish." [12] Man is naturally divine, and heroism and sainthood are merely two ways of expressing or exercising this divinity, and of lessening the gap between man and God through faith and suffering. Unamuno sees Don Quixote as the "Knight of Faith" (*Caballero de la Fe*), whose sorrow and faith often push him on to saintly, idealized heroism: "and he plunged himself into the saintly resignation of action which, unlike Lot's wife, never turns its face to the past, but rather orients itself always to the future, that unique dominion of the ideal." [13] Suffering and faith in an unrealized potential against reason and apparential circumstance are what make him holy, and it is this eternal striving that makes heroism a religion for Unamuno.

Any religion is, in principle, a noble thing, and all that which elevates the spirit of man separates him from the beast. This is why Unamuno states that suffering is the truest indication of the difference between the two, for it is a gift unique to man and is, for that reason, rewarding, since "the anxieties of the angel are a thousand times more savory than the tranquillity of the beast." Unamuno further clarifies this progression toward the greatest expression of the innate divinity of man in *La agonía del cristianismo*, when he says: "The man who agonizes lives a constant struggle, a struggle against life itself. And against death. It is the essence of Saint Theresa's ejaculatory prayer: 'I die because I do not die.' "

12. *Del sentimiento trágico*, O.C. 16: 332. Cf. Carlyle: "Thought, true labour of any kind, highest virtue itself, is it not the daughter of Pain? . . . In all ways we are 'to become perfect through *suffering*.'" *On Heroes*, p. 92.
13. *Vida de Don Quijote*, p. 301.

This is the saintly aspiration toward eternity. It exemplifies the suffering of the religious mystic in his ascent to God, and Don Quixote, the exemplary hero, feels in his heroic religion the same desire for death as the gateway leading from oblivion and nothingness to immortality and salvation; but more important, he sees it as the escape from the fear of futility which pursues him throughout his earthly life: "'I, Sancho,' continued Don Quixote, 'was born to live dying, and you, to die eating.' What a pregnant sentence! Yes, every kind of heroism was born to live dying." [14] Unamuno cannot believe that the selfless dedication of the true hero to a cause that he believes just, to the betterment and maximum development of his divinely endowed capacities, and to the enlightenment and ennobling of his fellow man, can be any less saintly than a more orthodox, dogmatic religious orientation like that of Saint Theresa and Saint Ignatius.

Saintliness is, for Unamuno, the goodness inherent in the man. Sincerity to oneself for the benefit of all is the only just criterion, and it may manifest itself in innumerable ways, including saintliness, but the closeness of the hero to a deeply rooted concept of God is no less than that of the saint:

> The root of your craze for immortality, the root of your longing to live through unending centuries, the root of your desire not to die, was your goodness, my Don Quixote. The good man does not resign himself to being wasted, because he feels that his goodness is a part of God, of that God who is the God, not of the dead, but of the living, since all things live for him. Goodness is not afraid of either infinity or eternity: goodness recognizes that only a human soul perfects and fulfills itself; goodness knows that the realization of Good in the process of the species is a lie. [15]

Unamuno believes in divine inspiration directed at the individual in heroic actions. He does not believe that society automatically progresses and, although the hero is to a large extent an instrument of God, or at the very least, of a greater will, he is charged with the specific mission of recognizing the needs of his historical con-

14. Ibid., p. 219; *La agonía del cristianismo*, O.C. 16: 463; *Vida de Don Quijote*, p. 303.
15. Ibid., p. 350.

text so that he may strive to fulfill them. William James, however, in his essay "Great Men and Their Environment," states:

> The mutations of societies, then, from generation to generation, are in the main due directly or indirectly to the acts or the example of individuals whose genius was so adapted to the receptivities of the moment, or whose accidental position of authority was so critical that they became ferments, initiators of movement, setters of precedent or fashion, centers of corruption, or destroyers of other persons, whose gifts, had they had free play, would have led society in another direction.[16]

Unamuno considers only the positive aspects to be appropriate to heroism, whereas James considers the broader question of all those who influence society. This difference notwithstanding, the similarity between the two men's views is striking.

Madness

The hero's task is more basic than the saint's in that he ministers to spiritual needs on all levels and, in effect, prepares man to some degree for the work of the saint. His task is to awaken all facets of man's individuality, with his apparent madness as a chief weapon; because he is in contact with all aspects of man's personality and consciousness, he cannot be dismissed as easily as the saint. A man for whom religion is not a momentous option may remain largely indifferent to the saint's efforts, but only the man who denies his very ego can remain unaffected by the hero. He does not concern himself with souls in the normal transcendental sense alone, but rather with the chore of spurring his sluggish audience so that it may be prepared to understand the more abstract values through his example. As a ground-breaker he appears mad only to the spiritually retarded.

Unamuno has a deliberately imprecise concept that calls anything opposed to all apparential and expeditious reason, mad. Madness is, then, a social judgment and not a clinical one. It is madness precisely because it is unique, but he also says: "And isn't anyone

16. William James, The Will to Believe (New York, 1922), p. 227. This passage is marked in Unamuno's copy of the work.

mad who takes the world seriously? And shouldn't we all be mad?" [17]
This is a bold challenge which may strike us as being dangerously
simplistic, for it leaves heroism open to being interpreted as simple
idiocy, while at the same time making any sort of irrational anti-
social behavior desirable; but Unamuno makes a distinction between
madness and what we might more precisely term foolishness. Don
Quixote and, by extension, the hero in general, may be mad, but
he is never stupid or foolish, for heroism and simple-mindedness are
mutually exclusive. Referring to Don Quixote, Unamuno points
out, "He wasn't a fool who rushed off half-cocked, but a madman
who accepted the lessons of reality." [18] The hero creates his own
reality, but as an improvement upon the existing one, and is always
receptive to the demands of external reality as seen, inevitably, by
his followers. Even Saint Ignatius in his militancy had to adjust to
the "impurities of reality," and indeed the order he established was
outstanding for its vital awareness of its social and historical context.[19]

Segundo Serrano Poncela explains the success of Don Quixote's
madness by characterizing it as an imposition of substance on mere
appearance. This upsetting of traditional values spreads, however,
unlike the madness of other literary characters (such as Raskolnikov),
and with it spreads the religion of Quixotism, which converts it
into a way of life: "And by dint of living his madness without
rationalizing it, making of it a complete vital experience — since it is
a madness of ideals and not of realities — he manages to establish
confusion in the areas of sanity he passes through in such a way that
there is a moment in which madness appears to be sanity and sanity
appears to be madness." [20] This is, however, a house built on shift-
ing sand, for Don Quixote succeeds in proving that his madness has
validity and that it is thus as true as apparent sanity. Madness —
uniqueness — is important for true heroism, but it must be supple-

---

17. *Vida de Don Quijote,* p. 225. See also "Glosas al *Quijote,*" O.C. 5:
596: "strictly speaking, madmen can scarcely be distinguished from sane men,
except in the sense that the latter think the follies of the former, but neither
say them nor do them."

18. *Vida de Don Quijote,* p. 100.

19. Ibid., p. 98.

20. Serrano Poncela, *El pensamiento de Unamuno,* p. 252.

mented with an awareness of apparential reality so that the hero
can judge the needs he is to fill.

Unamuno supports this praise of madness with examples taken
from the Bible. Saint Paul and Don Quixote went mad for essentially the same reasons, he feels, and this is used as a very strong
argument: "Saint Paul, for the praetor Festus, was a maniac: so
many letters, so much reading, had turned his head, perhaps they
had even dried up his brain, just as books of chivalry had done to
Don Quixote." [21] Saint Paul achieved a greater degree of sainthood,
heroism, and thus immortality than Festus, largely because of his holy
madness, so the point needs no further elaboration; but Unamuno
does add that "the most divine madman was and still is Jesus
Christ." [22] This provides a parallel that will be crucial for Unamuno's
sanctification of Don Quixote as well as for his thesis that heroism
is sainthood. The similarity between Don Quixote and Christ is
mentioned many times in the body of his work, as the maximum
extension of the parallel between mystics and heroic visionaries.

Christ the Hero

Although there are some similarities between the idea of Christ
as hero and Carlyle's first stage of heroism, the hero as god, it is
here that Unamuno differs so radically from the concepts of heroic
endeavor set forth by Carlyle, Nietzsche, and James; for in spite
of the ever-recurring doubts that haunted him, too, he could not
deny great admiration for Christ and the extraordinary effort he embodied. Christ was a symbol and inspiration throughout Unamuno's
life, the unspeakable beyond the glory of Don Quixote — particularly
since not even he had been able to escape the visible horror of
death, and this in itself was serious food for thought. His admiration never appears more movingly than in *El Cristo de Velázquez*
(1920), a poem of heroic qualities in itself, a lyric expiation in which
Unamuno tries to come to grips with the mystery of the Son of

21. "Comentario," *Cómo se hace una novela*, p. 50. Referring to Saint
Paul, in the *Diario íntimo*, Unamuno says: "And if he were mad, it would
be the saintly madness of Christ. Would that he suffered it!" p. 123.
22. "Comentario," *Cómo se hace una novela*, p. 50.

God, Son of Man, whose influence on man's fulfillment reaches beyond all calculation and all temporal limits.

He admits with enthusiasm, speaking directly to Christ, "You have been our support and encouragement!" for his triumph over death and his immortality gave man a hope that should be all but inconceivable. The tortures and trials of his life were human yet resoundingly joyful in their final results which must illuminate all men, since "from you we learned, / divine Master of sorrow, sorrows / which give birth to hopes [de Ti aprendimos, / divino Maestro de dolor, dolores / que surten esperanzas]." Yet the mystery remains: he passed through much of what could also be expected of us, yet his reward was an unquestioned eternity. Immortalized in Velásquez's painting, in the mind of men, and in the memory of God, Christ's progression led him from being man to being God himself, yet at the price of constant earthly suffering. Man's agony may lead him to fulfillment, but the pains of Christ led to true divinity: "You needed, / to become more godly, to pass through the anguishes / of the death struggle [Te faltaba / para hacerte más dios pasar congojas / de tormento de muerte]." [23]

El Cristo de Velázquez shows toward Christ a startlingly similar admiration to that expressed toward Don Quixote in the *Vida de Don Quijote* some fifteen years earlier. The difficulties, the ridicule, the agonizing self-doubts, the loneliness and isolation were fundamental to both Christ and Don Quixote, and, in their way, both succeeded where Unamuno's reason would see only failure. It is for this reason that he cannot feel anything but contempt for Nietzsche's rejection of the example set by Christ, seeing in it petty jealousy: "When you could not be Christ you cursed / Christ, the archetypal superman." [24]

Unamuno will not make the same error, for he shows throughout the poem that he chooses to follow the path laid out by Christ — but altered to the realities he sees around him, without doctrine, dogma, or organization. Toward the end of his life he still showed that this feeling had not begun to evaporate, and in the *Cancionero* was able

23. *El Cristo de Velázquez*, pt. 3, no. 15, l. 1982, O.C. 13: 767; pt. 1, no. 13, ll. 429–31, p. 673; pt. 3, no. 6, ll. 1711–13, p. 751.
24. "A Nietzsche," vv. 1–2, *Rosario de sonetos líricos*, no. 100, O.C. 13: 611.

to declare: "You made me find myself, my Christ; / by the blessed grace of your Father / I am what I am: a God, an I, a man! [Tú me has hecho encontrarme, Cristo mío; / por la gracia bendita de tu Padre / soy lo que soy: un dios, un yo, un hombre!]"[25] His philosophy had certainly gained in candor over the last quarter century. All heroism can be found in Unamuno's vision of Christ, as in his vision of Don Quixote. Christ serves as a link between the humanity of Don Quixote and the divinity of God, and Unamuno feels that through Quixotism and its application to circumstances he will be saved. Every detail becomes a symbol for salvation, and the Cross itself represents the superiority of the will over mere nature: "For your cross is the stairway to glory / and the sure lever with which man, / if he has faith, moves the universe / from all the mountains [Que es tu cruz gradería de la gloria / y es la firme palanca con que el hombre / si tiene fe traslada el universo / de las montañas todas]."[26] It was through Don Quixote, however, rather than through Christianity, with its heavy social and cultural ramifications, that Unamuno chose to approach his objective, for Christ always remained enigmatic.

The Religion of Quixotism

Don Quixote's efforts are only slightly less notable and grandiose than those of Christ, and even the laughter he must continually suffer is only a test of his faith, just as it was for Christ: " 'Behold the man,' they jeered at Christ Our Lord: behold the madman, they will say of you, my Lord Don Quixote, and you will be *the* madman, the unique, The Madman."[27] The individuality of Don Quixote reaches heroic proportions in Unamuno's thought, because he did not have direct knowledge of God as Christ did, but only the human virtue of faith. His madness is analogous, however, to that of Christ. Traces of the analogy can be seen starting with the Evangelists — whose record of the life of Christ was similar to Cervantes's description of the life of Don Quixote — and extending down through the Spanish mystics — especially Saint Theresa,

25. *Cancionero*, no. 32, vv. 1–3.
26. *El Cristo de Velázquez*, pt. 1, no. 25, vv. 959–62, p. 706.
27. *Vida de Don Quijote*, p. 175.

whose commentaries parallel those of Unamuno on the life of Don
Quixote. Pierre Emmanuel even refers to Unamuno as "the Apostle
Paul of Quixotism." [28] To dispense with these parallels by calling Unamuno presumptuous is irrelevant and probably inaccurate.
Unamuno's admiration for and devotion to Don Quixote knew virtually no bounds, as he saw himself in a similar light throughout
the greater part of his life, particularly during his long years of
exile. Don Quixote represented, not only the earthly ideals in which
Unamuno believed so fervently, but also the immortality for which
he hungered so desperately. His personal hope, then, was un-
doubtedly reinforced by seeing Don Quixote as a lesser Christ and
himself as another Don Quixote.

Don Quixote's principal obstacle was that, because he was considered to be mad, he was ridiculed and often ignored, not only in
the novel of Cervantes, but also through centuries of Spanish
thought. Unamuno's concern was to show that his madness is not
necessarily a negative or detrimental characteristic if properly applied
to the problems of the moment. For this reason he leans heavily
upon the statement of Saint Theresa found in chapter 16 of her
Life: "And she hit upon heroic madness, and even said to her
confessor: 'I beg your worship to let us all be mad, out of love
for him whom they called mad for us.' " [29] Unamuno was a consummate rhetorician, and such treasures as these found in the Bible
and the writings or lives of the saints and mystics he particularly
admired could not be overlooked, as they gave far too much strength
to his case — especially since he was aiming the majority of his concepts regarding heroism in general, and Don Quixote in particular,
to his Spanish audience. He continually exalts Don Quixote by
means of religious parallels. Speaking of Cervantes's novel, he says
that it "ought to be the national Bible of Spain's patriotic religion." [30]

Even Don Quixote's adventures form certain parallels with those
of Christ, especially his first one, while still alone. At the first inn
he is met by two prostitutes, and their kindness overwhelms both
him and Unamuno, who cannot refrain from saying:

28. Pierre Emmanuel, "La philosophie quichottesque d'Unamuno," *Esprit*,
24 (1956): 345.
29. *Vida de Don Quijote*, p. 215.
30. "Sobre la lectura e interpretación del *Quijote*," O.C. 3:842.

Two whores turned into maidens by Don Quixote — oh, the power of redeeming madness! — were the first to serve him with disinterested affection.

> Never was there a knight
> By ladies so well served . . .

Remember Mary of Magdala washing and anointing the feet of the Lord and drying them for him with her hair, so often caressed in sin; that glorious Magdalene to whom Theresa of Jesus was so devoted.[31]

The conceptual link remains intact. Don Quixote, like Christ, ennobles all he meets when they approach him with purity of heart. He, too, wins converts by the strength of his individuality and the force of his example. Even his adventures in the home of the duke and duchess are seen as parallels to the passion of Christ, because he is tortured and humiliated by those he has come to save, and the actions that are true results of his madness are saintly, as Unamuno points out: "upon returning to his sublime madness, that is when he returned to the magnanimous purity of intent with which he purified the world, his world . . . that is when, by sanctifying his actions, he became a saint." [32]

Neither can the stylistic element be overlooked. Unamuno constantly uses such terms as "sublime," "saintly," and "heroic" when speaking of the madness of his exemplary hero, whose actions are usually considered to be purifying and the result of his innate goodness and purity of intent. He unfailingly puts the supposed madness into a context of justification so that the reader cannot doubt the value of Don Quixote's heroism — the result of his faith — or his saintliness — the result of his goodness and childlike innocence. In his individualistic style he begs the question for his readers by crying: "Oh Don Quixote, my Saint Quixote! Yes, we sane men canonize your mad actions." [33] For Unamuno, then, all those who fully recognize Don Quixote's heroism and consequent saintliness must canonize him as he does. See, for example, the essay "San Quijote de la Mancha" (1923), where Unamuno says: "And we

31. *Vida de Don Quijote*, p. 95.
32. "Quijotismo," O.C. 5: 709.
33. *Vida de Don Quijote*, p. 258.

are going to undertake a campaign to canonize Don Quixote, making him Saint Quixote of La Mancha." [34]

But there is even more, for Unamuno is not one to satisfy himself with half measures. Don Quixote does not merely share certain parallels with Christ, he is the religio-heroic example for the entire Spanish race:

> And there is a figure, a comically tragic figure, a figure in whom we see everything that is profoundly tragic in the human comedy, the figure of Our Lord Don Quixote, the Spanish Christ, who summarizes and includes within himself the immortal soul of this my people. Perhaps the passion and death of the Knight of the Sorrowful Countenance is the passion and death of the Spanish people. Its death and its resurrection. There is now a Quixotic philosophy and even a metaphysics, and also a Quixotic logic and ethics, and a Quixotic religious sense — the Spanish Catholic religious sense. [35]

This is the apotheosis of the hero. We have seen that the hero should limit himself geographically in order to do his greatest deeds: just as Christ limited himself, Don Quixote should never have left his native La Mancha, for his defeat came in Barcelona. Nevertheless, although primarily Spanish, his example transcends all geography and can serve to illuminate all lives through all time. There is not, as we can see from the above passage, any conflict for Unamuno between this and orthodox Catholicism, just as there is none between the mission of the hero and that of the saint. They are complementary facets of a similar endeavor and can be mutually beneficial.

There are also innumerable comparisons drawn between the personality and actions of Don Quixote and those of Saint Ignatius of Loyola, all of which are intended to demonstrate that the two types of hero partake of similar character traits. These are particularly useful in illustrating the similarities between the monastic

---

34. "San Quijote de la Mancha," O.C. 16: 860.
35. *Del sentimiento trágico*, O.C. 16: 418. We should remember that the importance of such a concept is underscored by Carlyle's comment: "It is well said, in every sense, that a man's religion is the chief fact with regard to him. A man's or a nation of men's" (*On Heroes*, p. 2). The choice of hero reflects this fact.

vows of the Jesuits and certain of the heroic ideals. In his order, Saint Ignatius instituted the vows of poverty, chastity, and obedience, all of which were dutifully observed by Don Quixote, who, of course, shows an astounding disregard for his own material needs. This is a two-sided question, though, for on the one hand Unamuno states that this semivoluntary poverty, for example, is in itself heroic because "The most terrible enemy of heroism is the shame of appearing poor . . . to have to fulfill a rôle in the world while being poor!" [36] It is undignified to have to mend one's stockings in order to maintain a façade of well-being, but it also shows strength of character as another triumph of personality over circumstances. After all, "few things elevate Don Quixote more than his scorn for worldly wealth." [37]

The symbolism is appealing, for it reveals the hero to be concerned almost exclusively with things of the spirit, with his ideals, while making minimal concessions to social reality, thus proving his awareness of the true place of the individual. Such an attitude is also worthy of admiration because it inspires in the hero values similar to those of the saint. Of Don Quixote, Unamuno says: "Poverty made him love life, separating him from all satiety and nourishing him with hopes, and idleness must have caused him to think about never-ending life, about the disturbing life." [38] We have already seen that the staple diet of the hero is a never-dying hope, fed by deprivation.

Unamuno also reminds us that Don Quixote is chaste, as is his love for Dulcinea. Just as poverty stimulates heroism, so then may unrequited love: "Only unhappy loves are fertile in fruits of the spirit; only when love has its natural and usual course blocked does it spring like a fountain toward heaven; only temporal sterility gives eternal fertility." [39] We have seen the possibility that Don Quixote's heroism may be an outlet for the frustration of his amorous longings;

36. *Vida de Don Quijote*, p. 271. Carlyle sees no shame in poverty: "for a genuine man, it is no evil to be poor" (*On Heroes*, p. 166). His comments about Mohammed offer a striking parallel with Don Quixote: "They record with just pride that he would mend his own shoes, patch his own cloak" (ibid., p. 71).
37. *Vida de Don Quijote*, p. 117.
38. Ibid., p. 86.
39. Ibid., p. 138.

and the parallel with monastic vows is further emphasized when
Unamuno asserts that "one must save one's virility in order to engender children of the spirit." [40] All of this reaches its fullness
within the scope of the hero's obedience to his God.

This provides for the one great reality which alone is clear and
unmistakable and of which conscious man spends all his life being
aware. Some merely prepare for it (the saint), while others live
so that they do not merit it (the hero). This reality is, of course,
death. It cannot be repeated, and yet when it does occur there is
no doubt about it. Therefore, it is only natural that Unamuno should
be tempted to compare the death of Saint Ignatius with that of his
more earthly counterpart, Don Quixote: "Iñigo died as Don Quixote
had to do fifty years later, simply, without histrionics, without gathering people around his deathbed, and without making a spectacle of
death. This is how real saints and real heroes die, almost as animals
do: lying down to die." [41] His admiration is not for the quiet surroundings of a death in bed — it would seem likely that a hero
could also die in action — but rather for the fact that the true hero
dies with strength, dignity, and the confidence that have been his
throughout his life. If he was truly heroic in life, posterity and
God will recognize the loss — and that is the point. Heroism also
lies in knowing when *not* to act.

Solitude

In chapter 2 we touched upon the need for solitude in heroic
development, but solitude's contemplative and monastic elements
also give it a strong religious implication. We can see how it not
only brings the hero closer to mankind, but how it also strengthens
his bond with God. Christ said that those who followed him would
have to renounce all other relationships in order to devote themselves entirely to their mission with him, and Unamuno feels this
is also the doctrine of Don Quixote, since both he and Sancho are
solitary beings.

Like the saint, those who follow the heroic path must be alone.

40. *La agonía del cristianismo*, O.C. 16: 502.
41. *Vida de Don Quijote*, p. 354.

First, because it is imposed upon them from without — by society in its rejection of the hero, and by God — but also because the hero must voluntarily impose solitude upon himself so that he may have the essential opportunity of constantly reassessing his position, to be assured of its continued validity. The solitude imposed by society, by those who do not understand the hero or who feel somewhat removed from his aims is, then, just the first step. It is only a suggestion of the solitude he must eventually endure: "You are alone, much more alone than you think, and even so, you are just on the way to absolute, complete, true solitude." Unamuno goes on to explain that the hero must divest himself of all distractions (such as family and close friends, as well as the bad advice of any- one who does not understand) and approach his mission with absolute clarity and as little passion as possible so that he may be sure that he is not blinding himself. He must separate himself completely: "Absolute, complete, true solitude consists of not being even with oneself. And you will not be completely and absolutely alone until you shed your very self, on the edge of the grave. Saintly solitude!" [42] Human ties must be severed and he must look deep into his heart and communicate with his faith. This is the loneliness of the hero, but it is only apparential.

All heroes are alone, but independently they are working for similar goals and are united by their very solitude. It is here that we see how Unamuno views the hero as crusader. If heroism is a religion with a deep faith, it is also something that must be fought for: "Each one will think that he is going alone, but you will form a sacred battalion: the battalion of the holy and never-ending cru- sade." [43] From the awareness of a spiritual unity with others who believe in themselves and their faith as the only reliable source of self-extension, the hero derives much of his strength.

This unity among the solitary is difficult to overemphasize, for Unamuno feels it is a bond the roots of which run far deeper than the mediocre might expect. The hero alone knows what his task is: humanity at large is quite incapable of understanding it. Therefore,

42. "El sepulcro de Don Quijote," *Vida*, p. 82; Nietzsche's Zarathustra returns to the solitude of his cave after the disappointment of each journey among men.
43. Ibid., p. 81.

although they partially force solitude upon him, they also tend to misjudge its true value, just as they cannot estimate the true value of the hero himself: "It is a great and terrible thing that the hero is the only one who sees his heroic qualities from within, in his very depths, and that the rest see it only from without, on the surface. This is what makes the hero live alone in the midst of men and what makes this solitude of his serve him as comforting companionship." [44] All heroes feel similarly, and from this much of the salvation of mankind will come, since their power stems, as we have seen, from the depths of their own consciousness, and they alone are privy to the inspiration required: "no one understands anyone else better than solitary men understand each other. The crowning point of a good intelligence is a real monastery. And that is because their unity is born of themselves and is a brotherhood, and they are not united, like average men, by an external power." [45] This relationship between the solitary hero and the masses brings us to a seemingly paradoxical situation. Although Unamuno frequently stresses the need for solitude, he adds that it must always be coupled with constant contact with mankind in general, lest the hero, because of his individualistic and even incendiary ideals, find himself irretrievably severed from those he is to serve. He must, however, at the same time take advantage of the situation in order to plumb the depths of his own soul and continually reaffirm his faith.

Because the true hero is, in many ways, saintly, to be forced to deal with seemingly base material may seem like a lessening of his own grandeur, although in fact it is his very purpose. There is no room for vanity, for his two tragedies are his unrecognized greatness and his concomitant isolation: "And if the man who locks himself up — or rather, who is locked up — in a monastery is tragic, the monk of the spirit, the recluse who has to live in the world is even more tragic." Unamuno admits that "only the hermit approaches the ideal of the individualistic life," [46] but pure individual-

44. *Vida de Don Quijote*, p. 108.

45. "Fecundidad del aislamiento," O.C. 9: 84–85. See also "Solitario y desesperado," O.C. 10: 948–51. Cf. Carlyle, "Only in a world of sincere men is unity possible; — and there, in the long run, it is as good as *certain*." *On Heroes*, p. 125.

46. *La agonía del cristianismo*, O.C. 16: 521; 520.

ism without that vital contact with the society for whose salvation he is striving is not heroism.

Don Quixote lived very much among men, yet he cured himself of the afflictions of the world by retiring to the Sierra Morena so that he could strip himself to his barest soul and find strength. "To the spring of lost health / to the country, run, beneath the open sky, / to purge yourself of stimulants / which hold you trapped in their spells [Al manantial de la salud perdida / al campo corre, bajo el cielo abierto, / a purgarte de especias incitantes / que en tus hechizos te mantienen preso]." He is joined, nevertheless, by all other heroes in a spiritual union, each carrying with him his personal audience, and so he never allows himself to lose touch with the needs of individuals. Because of the profit man derives from this contact, Unamuno can say: "The greatest of solitary men have been, in fact, those who have most widely spread their spirits among men: the most sociable ones." The paradox, then, is only apparent, for we find that "only in solitude can you know yourself as a neighbor; and until you know yourself as a neighbor you cannot manage to see in your neighbors, other I's." [47]

We have come full circle. The hero must create his own example and at the same time show a sympathy in individual intercourse that is the basis, not only for heroism, but also for sainthood. Love is the unifying force for both, which leads them to the same conclusion: "from this love or compassion for yourself, from this intense desperation, . . . you pass to suffering with — that is, to loving — all those like you, brothers in apparentiality, unhappy shadows who pass from nothingness to nothingness, sparks of consciousness who shine for a moment in the infinite and eternal darkness." [48] This could be applied with equal aptness to either the doctrine of heroism or that of sainthood, for their paths are often parallel.

More specifically, however, what does the solitary man, be he hero or saint, discover in such lonely contemplation? The communication across a silence of brothers in the spirit gives man a deeper aware-

47. "Al campo" (1899), vv. 33–36, *Poesías sueltas*, O.C. 14: 684. Christ, Zarathustra, and Mohammed also separated themselves from the confusion of society. See Carlyle, *On Heroes*, p. 55; "Soledad," O.C. 3:900, 882.
48. *Del sentimiento trágico*, O.C. 16: 266.

ness of unity than he could achieve in the midst of the chaos of the masses, for it reveals to him an aspect of his being that would otherwise be hidden: "In isolation one finds in oneself not the primitive, prehistoric, or troglodytic man, since this man springs from the mass and is himself mass, but rather the new man, man himself." [49] He finds the most important setting for his individuality. The mediocre man is incapable of enduring such solitude, but the heroes are then most truly themselves and are able to reach each other internally, substantially, not through appearances alone: "Only in solitude does that thick layer of decorousness which isolates us from each other fall away; only in solitude do we find ourselves; and by finding ourselves, we find in ourselves all our brothers in solitude." [50] This is man demasked; this is the "holy battalion" that makes up the crusade.

From this monastic atmosphere comes militancy, for, like Zarathustra, the hero must now begin his down-going. There is no scorn, since he is searching for followers in his crusade, but there is vigor in his approach: "The solitary man, far from disdaining other men, seems to be saying to them: 'Be men!' He who insults a crowd is usually offering a tribute to each one of those who make up the crowd." [51] Unamuno himself spent his life provoking those he addressed in the belief that only anger can awaken the masses. In a speech delivered on April 12, 1931, during his attacks on the monarchy, he exhorted the crowd: "And now, a great deal of serenity and tranquillity; above all, let us be men! Let us not bow down before powers that lack authority." [52] The hero must do the

49. "Fecundidad del aislamiento," O.C. 9: 83.
50. "Soledad," O.C. 3: 882. Unamuno himself felt he lived in a sort of solitude that brought about his best work. In a letter to Joan Maragall, dated February 15, 1907, he says, "In your last letter you spoke to me of my campaign tent. Yes, in my life of struggle and fighting, in my life as a bedouin of the spirit, I have my campaign tent pitched in the middle of the desert. And there I withdraw and find peace. And there I am restored by the sight of my wife who brings me the breezes of childhood." Quoted by Manuel García Blanco in "Prólogo," O.C. 14: 92. Darío, in his article, "Unamuno poeta" (O.C. 14: 260), feels that Unamuno's very poetry is also his solitude.
51. Ibid., p. 897.
52. Quoted by Salcedo, *Vida de don Miguel*, pp. 335–36. Zarathustra's exhortation was, of course, quite different: "I teach you the Superman. Man is something that should be overcome. What have you done to overcome him?" Nietzsche, p. 41

same, and it is here that Unamuno tends at times to show the influence of the social determinists of the nineteenth century. He says, for example: "Heroes are those who live and fight and lead their people into battle, and sustain them in it. They are no less real and alive than those of flesh and blood, tangible and perishable." [53]

The hero must be militant and be carried on the shoulders of his followers; he must be prepared not only to anger for his cause, but also to astound; for he must have attention, he must never be ignored. He is in search of those who, by dint of their own individuality, are also looking for a means of expression, equally individualistic and imaginative. "Do you not think, my friend, that there are out there many solitary souls whose hearts are asking for some outrage, something that will make them burst?" [54] It is a romantic force that will mobilize a people. The crusade uses as its principal weapon "saintly madness," and is set against all the elements in man's existence that suggest or are linked to death or stagnation, for the crusade aims to conquer immortality itself. Its enemies, then, are "death's brothers in this life: apathy, sleep, unconsciousness, and peace." [55] The crusaders are hermits and monks in spirit who join with their own kind for the profit of mankind. It is indeed a religious war, the spirit of which is best conveyed in the following lines:

> Saddle up Clavileño for me,
> gentle shadow of Cervantes;
> I am going in search of the giants
> of the islands of sleep.
> Together on him rode
> Don Quixote and Sancho Panza;
> together with the same hope
> they embraced each other.
> Together the two of them, knights
> of wood, wood from the Cross,
> blindfolded saw the light
> of true dreams.

53. "El caballero de la triste figura," O.C. 3: 373.
54. "El sepulcro de Don Quijote," *Vida*, p. 76. Silence and secrecy earn few converts, for "The idea imprisoned within the glass / of logical husk / does not give the people food / to sustain them in the struggle." "La flor tronchada," vv. 55–58, O.C. 13: 269.
55. Blanco Aguinaga, *El Unamuno contemplativo*, p. 25.

Blindfold for me Spain's sight
and saddle up your machinery for me;
I am off to my last refuge,
I am off to my last conquest.

[Ensíllame a Clavileño
tierna sombra de Cervantes;
voy a buscar los gigantes
de las ínsulas del sueño.
Juntos en él cabalgaron
Don Quijote y Sancho Panza;
sobre la misma esperanza
juntos los dos se abrazaron.
Juntos los dos, caballeros
de leño, leño de cruz,
vendados vieron la luz
de los sueños verdaderos.
Véndame a España la vista
y ensíllame tu artilugio;
voy a mi último refugio,
voy a mi última conquista.] [56]

Faith and the Heroic Will

All heroism ultimately stems from a boundless faith, which Unamuno longs for and encourages in others throughout his writings. Don Quixote is the "Knight of Faith." His heroism is nourished by his faith in all aspects of his being and, according to Unamuno, this is all that anyone who would be heroic needs; it will be his strength: "Let your faith suffice. Your faith will be your art, your faith will be your science." [57] Life is action and action leads to faith. The examples that life presents will clarify the hero's concept of himself so that he may formulate a faith capable of sustaining

56. *Cancionero*, no. 1207, Aug. 4, 1929. Cf. Laín Entralgo: "human life . . . never stops being a question of living together, not even in the apparent solitude of the solitary or isolated man. . . . To whom other than God, supreme You, absolute You, is the voice of the desperate man directed, even though he may not know it, or even though in his soul he feels only the emptiness of God?" *La espera y la esperanza*, p. 385.
57. *Vida de Don Quijote*, p. 80.

him: "seek your life, for if you soak yourself in your life, with it, faith will enter into you." [58] Once again, he flees the abstraction and shows that, for him, and for the heroic, faith must be a concrete ideal. As Pierre Emmanuel explains, "The wages of faith is hope." [59] Once attained, it serves as protection from the forces that oppose heroic efforts or ridicule holy madness, for:

> To want — to believe — to be able; such is the holy
> procession which gives support to effort,
> between the "I want" and the "I can" of cement
> is forged the faith which shines on the hero.

> [Querer — creer — poder; tal es la santa
> procesión que al esfuerzo da sustento,
> entre el quiero y el puedo de cemento
> hace la fe que al héroe abrillanta.] [60]

Don Quixote, in his madness, projected his inner world outward and sincerely believed in it. It was his faith in it that convinced Sancho and won them both immortality and, for Unamuno, this is the proof of the strength of a sincere faith: "he believed to be truth what is only beauty. And he believed it with living faith, with the faith that gives birth to actions, and he decided to put into effect what his folly revealed to him, and by sheer belief he made it true." [61] If his madness combined with his faith gave rise to great deeds that impressed his memory upon the eternal mind of mankind, how can we say that he was wrong? Three of the principal sources for Unamuno's inspiration are Don Quixote, Shakespeare, and Calderón, because they were all conscious of the deeper aspects of the perception of external reality. Faith and dreams are similar in their power to create action and to project that inner world:

58. "La fe," O.C. 16: 100. Cf. Laín Entralgo: "This express and constant linking of believing with hoping determines the two cardinal points of the Unamunian concept of faith: its essential projection toward the future and its supposed virtue of creativity. To believe is, finally, to have faith in a person." La espera y la esperanza, p. 390.

59. Pierre Emmanuel, "La philosophie quichottesque d'Unamuno," p. 348.

60. "Fe," vv. 5–8, O.C. 13: 468. Cf. "Faith is trust before and above all else." "La fe," O.C. 16: 99.

61. Vida de Don Quijote, p. 88. A few years earlier, Unamuno had declared, "Give me faith, my God, for if I succeed in having faith in another life, it is because it exists." Diario íntimo, p. 35.

Compare Segismundo with Don Quixote, two dreamers of life. Reality in the life of Don Quixote was not the windmills, but the giants. The windmills were phenomenal, apparential; the giants were noumenal, substantial. The dream is what is life, reality, creation. Faith itself, according to Saint Paul, is just the substance of those things that are hoped for. And faith is the fountainhead of reality, because it is life. To believe is to create.[62]

If Don Quixote's sublime visions could give birth to specific results beneficial to humanity, they were as real as the visions of the mystics and more real than the abstract a priori assumptions of Sancho and other rational men. Faith, by its very nature, is opposed to pure reason. It is, according to Unamuno, an act of the will; and William James says: "The essential achievement of the will, in short, when it is most 'voluntary,' is to ATTEND to a difficult object and hold it fast before the mind." [63] This is certainly true of the heroic will, for we know that the hero must be obsessed in order to be able to continue with his mission. Unamuno says of Don Quixote's faith: "In sustaining that fight between heart and head, between feeling and intelligence, and in making the former say 'Yes!' while the latter says 'No!' and 'No!' when the other says 'Yes!' — in this, and not in making them agree, consists fertile and saving faith. At least for the Sanchos. And even for the Quixotes." [64] Faith is, then, not merely the predominance of instinct over intelligence, but actually the triumph of one over the other. (Once more we see the parallels with Kierkegaard and Bergson.) Faith cannot be acquired without an exercise of the will, and it is thus that Don Quixote succeeded in convincing himself and others of the truth of his visions.

As the development of the ego is a volitive process, so too is the winning of followers who come to believe in a hero's particular inner world. James seems to feel that faith based upon the will is as

---

62. "Prólogo," *Tres novelas ejemplares y un prólogo,* O.C. 9: 418.
63. William James, "The Will," *Selected Papers,* p. 69.
64. *Vida de Don Quijote,* p. 225. Unamuno has marked the following passage from James in red: "Faith means belief in something concerning which doubt is still theoretically possible; and as the test of belief is willingness to act, one may say that faith is the readiness to act in a cause the prosperous issue of which is not certified to us in advance." *The Will to Believe,* p. 90.

justifiable as a more empirical type of faith, as long as it involves what Unamuno would call one's mission: "In truths dependent on our personal action, then, faith based on desire is certainly a lawful and possibly an indispensable thing." [65] The hero, however, holds no magical powers. He cannot, by strength of his will, cause another man to achieve his mission, but he can motivate him to do it. Therefore he can use his faith, based upon desire, to reach his own fulfillment and can offer it as an example, or what James calls a "living option," for others to follow. Then it rests with their own wills to decide whether they will accept it. The hero's faith can reach to the edge of his potential follower's faith in the hope that the spark will be transmitted, but the two faiths do not overlap: the hero cannot have faith for two.

The faith he does have, however, makes him all but invulnerable. Benardete says, "Faith is protection against the opposition forces that ridicule." [66] If, as we have seen, it is the result of sincere self-examination, it justifies all the hero's actions, because the intention with which they were carried out negates the apparentiality of the result, which may not truly reflect the intention: "He who has the law lodged in his heart is above the law dictated by men." [67] When Don Quixote is in danger of being arrested for having released the galley-slaves, for example, he resists, confident of the justness of his actions (pt. 1, chap. 45). Unamuno cries out gleefully: "Bravo, my Lord Don Quixote, bravo! The law was not made for you, nor for those of us who believe in you: our statutes are our will." [68] While reasonable men may be tempted to question the social wisdom of such anarchic actions, Unamuno feels that if all men conducted themselves according to their hearts, society would not harbor fears of people like Don Quixote. All men desire the good, but they must have knowledge to guide them. Self-deception is the social enemy.

This self-assurance, this feeling of invulnerability, of course permits the hero to view anything without alarm. He feels confident

65. James, "The Will," p. 25.
66. Benardete, "Personalidad e individualidad en Unamuno," p. 32.
67. *Vida de Don Quijote*, p. 123. Indeed, as Unamuno points out in a letter to Joaquín Maurín, dated January 4, 1918: "One must light the cult of sincerity and even of indiscretion. Freedom of conscience. He is free who knows the law by which he is governed." *La Torre*, 1, no. 2 (1952): 189.
68. *Vida de Don Quijote*, p. 200.

his faith will see him through, since "faith is the creative power of man," and conquers all personality weaknesses by pointing directly to the ideal, the fulfillment of the mission. In chapter 2 we saw that the hero can never know any satisfaction and that Unamuno's concept of faith, which is an active pursuit and therefore a sort of tension, is directly related to this tragic feeling: "Faith feeds on the ideal and only on the ideal, but on a real, concrete, living, incarnate, and at the same time inaccessible ideal; faith seeks the impossible, the absolute, the infinite, and the eternal: the full life." Meyer further clarifies this idea by saying: "It aims at the *ideal,* which, in essence, is not and *cannot be;* its categories are neither those of the real nor even those of the possible . . . but rather the category of wanting to be and of having to be." Faith, then, is not a concept intended to lull but to agitate, because the very nature of the heroic mission is always to seek more. Only by having faith in his ability to strive continually can the hero fight death. Effort always renews itself in the hero's existence, pushing him constantly onward, and faith itself is ultimately aimed at humanity so that it, too, is in a state of constant renewal and revitalization in its capacity to generate compassion for other men: "For such is the condition of living faith: it grows by being poured out and by being dispersed it grows. Since it is, when true and alive, love!" That is to say, it, too, is an extension of the ego toward others, and just like all other elements in the existence of the hero, it is in tension. It is a bridge between the hero and his follower, for they have faith not only in themselves, but in each other: its only justification is a human one, and it can be maintained as long as the human objective is kept alive in the hero's impulse. It is one of the highest exercises of the will, for "faith is, above all, sincerity, tolerance, and mercy." [69]

Inevitably, tolerance is an important aspect of faith, for it reveals a quid pro quo attitude that implicitly recognizes another's individuality. Unamuno points out that diversity has not necessarily meant division since the earliest days of the Christian church, and that although two men have distinct faiths, they need not enter into active and mutually destructive opposition. The hero must never

---

69. *Del sentimiento trágico,* O.C. 16: 319; "La fe," O.C. 16: 100; Meyer, *La ontología de Miguel de Unamuno,* p. 115; *Vida de Don Quijote,* p. 114; "La fe," O.C. 16: 112.

believe that his is the only valid faith — only that it is still the best for him. He must retain an open mind so as to benefit from the example of others, just as they may profit by his. Unamuno counsels his readers: "But do not condemn any faith when it is spontaneous and artless, even if it finds itself forced to take on shapes that deform it. All faith is sacred." [70] Just as the right to believe is sacred, so is the right to differ, especially when put into the proper perspective. Nevertheless, Unamuno sees two types of faith, *pistis* and *gnosis*.[71] The first may be called live faith — hope — whereas the second is frank conviction — doctrine, dogma. Needless to say, he prefers the former, considering it a younger and more fruitful idea, as it makes the mind receptive to new aspects, and he feels that from the times of early Christianity to the present day it is essentially what links diverse Christian faiths. The true hero and the heroic saint hold a dynamic faith, and it is this type of faith that Unamuno feels provides a more liberal justification and a deep sense of mission, because it is more flexible yet exists within realistic limits.

This avoidance of doctrine is characteristic of Unamuno, who feels that it is as essential for the hero to doubt as it is for him to have faith. Doubt, thought, has to be limited, for the genuine hero cannot really err; radical about-faces are not necessary for him who has kept in direct touch with the needs of his audience. We know, though, that the very tension of faith holds the hero in a state of suspension between dogmatism and doubt. This is essential to keeping his faith active, since "a faith which does not doubt is a dead faith." [72] Doubt is, as Descartes recognized, an indication of existence and proof that the hero has not sunk into complacency; he must care even to doubt. This is an exercise of the will and, as such, an indication of his capacity to believe truly: "only those who doubt really believe, and those who do not doubt and feel no temptations which go against their faith do not really believe. . . . Faith is maintained by resolving doubts and by again resolving those which have arisen from the resolution of previous doubts." [73] Doubt is,

70. "La fe," O.C. 16: 109.
71. Ibid., p. 102.
72. *La agonía del cristianismo*, O.C. 16: 468. Cf. "Life is doubt, / and faith without doubt is only death. / And death is the support of life, / and doubt, of faith." "Salmo II," vv. 22–25, O.C. 13: 287.
73. *Vida de Don Quijote*, p. 224.

at the very least, an indication of awareness. It shows a resistance to spiritual blindness and keeps the hero pure in his actions. If faith is never tested, it becomes complacency and gnosis, knowledge or dogma. It must find itself constantly shaken and reaffirmed in order to be constantly a source and impulse for the projection of the hero's peculiar inner world. As long as he is subject to questioning even his most basic values, the hero is sincere: "He who affirms his faith on a basis of uncertainty does not and cannot lie." [74] As long as he can be assured of his faith, he can also maintain hope: "And our faith is built and rests/ upon hope,/ and our faith is just hope [Ye se construye nuestra fe y estriba/ sobre esperanza,/ y es esperanza nuestra fe tan sólo]." [75] Nevertheless, to maintain his heroism he must always work with some measure of conviction, for as Carlyle said: "when Belief waxes uncertain, Practice too becomes unsound." [76]

Unamuno sees all these elements — faith, doubt, suffering, re-affirmation, fear, and despair — as part of the same question. The hero spends his entire existence passing through all these over and over again, while his faith in the possibility of immortality becomes ever more secure. Unamuno offers consolation by saying that faith surmounts all the obstacles of this life with the promise of ever greater fulfillment: "Do not get angry over what may happen to you in this apparential world; wait for the substantial world or hold on to it, in the depths of your madness. That is the profound and true faith." [77] The religious coloring is clear. The hero must have faith that all his efforts lead somewhere, and in fact that they are directed or inspired by a conscience more enlightened than his, how-ever great his own extension and fulfillment. Faith, like heroism it-self, is a special ability; however fundamental the need for the will, it alone and untapped cannot suffice, although without it faith is impossible: "Faith is not held by he who wants to have it, but by he who can; that one to whom his life gives it, because faith is a

74. Del sentimiento trágico, O.C. 16: 324.
75. "La esperanza," vv. 22–24, O.C. 14: 801. See also "Salutación a los rifeños," vv. 176–78, O.C. 14: 799; "Ateísmo," vv. 9–14, O.C. 13: 569; Cancionero, no. 959.
76. Carlyle, On Heroes, p. 118.
77. Vida de Don Quijote, p. 147.

living gift and divine grace, if you will." [78] For a moment, Unamuno seems to teeter on the edge of orthodoxy, but although he admits the possibility of grace, in that faith is bestowed by a divine hand, one must remember that so is the heroic mission itself, and that the two are inseparable. The mission gives the individual the opportunity actively to extend himself, and from this active extension comes his faith. It, too, must be developed even though the seeds have been planted from without.

God and the Hero

This brings us to the unique relationship between the hero and his God, for it is now clear that he enjoys a sort of personal communion with God. A great deal of energy has been expended on the question of whether Unamuno believed in God in the conventional sense. Much of his thinking in this regard is the outgrowth of his reading of Kierkegaard in 1900 and 1901, when the question of immortality had become more critical for him than at any time before the crisis of 1897 and his questioning became a vital part of his agony. According to many, Unamuno simply did not believe. This is to overlook or even to deny the very fiber of his philosophy, for he dedicated himself to writing and formulating theories *as if* God existed and *as if* he himself believed in him. This was later to be the lesson of *San Manuel Bueno, mártir,* because some concept of God pushed him forward and was always a momentous option for him. Sánchez Barbudo says: "The greatest falsehood consists in calling 'God' what was only a desire for God, and 'faith' what was only a longing for faith, if it was even hope," [79] but this is a simplification predicated upon a false evaluation of the problem and stylistic double talk.

Absolute certainty about God and the essence of God was impossible for Unamuno, as it is for most men, and yet the concept itself is undeniably real. Unamuno was constantly moved by it, and so God never ceased to be a real force for him. As for hope, the

---

78. "La fe," O.C. 16: 99.
79. Sánchez Barbudo, *Misterio,* p. 206n. See also the explanation of Luis Granjel, *Retrato de Unamuno* (Madrid, 1957), p. 255.

very fact that Unamuno never renounced the struggle reveals his hope, as Laín Entralgo has demonstrated. It would be difficult to give any value whatever to his work, beyond a questionable literary one, if all this were denied. He did indeed doubt constantly, but we know that he considered this to be characteristic of all who deeply agonize at the thought that they could be in error. Unamuno's concepts of God, immortality, faith, and belief are not orthodox, but neither are they blind; and had they been so, his philosophy would have acquired a static quality that would destroy any possibility of eternal validity — the one thing for which he strives, deeply aware of the inescapable need for sincerity.

God was a living concept and fundamental to his idea of the hero. In "Nicodemo el fariseo," written in 1899, and the product of his greatest religious crisis, he demonstrates the tension that exists between the hero's sociohistoric context and his rôle as an instrument of a transcendental will: "There is a process of growth from within to without, a growth which comes to us from God, who dwells within us, and there is another one from without to within, which comes to us from those layers of alluvion which the world deposits around our eternal nucleus, trying to smother it in time." [80] God is the initial impulse for the extension of the ego, but also the ultimate objective. Society or human interaction gives us the awareness of the specific historic needs we are to fill. The recognition and reconciliation of these two forces is the true heroic ideal. If we exist in a substantial way, it is possible and even probable that God does, too, for our strength must come from somewhere: "Faith in God stems from faith in our own substantial existence." [81]

Conversely, if God exists, then the effort expended to direct our energies toward some useful end redeems us and justifies our presence. The more one believes in God (once again we see the parallel with sainthood), the more one believes in oneself and the greater one's heroic potential, for the purpose is proportionately clearer: "And the fact is that there is no faith in oneself like that of one of God's servants, since he sees God in himself; nor a faith like that of a man who, like Don Quixote, though he may be lured by fame,

80. "Nicodemo el fariseo," O.C. 3: 134.
81. "¡Plenitud de plenitudes, y todo plenitud!" O.C. 3: 768.

seeks above all the kingdom of God and his justice. You can just toss everything else into the bargain, for above everything else is faith in oneself, which is essential if one is to act." [82] Immortality is a real possibility; no other encouragement is needed. We know, of course, that regardless of the strength of his faith in God, the hero must always maintain the struggle to keep that faith alive and productive, a quality that distinguishes him. His capacity for enthusiasm and devotion sets him apart from, and above, the norm: "The enthusiast is inspired by God, he is one who becomes God, who fills himself with God. This is something which could occur to a poet, to a creator, but not to a normal man or to an average man." [83]

The hero is, finally, the man who feels God within himself and identifies himself with God. He has received his outstanding qualities from a superior force and feels the impulse of this force within him, since it gains strength as he does. Greater effort leads to greater enthusiasm, greater devotion, greater faith, greater security, and greater contact with God. He is the individual chosen to enter into a pact with God and to act as his instrument in society: "And since the hero is the only one who hears it and knows it, and since obedience to this mandate and faith in it are what make him what he is, what make him a hero, he may very well say, 'I know who I am, and only my God and I know and the others do not.' Between my God and me — he may add — there is no mediating law; we understand each other directly and personally, and for that reason I know who I am." [84]

Now the question of the hero's solitude becomes clearer. His company consists not only of other heroes, other solitary men, but also of God himself. The sense of mission does indeed come from the hero's consciousness, his soul, but this is the very presence of God within him, an awesome burden which only the hero fully comprehends. His duty is partly to make others aware of it, but the

---

82. *Vida de Don Quijote*, p. 174.
83. *La agonía del cristianismo*, O.C. 16: 491.
84. *Vida de Don Quijote*, p. 108. An excellent explanation of this idea is contained in the poem "En el desierto," O.C. 13: 299–301. Carlyle, too, speaks of the great man's "free force direct out of God's own hand." *On Heroes*, p. 13.

loneliness of this knowledge only contributes to his image of madness: "It is a thing as terrible as it is great to have a mission known only to oneself and in which others cannot be made to believe; to have heard in the inner recesses of one's soul the silent voice of God saying, 'You must do this.' " [85] The mission consists of the maximum extension of the ego for the positive benefit of man through a concrete example. To be chosen is in itself awesome, but to strive to meet the challenge is agonizing.

Man does have free will, according to Unamuno, in the sense that although his duties may be imposed upon him by God, he has the freedom to accept or reject the duty and to succeed or fail in its accomplishment. The vision is the idea the hero has of how to reach his plenitude, but although the means of reaching it depend upon him, the goal itself is largely predetermined, since "what you want to be is your idea in God, Consciousness of the Universe, it is the divine idea of which you are a manifestation in time and space. And your longing impulse toward what you want to be is just the nostalgia that pulls you toward your divine home. A man is only a complete man when he wants to be more than a man." [86] The hero achieves the idea that God has of him in his sociohistoric context: he sees God everywhere in all things and there is no pure chance. Even while he is exercising his free will, he does so within the limits foreseen by God, and for that reason he must rise to the challenge presented to him and not create needs that should not exist. His heroism or his usefulness stems largely from filling a specific need, and rather than try to make the challenge easier for himself by fighting his destiny, he should rise to the challenge that lies before him: "Instead of seeking to do some-

85. *Vida de Don Quijote,* pp. 107–08. For this reason he can cry "Fight, fight, brothers, for the soul, / without expecting the palm / of human justice!" "Salutación a los rifeños," vv. 139–41, O.C. 14: 798. See also *Diario íntimo,* p. 156: "God has called me, I must hear him. Although the others will not understand that call, am I to live a slave to them? One must live in the reality of oneself and not in the appearance which others make of us for themselves; in our own spirit and not in the concept of another."

86. *Vida de Don Quijote,* p. 109. The relationship between man, God, and human will is considered several times in the *Diario íntimo,* e.g.: "Free is he who can receive divine grace, and be saved by it" and "Our will without grace is nothing." P. 138.

thing other than what you are doing, struggling against your own nature, convince yourself that in all that you do, whether it seems good or bad to you, you are God's minister on earth and the arm by which he carries out his justice, and it will come to pass that your actions will end up by being good." [87]

Thus, the actions of Don Quixote become especially significant, as he allows himself to be guided by Rocinante and to right the wrongs that present themselves. Unamuno suggests that it would be excessively proud for Don Quixote to presume to be able to choose his adventures, since God must know more about what is necessary than the hero, and since he must also be concerned with preserving the hero and giving him the immortality he seeks, so that he may continue to believe. While the hero can choose whether to act, and while he has great liberty to make errors or to be successful, the hand of God is never far away, in the sense that he sets out the choices and the hero must then trust his own intuition. Unamuno does not believe in luck or chance where the hero is concerned: "when we imagine that we are doing something in jest is when the Supreme Power, who uses us for his occult and inscrutable ends, is making us do it in earnest." [88] Heroism is a rejection of chance, insofar as is possible, and Don Quixote's confidence in his own ability successfully to bring to fruition any task is what Unamuno calls the heroic spirit: "His heroic spirit would have acted equally well in any adventure: in whichever one God had seen fit to set for him. Like Christ Jesus, of whom Don Quixote was always a faithful disciple, he was ready for whatever the chances of the road might bring his way." [89]

Unamuno himself seems to believe in this devotion. He tries to deliver himself to a divine will with a fervor that is impressive, regardless of his intentions. He calls out in despair:

87. *Vida de Don Quijote,* p. 131. Cf. "only the one whom you stamp with your seal, marking the route for him, enjoys freedom." *Romancero del destierro,* no. 25, vv. 12–14, O.C. 14: 656.

88. *Vida de Don Quijote,* pp. 261–62. Cf. Carlyle, "Great souls are always loyally submissive, reverent to what is over them; only small mean souls are otherwise." *On Heroes,* p. 179.

89. *Vida de Don Quijote,* p. 92. An illuminating discussion of the hero's independence of action appears in the *Diario íntimo,* pp. 176–82.

Look, Lord, we are tiny,
we do not know how to walk along your paths;
extend, Lord, a finger, a single finger
of your hand
with which you have just molded the universe
and holding on to that finger
we shall cross through life.

[Mira, Señor, que somos pequeñuelos,
no sabemos andar por tus caminos;
tiende, Señor, un dedo, un solo dedo
de esa tu mano
con que acabas de heñir el universo
y a ese dedo cojidos
la vida cruzaremos.] [90]

Many times the hero's feelings and ideas do not make sense even
to him; he may feel himself irresistibly swept along by a greater
force, but his gift lies in being able to distinguish between a purely
human or social force and a divine one, and in his ability to adapt
himself to it. This clarity of judgment gives the hero his invulnerability. Applying this to himself, Unamuno says: "The meaning of
many of the things that occur in my spirit and that I confide to you
is not known to me, or at least, I am the one who does not know
what they mean. There is someone within me who dictates them
to me, who tells them to me. I obey him and I do not look inward
to see his face or to ask his name. I only know that if I were to
see his face and if he were to tell me his name, I would die so
that he might live." [91] The influence of the mystics is patent here.
The hero is no less divinely inspired and no less obsessed than
they. His rôle is inescapable and he must awaken the masses to
the fact that many of them, too, may be similarly endowed.

To fulfill his task in this tension between God and his sociohistoric context, and to maintain some sort of equilibrium, is the
agony of the believing man and the "tragic feeling" of the hero.
He must keep close contact with God so that he will not err with
man, for it is God who is stronger, yet he must conform to certain
human and temporal standards in order to gain an audience and

90. "Salmo de la mañana" (1907), vv. 23–29, O.C. 14: 733–34.
91. "El sepulcro de Don Quijote," *Vida*, p. 74.

followers among men. Equilibrium can be maintained only with the constant support of God, without which there is oblivion and annihilation: "If I aspire to you, I shall live in you; if I turn away from you, I shall end up in what is not yours, in the only thing possible outside of you: in nothingness." [92] The hero can afford to appear mad to the masses, for eventually some may understand and a few may even appreciate his worth immediately. For them he continues. However, God can bestow on him not just the apparential immortality — fame — of the masses, but the substantial immortality of constant effort. Thus Unamuno counsels his reader: "Cure yourself of the affliction of caring how you appear to others. Care only how you appear before God, care about the idea God may have of you." [93]

This aspiration to God is the aspiration to be all (*querer serlo todo*). The actions of Don Quixote made him indispensable because, although they had their redeeming social aspects, their value was transcendental. His example is as pertinent now as it was then — perhaps more so — and there is no reason for it to diminish in value, for we have seen that society is, for Unamuno, a collection of individuals who must not be motivated as a homogeneous unit. The hero cannot raise all mankind at once, but only individual men who will pass the lesson on. Don Quixote passed his example on to Cervantes and Sancho, and from there it has spread, until now he has a battalion of followers much wider than he knew before.

Ultimately, then, he succeeded, and that is the criterion. To achieve a relevance that lasts for innumerable lifetimes is to achieve immortality, but there is more, for in itself it is to achieve God:

And if human history is, as I have said and repeated, the thought of God on the earth of mankind, to make history and to make it

92. *Vida de Don Quijote*, p. 320. Cf. Charles Moeller, *Literatura del siglo XX y cristianismo*, trans. Valentín García Yerba (Madrid, 1960), p. 128: "Thus, Unamuno is going to strive to build his faith on a nothingness of philosophical certainty. Of the 'living God who dwells within us, and who reveals himself to us through acts of charity and not through vain concepts of pride,' he will not be able to know that he exists and that he saves him from death *except in the interior of faith itself*, in the light that segregates, once all the props are knocked out, once all the rope ladders that facilitate the climb to the citadel of clouds are thrown into the dark abyss."
93. "El sepulcro de Don Quijote," *Vida*, p. 82.

forever is to amass eternity. . . . And the fact is that the Kingdom of God, for the coming of which simple hearts ask daily —
"Thy kingdom come!" — that kingdom which is within us, is
coming to us from moment to moment, and that kingdom is the
eternal coming of it. And all history is a commentary on the
thought of God.[94]

History is deeply influenced by the heroes, who in their turn are
instruments of God in a specific context. Their successful or truly
heroic actions are thus the expression of God's will and bring him
closer to earth. The relevance of their work stretches across time
and gives them an apparential immortality for their lasting fame
among men, and a substantial immortality for their continuing
contribution to God's wishes, even after they have left the earth.
Unamuno, like Hegel, believed that the hero could die or suffer
defeat, but that history would vindicate him.

Don Quixote's immortality is such as to deify him, both for the
inspiration he showed and for his everlasting pertinence to the
spirit of man. Like Christ, he may have arisen from the dead to
roam the earth again, perhaps as the shepherd Quijotiz, or perhaps
as a poet or orator (or perhaps, one always wonders, as Unamuno?).
The truth is, of course, that he never died, and Unamuno devotes
himself to his ideals with the cry: "Madden me, my Don Quixote!" [95]
If Unamuno bestows immortality upon Don Quixote because of his
sincerely felt faith, then all heroes achieve their fulfillment as
martyrs to their mission: "I have already told you, reader, that it is
the martyrs who make the faith rather than the faith that makes
the martyrs. And faith makes truth." [96] His followers make the
hero what he is from age to age and adapt their vision of him to
meet the changing needs of individuals. Even the apostle Cervantes
was raised beyond his own limitations through Don Quixote's inspiration in transmitting his example to the ages:

---

94. "Comentario," *Cómo se hace una novela*, pp. 46–47.
95. *Vida de Don Quijote*, p. 323. Sure of his purpose, he also says, "Your
Gospel, my lord Don Quixote, / in the breast of your people, like a javelin /
I threw." *De Fuerteventura a París*, sonnet 17, vv. 1–3, O.C. 14: 493.
96. *Vida de Don Quijote*, p. 301. See also p. 195; *Del sentimiento trágico*,
O.C. 16: 318, and *Paz en la guerra*, O.C. 2: 320

Must we not consider as Don Quixote's greatest miracle the fact that he caused the story of his life to be told in the way that it was, by a man who showed in his other works, as Cervantes did, the weakness of his imaginative powers and how inferior he was to what would have been needed, in the natural order of things, to tell of the feats of the Ingenious Gentleman? [97]

In other words, Don Quixote has attained the immortality that Cervantes can never have because Cervantes chose to create a truly autonomous character. Cervantes the man inspires few, while Don Quixote, the fictive entity, teaches by means of an awe-inspiring reality.

97. *Vida de Don Quijote*, p. 360. It is interesting, though, that Carlyle should have asserted that "Shakespeare and Dante are Saints of Poetry." *On Heroes*, p. 85.

5. The Hero in History and Fiction

Fiction versus Reality

Certainly the most important test for Unamuno's theories of heroism is their successful application to specific realities drawn from his own creative surroundings, for he repeatedly stressed the belief that only what is true in the concrete sense is valid, that abstractions are of no use in themselves. Simply stated, whatever works is real. This is no less true of philosophy and literary theories than it was of Don Quixote. That which functions, has an effect, a continuing value, or usefulness, is authentic, whether man or myth. This idea directly derives from the pragmatism of William James, who expressed it as follows: "All the *sanctions* of a law of truth lie in the very texture of experience. Absolute or no absolute, the concrete truth *for us* will always be that way of thinking in which our various experiences most profitably combine."[1] It is a question of fruitfulness, whether of people or ideas: both partake of a certain degree of reality in direct proportion to their lasting qualities. We have already seen that man is immortal as long as he is remembered or as long as some aspect of his personality is exercizing an influence; this is the potential benefit to be derived from having blood descendants. However, the same may also be said of concepts and ideas and Unamuno expresses it as follows: "Everything is true insofar as it nourishes generous longings and brings forth fertile works; everything is false when it smothers noble impulses and aborts sterile monsters. By their fruits will ye know men and things. Any belief that leads to living works is a true belief, and it is a

1. James, "Humanism and Truth," *Selected Papers*, p. 229.

false belief that leads to dead works." [2] Reality is a piece of eternity for both men and ideas.

We have seen that heroism demands immortality of its followers and that this is indeed its primary goal. The hero, then, is he who has achieved immortality (as opposed to notoriety, which Unamuno rarely considers because it is based on fame through some evil accomplishment) on the strength of his personality, and has made that personality eternally significant. As long as his personality represents an active contribution to the improvement of mankind, he himself exists, is real and immortal. In an important chapter for the full understanding of the implications of reality for Unamuno, José Ferrater Mora says:

That which lasts — or, if one prefers, that which is everlasting — is also real. Not, of course, the intemporal and abstractly eternal, but the permanently concrete. This last can be understood in two ways. First, as something whose permanence is being continuously produced or created; true permanence is, Unamuno believes, the result of an effort, of an act of will, of a *conatus*, to such an extent that there is no fundamental difference between being and wishing to be. Second, as something whose duration is constantly threatened by annihilation; just as war is the guarantee of peace, death — the imminence of death — is the guarantee of life. To last forever is not to go on existing, to continue to be; it is the unceasing conquest of one's own being. This explains why for Unamuno to live was primarily "to agonize," that is, to fight against death.[3]

This is indeed the crux of heroism and the effort of the heroic will to endure. One is not endowed with reality but must first achieve it and then maintain it. The efforts of the will, the suffering, isolation, and ridicule now become firmly grasped means to this end, and we shall see that this same desire to persist is also the key to the heroism of Unamuno's fictional characters.

The person who brought these concepts to life in Unamuno's mind was, of course, Don Quixote who, says Unamuno, was resur-

2. *Vida de Don Quijote,* p. 181.
3. José Ferrater Mora, *Unamuno: a Philosophy of Tragedy,* trans. Philip Silver (Berkeley, 1962), pp. 119–20. I am grateful to Professor Ferrater Mora for his help in this matter.

rected so that his spirit might continue to function in the minds of men. He is a real person, not a myth, because he fulfills all the qualifications mentioned by Ferrater Mora. As the perfect hero, he exemplifies heroic reality: "Your worship must surely know from his studies that saying *operari sequitur esse,* working follows being, and I add to that the idea that only what works exists, and to exist is to work, and if Don Quixote works for those who know him, and does life works [*obras de vida*], Don Quixote is much more historical and real than many men who are just names and who wander through those chronicles. . . . Only what works exists."[4]

His death prefaces a period of continual resurrection, as his importance repeats itself with each individual and with each generation. In an essay appearing in 1905, just a short time before the publication of the *Vida de Don Quijote y Sancho,* Unamuno explains that he feels quite capable of insisting upon the reality of Don Quixote, whose *conatus* demands repeated resurrections: "but one can and must maintain that Don Quixote existed and continues to exist, that he lived and continues to live with an existence and a life which are perhaps more intense and effective than if he had existed and lived in the common and ordinary manner," for "each successive generation has kept adding something to this Don Quixote, and he has kept transforming and enlarging himself."[5] He is still active and continues to enrich himself and others. In concrete terms, the extension of his life has not substantially changed.

One might accuse Unamuno of deliberately confusing illusion and concrete reality in order to serve his own purposes, but he demonstrates that much of what is normally called illusion can be called real, when the criteria are based not on purely phenomenological grounds, but rather on what Unamuno calls practical ones:

> And regarding this business of hallucinations, I have to tell you that everything we perceive is just that, and that all our impressions are just hallucinations. The difference is of a practical order. If, consumed by thirst, you go through a desert and hear

4. *Vida de Don Quijote,* p. 94. Cf. "The name is what makes the man; / but renown / is a mere trifle." *Cancionero,* no. 541, Dec. 8, 1928.
5. "Sobre la lectura e interpretación del *Quijote,*" O.C. 3: 848.

the murmuring of water in a fountain and you see — water! — none of this is more than a hallucination. But if you put your mouth up to it and you drink and your thirst is quenched, you call this hallucination a true impression, a reality. All of which means that the value of our perceptions is determined by their practical effect.[6]

This is, as always, the triumph of feeling over reason, because only what we feel has any practical value for us. Very much a man of his time, Unamuno makes a good case for his distinction and finds that it can be successfully applied to virtually anything and clarify the relationship between man and that which affects him: "What we call reality, is it anything more than an illusion that leads us to work and that produces works?"[7] Were the forces that drove Segismundo and Don Quixote unreal? Certainly not for them. It is no longer a distinction based upon reason, but Unamuno does not feel that there is any necessary link between reason and reality anyway, for "there are many of us who . . . still believe that what is real, what is really real, is irrational."[8] He calls for a suspension of idées reçues and asks us not to depend on the purely phenomenological if it has no practical effect or meaning in our personal circumstances now.

Fiction and History

Thus can Unamuno insist that the mere fact that a man existed at any point in history does not necessarily endow him with a lasting reality, although at that particular historical moment he may have had some passing reality which has since evaporated through a lack of continued relevance. "Pure names" are not real by dint of their limited temporal existence since that has now ceased. As Julián Marías says: "strictly speaking, there is no historical reality without some knowledge of it, as there is no temporal person without memory."[9] Even a reading of the names of those who may

6. "El que se enterró," O.C. 9: 199.
7. Vida de Don Quijote, p. 244.
8. Del sentimiento trágico, O.C. 16: 131.
9. Julián Marías, Miguel de Unamuno, p. 24. This is a two-edged sword, for Unamuno also observes, "How many useless heroes have been made heroes of legends and subjects of songs!" Diario íntimo, p. 162.

have lived brings them a step closer to continuing reality than they would otherwise be, but it does not give them the fullness that is Unamuno's aim.

It is, then, a question of degree. We know that Cervantes existed, but if the personality of Cervantes has no effect upon us as a temporal group, he is purely historical. On the other hand, Don Quixote succeeds in transcending both his historical and literary contexts by imposing himself more directly on a greater number of individual followers. Just as Cervantes would now be unreal had he not developed beyond infancy, so would Don Quixote, had he not developed beyond his literary origins. As Marías says: "The being of the literary character, like that of man himself, is a result." [10] What the person or character becomes is more important than what he started out as.

This creates another source of possible confusion, for until now we have seen that the only part of a hero's actions that matters is his intention, not the results. Now we must realize that, on the other hand, his immortality (and therefore his enduring reality) does depend upon the final outcome of his intentions, their concrete results. The hero must, in order to remain real, move from the merely potential personality he has, to the fully realized self that can endure, from the desire to be, to the actual being — although without ever losing that motivating desire.

Thus it is that Unamuno can feel that all men "without a history" are essentially indistinguishable, individuals without personality. Whether their origins be literary or physical, all entities must ultimately be judged on the same scale in order to determine their reality. In Del sentimiento trágico de la vida, he lists those whom he considers to be the great tragic figures,[11] and the list is particularly noteworthy for its mixture of men who lived in the phenomenological sense and those who started as literary creations: Marcus Aurelius, Saint Augustine, Pascal, Rousseau, René, Obermann, James Thomson, Leopardi, Vigny, Lenau, Kleist, Amiel, Quental, and Kierkegaard. No distinction is made as to their origins;

10. Marías, p. 23.
11. Del sentimiento trágico, O.C. 16: 144. Another example could be the literary hoax, Luis Maldonado's "blind man of Robliza" who was perfectly real for Unamuno. See "Romance" (1894), especially vv. 84–87, O.C. 14: 677.

they are all real to Unamuno to approximately the same extent. To separate René or Obermann from the rest would be to underestimate the lasting significance they have in Unamuno's thought, their beginnings in fiction notwithstanding.

If Don Quixote was responsible for making Unamuno see the arbitrary distinction commonly made between fiction and reality in history, then it was Calderón's Segismundo — "brother to Don Quixote" [12] — who served to support what Unamuno could only suspect when he first approached the problem. Calderón attempted to show that man is God's dream and that man can in turn dream other characters but that the fictive characters of man's creation will be no more lasting than he is. Unamuno, we shall see, came to feel that the creature could in many ways be equal and even superior to his creator. There is no such thing as objective reality. Reality depends upon the powers of creation that a person has: God creates man, who re-creates God and thus gives him reality so that they both exist. No one can exist in a void, so the hero also creates an audience that will be self-perpetuating and self-fulfilling; it, in turn, will re-create him and give him continuing reality. At the same time he maintains the reciprocal arrangement with God so that he can be immortal both with men and with God. Reality is dynamic.

Since reality depends on the completeness of a personality, this plenitude must be such that it cannot be concealed or dimmed by social changes or conventions. This is clear, for reality–immortality–re-creation presupposes that the personality is bigger than life and greater than society so it may maintain itself. As José Ferrater Mora says: "the 'real' man — the 'authentic' man — is not the one who hides behind his social cover, his everyday gestures, and conventional words, but he who reveals himself abruptly in all his contradictory being." [13] Personality is, in large part, this work of transcending limits, and to determine reality on the basis of an individual's ideal or abstract qualities would be self-defeating since it would effectively deprive him of the very dynamism that is his personality, his heroism, and his reality. To reduce the problem to an

12. *Vida de Don Quijote,* p. 294.
13. Ferrater Mora, *Unamuno,* p. 118.

abstract common denominator would be a major falsification: "Only by killing life, and true truth with it, can the historical hero be separated from the novelistic one, from the mythical one, from the fabulous one, or from the legendary one, and only thus can it be maintained that one existed completely or almost completely, the other, partially, and the third, not at all; because to exist is to live, and he who acts, exists." [14] And so we find ourselves faced once more with the unavoidable problem of ontological distinction based uniquely upon practical effects, since it is the only distinction with a thread of true consistency. It alone is based upon a consideration of the totality of the person.

To a certain extent, however, we all are the result of a literary creation. Unamuno feels unequivocally that to some degree we must belong to either an oral or a written tradition, and it is inconceivable that there could be people without this tradition: "Are there men who are not from a book? Even those who do not know how to read or write. Every man who is truly a man is the child of a legend, either written or oral. And there is nothing other than a legend, that is to say, a novel." [15] This type of observation is never meant to indicate any sort of contempt since legend and fiction are as valid as history — more so, perhaps, as "Legend is true history, since legend is what men believe has happened. And what one believes has happened influences one's action more than what really happened." [16] As in all things of men, to believe is to want to believe. Thus, if it would be difficult to separate us by our literary or phenomenological origins, it would be especially so for exactly those who might be interested in the question of the respective degree of reality of individuals — people whose knowledge and culture is derived principally from books that bestow the same physical reality on everyone.

A division between fiction and history becomes impossible, because "all of us who live primarily from reading and in reading are unable to separate the poetic or novelistic characters from the historical ones" [17]; and indeed such a separation would be all but

14. "El caballero de la triste figura," O.C. 3: 372.
15. "Continuación," *Cómo se hace una novela,* p. 149.
16. Note to sonnet 54, *De Fuerteventura a París,* O.C. 14: 533.
17. *Cómo se hace una novela,* p. 67.

meaningless, since pure history rarely is an accurate reflection of the imposition of the will upon circumstances: "History is nothing more than a cinematographic kaleidoscope moved by the endless belt of Chance." [18] Unamuno sees history as little more than incidental mindlessness, the most important element of which is time, which obscures and equalizes individuals. History is important, but in and of itself it does not live. Its movement is a self-limiting one with no aim beyond its own continuation, and whereas the purely historical aspect of a person is not real or alive, his individuality may well be. The lesson does not lie in the historical fact, but rather in its evaluation: the subjective analysis of one's individuality in its time and place, the heroism that goes beyond the limits of the historical lesson.

Thus, the existence of a once great man in history does indeed give him a certain amount of immortality and reality, but not necessarily more than that of a great figure who has emerged from the pages of legend or literature. The historical dimension is an end in itself, but its very objectivity keeps it from being the medium in which to perpetuate the qualities of a man's heroism, whereas literature can be. Literature, however, is not necessarily self-perpetuating and needs to fit into the historical context in such a way that its significance can last. Heroism and its subsequent reality, then, are dependent upon what we may call a confluence of spiritual (literary) and phenomenological (historical) significance which the hero must be able to bring about in order continually to re-create himself: "History, the only living thing, is the eternal present, the fleeting moment that remains by passing, that passes by remaining, and literature is nothing more than death. A death from which others can pluck life." [19] Thus, history may be factual, but if literature can be historically or even "intrahistorically" significant, it can be more real because it can perpetuate the confluence. It is for this reason that, "on the eternal scale, legends and fictions are more truthful than history." [20]

Literature, and therefore literary creations such as Don Quixote,

18. "Mi libro," O.C. 8: 589.
19. "Introducción," *Cómo se hace una novela*, p. 14.
20. *Vida de Don Quijote*, p. 184. Cf. "To live for history! How much simpler and healthier to live for eternity!" *Diario íntimo*, p. 278.

Segismundo, René, and Obermann, who maintain their place of importance in a historical setting that was not their original one (such as, for example, in the mind of Unamuno), are indeed real; and to base an evaluation of their reality upon the terminology used to distinguish genres (i.e. chronicles, novels, legends, epics, biographies) reduces them to their purely apparential or formal aspects and not to their effective or practical worth. If they are actively believed in, they are real, regardless of circumstantial considerations. Their effect upon the will of future generations determines their reality: "The more things are believed, the truer they are, and it is not intelligence, but will, that imposes them." The break between reason and reality is complete and it should no longer be necessary to consider reason as the prime criterion. Just as Don Quixote is heroic for what he believes and not for his reason, so "truth is not the logical relationship between the apparential world and reason, which is apparential also, but rather the intimate penetration of the substantial world into consciousness, which itself is also substantial." [21] The distinction, then, can be restated as occurring, not between history and imagination, or between intelligence and intuition, but rather between appearance and substance.

Fiction as Reality

We have seen how great a part of our historical relevance may be determined by our position within some sort of literary tradition and how the reality of a hero may depend upon the literary aspects of his immortality. If the literary works that gave birth to Obermann, René, Don Quixote, and Segismundo are their biographies, it is also true that the life of each individual is a novel or drama, perhaps as yet unwritten. This is, of course, a commonplace, but nonetheless true for being so. Unamuno states: "Is the life of each one of us more than a novel? Is there any novel more novelistic than an autobiography?" In other words, the very business of living is the writing of that novel. Similarly, all novels are also history: "Whoever says a novel says a history." [22] The accepted divisions grow continually more indistinct.

21. *Vida de Don Quijote*, pp. 194; 205.
22. "Comentario," *Cómo se hace una novela*, p. 47; Ibid., "Prólogo," p. 14.

If a novel — any novel — is history which, we have seen, is alive, and if any life is a novel, the important common denominator is life itself. In order for a hero to emerge from a novel, the novel itself must live, but "a novel, to be alive, to be life, has to be, like life itself, an organism and not a mechanism." [23] The flesh-and-blood hero must live an active life, and the hero who emerges from fiction must come from a novel-history-biography which is itself vigorous and in which his existence is similarly threatened. This type of novel, like life, is in a state of eternal tension. It is continually re-creating its characters, whose very existence reaffirms the existence of their creator, much as that of man reaffirms the existence of God. The author gives life to the characters, but they respond, if they are to live, by developing beyond the limits of their creator (much as the flesh-and-blood hero transcends the limits imposed by space and time) and by adding facets to the reality of the author.

Thus the novel becomes autobiographical, for "all novels that make themselves eternal and that last by being eternal and by making their authors and their antagonists last, are they perhaps not autobiographies?" That is to say, they are doubly autobio-graphical. If they are organic, they represent the creation, self-development, and re-creation of the character and are in that way the character's own story; but they are also the story of the author himself, at least to a small extent, since all characters for a novel must be in part torn from the author's flesh and thus tell a portion of his story, too: "Every being in fiction, every poetic character that an author creates is part of the author himself." In the case of Cervantes, this is somewhat less true, for he virtually disappears behind the personality of his hero; Unamuno tried to overcome this threat by making himself the subject of all his work. Thus, all his work is frankly autobiographical and his characters are usually either himself or an alter ego. He justifies this by saying that he writes about what he knows best, and only a hero can truly claim to know himself: "When someone tosses in my face — and it has happened — the fact that I talk and write a great deal about myself, I always reply with this, which is that I prefer talking too much about myself to talking about others, and that it is much better to spend life

23. Ibid., "Continuación," p. 147.

writing one's autobiography rather than to spend it murmuring about one's neighbor, which is the way that those withdrawn and worthy men who carefully hide their intimate selves spend it." [24]

Unamuno was conscientiously heroic at every opportunity. For this reason it is quite natural that he sometimes regretted having taken the trouble to create characters to express himself rather than speaking directly: "I am ashamed to admit that on occasion I have invented fictional entities, characters in novels, so that I might put in their mouths what I did not dare put in my own and make them say in jest what I feel very seriously." [25] This is, however, a justifiable practice in some instances. Jorge Luis Borges admits that his more successful metaphors are more readily accepted if he attributes them, not to his own ingenuity, but rather to that of an obscure Persian or Norse poet. Unamuno does essentially the same thing to protect himself while testing the ground before he takes a stand on an issue, or when he wishes deliberately to cloud the matter in order to force the reader into taking a more active part. It is often better to feel the idea first through a character of one's own making before accepting it for oneself. Unamuno frequently used this device to sample many things, but especially death itself. The reality of his characters permitted him to have a more vivid experience than he could have had by way of mere abstractions, since each was intended to be an organic part of himself. God did likewise, claims Unamuno, when he sent Christ to the cross.

Therefore, the characters can express a vivid reality for the author, but does the reader encounter the same reality? We can say no, since we have seen that it is a purely subjective impression that must vary from person to person. Moreover, Unamuno feels that it is unimportant whether his feelings and those of the reader coincide: "What difference does it make to me, reader, if you do not read what I wanted to put in [my work], provided you read something that sparks you into life? It seems idiotic to me that an author should amuse himself by explaining what he wanted to say, when what matters to us is not what he wanted to say, but what he did say, or rather, what we hear." [26] Since the novelist's prime

24. Ibid., p. 64; p. 65; "A lo que salga," O.C. 3: 796.
25. "El sepulcro de Don Quijote," *Vida*, pp. 74–75.
26. "Comentario," *Cómo se hace una novela*, p. 41.

concern is to create characters whose reality will enhance his own, it makes little difference what the reader finds in the novel; for, after all, anything that makes the novel or its characters significant moves the author nearer to immortality, and the sensitive reader will add unforeseen dimensions. History ideally gives each person the same sense of reality because it is objective, but literature lets each choose and make his own decision, and there is no way that the writer can predict what that decision will be. In his heroism and in that of his characters the author must do what he feels is necessary and somehow rewarding; but, like any other hero, he fails only if future readers find nothing of meaning. Cervantes gave birth to the greatest of heroes, but in so doing, he submerged his own personality and became less heroic and less immortal as a man. His loss of heroism, however, was caused less by the strength of his characters, than by his inability to judge his own individuality and to reach a personal plenitude directly instead of through Don Quixote.

Unamuno, then, wants his characters to emphasize his personality and reality rather than to obscure them. His novelistic efforts, therefore, were made with this in mind: that the ultimate creation be Miguel de Unamuno. As a hero, he must convince his audience and win converts, not, to be sure, by means of mere logic and reason, but rather by creating a believable atmosphere around his characters so they may be real for the reader and form a lasting part of his spiritual life: "One does not enjoy a character in a novel until one has made him one's own, when one agrees that the world of fiction should form part of the world of permanent, intimate reality."[27] The key words are, of course, "permanent, intimate reality." Unamuno must urge his readers into active participation in his own re-creation through their re-creation of his characters.

It is for this reason that *Cómo se hace una novela* (1927) may truly be considered the key to his work.[28] As a result of its technique of a novel within a novel within the novel of life, the reader, as Zubizarreta points out, is required to abandon his traditional position of spectator and recipient of fixed ideas and to become an

27. "Prólogo," *San Manuel Bueno, mártir*, O.C. 16: 569.
28. See Julián Marías, *Miguel de Unamuno*, p. 59; Armando F. Zubizarreta, *Unamuno en su 'nivola'* (Madrid, 1960), passim.

integral part of the processes of creation and re-creation: "Unamuno addresses the reader, demanding that he be an authentic reader, a reader-author. He wants his reader to be author, actor, and character — and his own public — in the comedy of life, and he invites him to make his independent stand [*lanzar la morcilla*] as a rebel in the cause for immortality." [29] Without this participation the author — and his characters — have practically no hope of escaping oblivion, and if he becomes passive, the reader himself is in danger. He must make the novel his own autobiography by re-creating and inspiring himself in its reality (presupposing, of course, that the novelist or dramatist has succeeded in his attempt to give it some reality) and thus enrich the novel of his own life. There is, then, a mutually fruitful progression: the writer saves himself by enhancing his own reality through successfully real characters and he aids the reader by helping him to fulfill his own reality. This is the writer's heroic effort. The reader responds by continually re-creating the author and his characters: "and only when one becomes both the creator and the reader of the novel can both be saved from their deep-rooted solitude." [30]

This work of creation and re-creation and active participation is not, however, a literary endeavor in any meaningful sense of the term. As always in the work of Unamuno, it is an attempt to reach the very depths of the human spirit so that one may learn to perpetuate it. What one sees in others can be essential to one's own immortality, and only through an exercise of the will can this insight be fully developed and put into motion.

To be impeded by the merely apparential aspects of literature not only removes any genuine sense of reality, as we have seen, but also sets up a barrier between souls, be they of literary or biological origin. The letter is essential, but it is not an end in itself, as Blanco Aguinaga points out: "In comparison with the spirit, the letter is dead wood that impedes penetration, the 'overflowing' of souls and, in the final analysis, all communion; the letter is dogma,

---

29. Zubizarreta, p. 221 and passim. The essential creativity of the reader is also present in Carlyle: "We are all poets when we *read* a poem well" (*On Heroes,* p. 82). Carlyle's concern, however, is more deeply rooted in aesthetics.

30. "Continuación," *Cómo se hace una novela,* pp. 157–58.

that which does not act, the domain of intellectuals, that which acquires life only when it receives in its interior the breath of the spirit." [31] This is Unamuno's aim: to give the "breath of the spirit," the continuing reality, to literature so that it will live — both for future readers and as an integral part of Unamuno — organically.

The Illusory Reality of Author and Characters

The division between Cervantes and his characters is arbitrary, as Cervantes has scarcely any reality at all for us now; and the same could probably be said of Chateaubriand and René, Senancour and Obermann. Obviously, this is an ontological question of the first magnitude, for the writer is faced with the task of deciding whose will shall triumph, his own or those of his characters; more difficult yet is the matter of controlling this, if at all possible. Unamuno examines the question in a short story, "Y va de cuento," included in *El espejo de la muerte* (1913), in which he firmly ties his concept of the hero to a literary tradition:

Q. — What is a hero?
A. — One who provides the opportunity for writing about him an epic poem, an epinicion, an epitaph, a story, an epigram, or even a brief notice or a mere phrase.[32]

The hero causes his name to be immortalized; it is a conscious act of the will, designed to add a dimension to his existence and give him some lasting personality, however small.

Unamuno, in his godlike view of the writer's craft, abrogates some of this power, however, through an act of his own will; and the struggle between creator and creature is made concrete. He feels that it is within his domain to bestow heroism upon his characters: "We writers, then — oh, noble priesthood! — are the ones who make heroes for our use and satisfaction, and there would be no egoism if there were no literature. The idea of unknown heroes is

31. Carlos Blanco Aguinaga, *El Unamuno contemplativo*, p. 150. See also *La agonía del cristianismo*, chap. 4; Ferrater Mora, *Unamuno*, chap. 5; Barry Luby, *Unamuno a la luz del empirismo lógico contemporáneo*, p. 124; and of course throughout *El Cristo de Velázquez*.
32. "Y va de cuento," *El espejo de la muerte*, O.C. 2: 774.

a placebo to console the simpletons. To be a hero is to be *sung!*" [33]
The heroes are used by the writer in the sense that they add to his
own heroism. In other words, he himself can be immortalized because he is writing autobiographies, whether they be novels, dramas,
or short stories. Such braggadocio makes us wonder: is Unamuno
really sure of his ability to avoid Cervantes's fate? Already in 1902,
speaking of *Amor y pedagogía*, he admits that, "it is not I who
have given life to don Avito, Marina, Apolodoro, but rather they
who have taken on life in me after having wandered about in the
limbo of nonexistence." [34] This suggests the danger that the writer
may become a mere tool for a character's heroism, and we see Unamuno grappling with the thorny problem of the autonomous character.

The autonomous character has a long history in European literature and has made particularly frequent appearances in Spanish
literature. It originated, says Benavides,[35] in Arabic literature whence
it entered into Spain, in the *Libro de buen amor* (1330–43). The
difficult question of fiction versus reality passed into *El corbacho*
(1438) of the Archpriest of Talavera, the works of Diego de San
Pedro, Juan de Flores, Francisco Delicado — and, of course, Cervantes, from whom Unamuno took his greatest inspiration. Many
of the tricks he used to give life to his characters came from the
second part of the *Quijote* (1615), but in the nineteenth century,
there were two more great influences on Unamuno: Carlyle's *The*

33. Ibid. Although Carlyle never considers the problem of *logos* as con-
cernedly as Unamuno does, literature as remembrance is an element of heroism: "Why, in thirty or forty years, were there no books, any great man would
grow *mythic*, the contemporaries who had seen him, being once all dead." *On
Heroes*, pp. 25–26.

34. "Epílogo," *Amor y pedagogía*, O.C. 2: 568. The same problem reappears in *Teresa*, when Unamuno finds himself falling under the influence of
Rafael. See "Presentación," *Teresa*, O.C. 14: 275. However, in the *Diario
íntimo*, a more resigned Unamuno had observed: "I leave a name. What is
more than a name? What more will I be than the fictitious characters that I
have created in my inventions? What more, today, on earth, is Cervantes
than Don Quixote?" *Diario íntimo*, pp. 33–34.

35. Ricardo Benavides Lillo, "Para la genealogía de Augusto Pérez," in
Unamuno (Santiago de Chile, 1964), pp. 158–59. Benavides relies heavily
upon Américo Castro's *España en su historia*. See also Joseph E. Gillet, "The
Autonomous Character in Spanish and European Literature," *Hispanic Review* 24 (1956): 179–90.

French Revolution: A History (1837), which Unamuno translated into Spanish around 1900 [36] and in which Carlyle engages in conversations with his characters; and the novels of Galdós. In at least three novels — *La sombra* (1866–67), *El Amigo Manso* (1882), and *Realidad* (1892) — Galdós gave birth to partially autonomous characters, and in *Misericordia* (1897), one of his own characters creates an autonomous character.

It was, though, *El Amigo Manso* that most impressed Unamuno, who said in a letter written to Galdós on November 30, 1898: "If you knew how many times I remember your Friend Manso! It is not that I have seen him, I have felt him within me!" [37] Galdós, to give himself greater flexibility as a novelist, created a metaphysical entity whose very existence is false and deceiving from a phenomenological viewpoint. Manso wants to strip other people's souls in order to set up a valid educational system, but he fails because he cannot appreciate their intimate human characteristics. His rôle in life is gradually defined through an understanding of the distinctive gifts of his student, whose influence on his master is no less than that of the master on him. Consequently, he can claim that he does not exist since he is scarcely real for those he is most trying to influence. At the end of the novel, he disappears almost as he came: he is destroyed by life, by reality.

Unamuno's interest in this novel is understandable considering that one of his principal preoccupations is the search for the absolute by means of the relative. In the next chapter we shall see more concrete links between the novel of Galdós and *Amor y pedagogía*, written in 1902. Unamuno further extended some of the concepts employed by Galdós when he wrote the *Vida de Don Quijote y Sancho* in 1905, and it was during the next decade, leading up to the publication of *Niebla* in 1914, that he succeeded in clarifying his ideas regarding this relationship between the creator and the creature. We have seen how he freed the characters of Cervantes from their strictly literary framework, and in our discussion of *Niebla*, we shall see to what extent he freed his own.

36. The poem "Hero-Worship" was written about this time, and almost certainly is the result of Unamuno's readings of Carlyle. See O.C. 14: 697.
37. Quoted by H. Chaim Berkowitz, "Unamuno's relations with Galdós," *Hispanic Review* 8 (1940): 322.

It is also essential to mention the parallels that exist between Unamuno and his contemporary, the Italian dramatist Luigi Pirandello. Many references have been made to the similarities in their literary techniques, but startlingly little investigation has been made in depth. Both men were innovators in the use of autonomous characters, but as Américo Castro pointed out in 1924,[38] both of them were mainly influenced by Cervantes and the curious game of mirrors that he played with Don Quixote and Sancho in the second part of his novel. The two twentieth-century writers, however, did not profoundly influence each other, but were merely writing along similar lines when the intellectual climate in Europe was such as to make certain techniques necessary to dramatize the crises of existentialism. Both were deeply aware of the ambiguous and arbitrary aspects of all concepts of truth and tried to exemplify the subjectivity of reality in similar ways.

Pirandello did most of his innovating on the stage, although not all of it (see, for example, *Il fu Mattia Pascal* (1904), which in many ways represents the reverse of Galdós's *Misericordia*), while Unamuno's new techniques were better adapted to the novel. Only late in his career, in *El otro* (1932), did he use in the theater techniques similar to those of Pirandello. Personality was the crucial question for both writers, as Luis Leal points out: "Both Unamuno and Pirandello believe that each individual has as many personalities as there are individuals in the world; that is to say that personality, for them, is a result of the evaluation others give to our way of being; the concept that the individual has of himself is only one of many aspects of his personality, and not necessarily the true one." [39] Unamuno describes his attitudes toward this idea in the prologue to *Tres novelas ejemplares,* and we shall see in the next chapter how he gave concrete form to the problem in his fiction.

The point is, though, that Unamuno as creator wanted his char-

38. Américo Castro, "Cervantes y Pirandello: un estudio comparativo," *La Nación* (Buenos Aires), April 16, 1924.

39. Luis Leal, "Unamuno y Pirandello," *Italica* 29 (1952): 194. See also Frank Sedwick, "Unamuno and Pirandello Revisited," *Italica* 33 (1956): 40–51, and José Monner Sans, "Unamuno, Pirandello y el personaje autónomo," *La Torre* 9, nos. 35–36 (1961): 387–402. See also Unamuno, "Pirandello y yo," O.C. 10: 544–48.

acters to affirm his own reality and to immortalize him; and to protect himself from their vitality, he established a vertical distance between them and him. This was done partly in order to convince himself of his own superiority, for in *Del sentimiento trágico de la vida* he says: "We need others to believe in our superiority to them so that we ourselves may believe in it, and thereon base our faith in our own persistence, or at least in the persistence of our faith." [40] Like God, but unlike Galdós and Cervantes, Unamuno creates his characters for his own glory. They are an audience whose applause will attract attention to him, but whose dependence, vagueness, and obvious inferiority, particularly on the scale of reality, will not endanger his own immortality. When he actually makes an appearance in his novels, he hopes to acquire whatever reality his characters may have, as well as hold on to that which he may have in his own right. Since immortality is at best a chancy thing, he scoffs at no opportunity to reinforce it. Thus the work of fiction becomes doubly autobiographical, and he can flaunt the duality of his existence: "I . . . like the hero of my story, am also a hero and professor of Greek" and "I, Miguel de Unamuno, fictional (*novelesco*) too," and "who is he who signs himself Miguel de Unamuno? Well, . . . one of my characters, one of my creatures, one of my agonists." [41] In this way he manages continually to test reality in all its manifestations and to create himself throughout his life in his novels / autobiographies, just as he continues to create his characters.

The fascination Unamuno may hold for his audience, like that of his characters, is that he is in an eternal state of development and can repeatedly test new dimensions on his readers. Since he is primarily concerned with reality, his autonomous characters tend to give an appearance of reality while still, in fact, depending on him for their life. As José Ferrater Mora puts it: "If the characters were simply fictitious, their independence of the author would be illusory; the author would always lead them by the hand. If they were merely real, on the other hand, their dependence on the author

40. *Del sentimiento trágico,* O.C. 16: 180.
41. "Y va de cuento," O.C. 2: 778; *Cómo se hace una novela,* p. 76; "Prólogo," *Tres novelas ejemplares,* O.C. 9: 420.

would be abolished; they would become so completely detached from him that they would no longer be characters, but 'things.' " [42] This is why Unamuno's characters are so generally criticized for being mere puppets. They are indeed. However, Unamuno did not, it would appear, always want the strings to be quite so evident.

His feeling that he is like a god to his characters can hardly be overemphasized, and this reaches the extreme of giving him a feeling of superiority over his vision of other contemporaries. All substantial human contacts are re-creations, and we are each of us the product of another person's creativity: "Is it not true that my Alphonse XIII of Borbón and Hapsburg-Lorraine, my Primo de Rivera, my Martínez Anido, my Count Romanones are just other creations of mine, part of me, as much mine as my Augusto Pérez, my Pachico Zabalbide, my Alejandro Gómez, and all the other creatures in my novels?" [43] Just as for himself he creates the reality of his characters, so he does with all those who are real for him, and this is the sublimity of writing, "Because which is the supreme heroism if not that of making heroes, that of singing about it?" [44] Instead of merely having to search for an audience and followers, Unamuno has it in his power to create them all and to imbue them with enough reality to participate actively in the re-creation of their creator.

We may say, then, that there are several planes of mutual re-creation: God, who creates man to applaud him and reaffirm his existence; man, who may find or, in the case of the writer, create, an audience or fictive characters who applaud him and reaffirm his reality; and finally the reader, who has two functions: his special importance for the writer as well as his relationship as a man with God. The reader, then, as exemplified in *Cómo se hace una novela,* finds himself in the provocative position of applauding the "real" characters who, in their turn, applaud their creator, who, in his turn, applauds his Creator. And so it goes, in a state of dynamic tension, from one pole to another.

So it is that, with this goal, Unamuno finds himself in need of autonomous characters. If they are to contribute to his reality

---

42. Ferrater Mora, *Miguel de Unamuno,* pp. 110–11.
43. *Cómo se hace una novela,* p. 67.
44. "Y va de cuento," O.C. 2: 778.

and immortality, they must have an initial inherent reality of their own before the reader encounters them. And so, he explains, speaking of *Tres novelas ejemplares:* "Its agonists, that is to say, its fighters — or if you prefer, we'll call them characters — , are real, very real, and with the most intimate of realities, the reality that they give themselves, purely by wanting to be, or purely by wanting not to be, and not with the reality readers may give them." [45] To be convincing, they should be independent both of their readers and of their creator. They are active, they fight, they have wills and are capable of heroism. Regardless of whether they want to be or want *not* to be, they can be heroic in their own right; for, after all, "there are heroes who want not to be, heroes of *will not [no-luntad]*." [46] The novelist or dramatist, however, must first give his characters a will, if they are to be real. The problem is to determine how strong that will must be. God gave man a will and thus the ability to deny him; but even so, God must still exist, for the very action of negation by man is an affirmation of God's reality. Unamuno parallels this situation in *Niebla,* and, like God, is forced to kill Augusto Pérez in order to protect himself. The dividing line between God and man, however, is ultimately much clearer and more rigid than that between the author and his characters.

The Motivation for Literary Creativity

Unamuno's scorn for the problem of literary genres is well known, and the dangers involved in relying upon such arbitrary classifications have already been outlined in this chapter. In a letter to Juan Ramón Jiménez, dated October 31, 1915, he says: "I am not, in general, a man who succeeds by the force of his will to choose the genre of what I write. It has to come to me on its own. There are long spells in which I do not write a verse, and others in which a story does not occur to me. The most spontaneous thing is the *essay*." [47] Nonetheless, Julián Marías points out an important dimension in the novel that makes it especially useful for Unamuno:

45. "Prólogo," *Tres novelas ejemplares,* O.C. 9: 415.
46. Ibid., p. 417.
47. Letter to Juan Ramón Jiménez in the library of the University of Puerto Rico.

"the novel is the proper instrument for showing us something which also takes place temporally. Both novel and life consist essentially in temporality." [48] The novel can be a valuable tool for showing heroism since this, too, is largely a temporal question. However, the same can be said of drama and the shorter prose forms employed by Unamuno, and we shall consider them basically as one. This is, perhaps, to deny certain of the artistic values of Unamuno's work, but his main purpose in writing was not aesthetic. His work relies heavily on philosophical considerations, and the artistic form was important to him only insofar as it made his ideas clearer or lent credence to them. In trying to bring the substantial out of the chaos of the apparential, he was not trying to lend aesthetic brilliance to the cosmos, but to make it more readily comprehensible by man and to show the deepest truths about the human soul.

Much discussion has been carried on regarding Unamuno's division of fiction-writing into viviparous and oviparous — that which is spontaneously brought into being and that which is slowly and laboriously created. *Paz en la guerra,* his first (1897) major fictional work, is by his own admission an oviparous product. He was moved to write it above all by patriotic impulses, although its philosophical roots are also far-reaching. After this novel, though, he moved away from the heavily documented type of fiction and turned toward what Julián Marías chooses to call the "personal novel," in which Unamuno claims he writes without a plan so that the work will have the organic quality he strives for. It has been frequently stated that his works are didactic in nature and are mere vehicles for his thought. This is true, but the viviparous quality of them is also true, for it seems that he hit upon a theme first and then let the work emerge under its own power. When he explains this division in his techniques, he says of writing viviparously: "This is to go without a preliminary plan, and to let the plan spring up. It is the most organic way, as the other way is mechanical; it is the most spontaneous way." [49] He was always more concerned with how things worked than with what their results would be, and his fiction was really nothing less than character studies designed to show how the human

48. Julián Marías, *Miguel de Unamuno,* p. 61.
49. "A lo que salga," O.C. 3: 791.

soul functions. In a letter to the Puerto Rican critic José Balseiro, dated February 27, 1928, he writes: "I am more concerned by what I would call the *metablema*. The road and not the goal. In a work of art — and even of science or philosophy — I stroll and do not go to a goal. And the fact is that there is only the road." [50] To rely solely on the target to justify the trajectory would be to deny active participation by becoming a mere spectator. Therefore, to make the path itself important, the characters and their actions are the center of Unamuno's focus. What they do is important because it shows something about their personalities and helps to make them real.

Just as anyone who wishes to become a hero must look into another's soul in an attempt to understand his own, so the reader is urged to fix his attention upon the characters in order to derive any lesson he can from the reality the writer may have given them, as well as any he himself may see. That way, he should cease to be interested in the purely circumstantial elements of the story at the expense of the significance they may also have for him: "Any reader who, when reading a novel, worries about how the characters in it will end up without worrying about how he himself will end up, does not deserve to have his curiosity satisfied." [51] Unamuno must convince the reader to turn away from appearances and look deep into the heart of reality as reflected — or, hopefully, even generated — in his characters. He speaks of "my purpose of addressing myself to the intimate individuality, to the individual and personal intimacy of the reader of [the novel], to his reality, not to his apparentiality." [52] Thus, he wishes to inspire life, effort, heroism in his reader by making him think about, participate in, and even doubt, his own existence, so that he may strive to affirm it. On many occasions he states that he will be satisfied if he has at least managed to bring the reader somewhat closer to himself.

The novel provided Unamuno with an opportunity to extend himself, to engender spiritual children who would be part of him, but also separate. It was his opportunity to "be himself and to be

---

50. Quoted by José Balseiro, *Blasco Ibáñez, Unamuno, Valle-Inclán y Baroja: cuatro individualistas de España* (Chapel Hill, N.C., 1949), p. 105.
51. *Cómo se hace una novela*, p. 110.
52. "Prólogo-Epílogo a la segunda edición," *Amor y pedagogía*, O.C. 2: 431.

all." He did not, however, allow them to get out of hand, and one may read the entire body of Unamuno's work without ever finding one character more powerful than he. Even Don Quixote is kept under control by his rigorous vigilance and by the highly personal interpretation he gives of him, which, rather than making Don Quixote even more powerful than he was before, makes him more dependent than ever — but now on Unamuno.

In many ways, his attempts at characterization were part of Unamuno's search for some kind of proof of perpetuation. He uses his characters to live many lives at once and to enter into different levels of existence. As he admits, "I have always been bothered by the problem of what I would call my 'ex-future I's,' those that I could have been and stopped being, the possibilities that I have been leaving along my life's road." [53] There is always the fear that the wrong road may have been chosen, and the more levels of existence he can savor in his fictional characters, the more lasting facets there can be to his own reality. He can live not just one life but all those he has created, if he can succeed in living *through* them and not *behind* them as Cervantes did. He can then impose himself upon history in his fiction, by adding to it: "To live in history and to live history! And one way of living history is by telling it, creating it in books." [54]

By living the story of each character in his novels, and especially the more real or heroic ones, Unamuno penetrates to the core of their existence, since "the essence of an individual and that of a people is its history." [55] Not only does the novel permit him to live several times but, even more important perhaps, in all his fellow men and fellow characters he can recognize the man who might have been, had the elements that form him combined differently.

---

53. Note to sonnet 56, *De Fuerteventura a París*, O.C. 14: 536. See also the poem "Oh, si hubiera salido . . . !" (1908), O.C. 14: 778. Zubizarreta says: "That is to say that Unamuno developed in each of his characters one of his *possibilities of existence* on the basis of a real, historical self, a psychological self, the self of a possibility that was not realized, or a self born of the multiple perspectives of human relationships, dressing them up slightly, within the starkness of his works, with circumstantial events, making them live in these events." *Unamuno en su 'nivola,'* p. 82.

54. *Cómo se hace una novela*, p. 68.

55. Ibid.

He insists that "our other ex-future I's, which were possible, are other men." [56] Writing the novel deepens his understanding of others as well as of himself.

Unamuno's Characters

Unamuno's characters are his spiritual children. Each represents a potential of the ego in general and, inevitably, of Unamuno's in particular. The situation or plot is a mere convention to give the character — Unamuno's alter ego — an opportunity to perform on a stage that permits both the author and his reader to peer deep within him. The events do not matter, just the totality of the developing character's being, and the outcome should be of scarce interest because the subject is life, and its only possible outcome is death. Unamuno rarely tries to penetrate the obviously enduring aspects of his characters, or their immediate success at achieving immortality. Not even the emotional side is important except as a device to cast light on their personalities. He aims directly at the subconscious, the murky nucleus of the intimate self, the personality and consciousness which the apparential world masks and deforms but which are captured and laid bare in a gesture or word from the character. This is a revolutionary step in the development of fiction and is the basis for the personal novel. The gesture or phrase is uniquely Unamuno's, though, regardless of how real his characters may wish to seem. They are torn from the depths of his ego and serve as his emotional release. He claims that Cervantes used the same device: "And if Cervantes did not go mad . . . it was because . . . the romantic poison of his soul alleviated his madness in Don Quixote." [57]

Unamuno is consciously taking his revenge on God. All his anguished preoccupation with man is exhibited in his characters. For that reason he made every effort — short of making them stronger than he — to give them consciousness and volition, the distinguishing and eternal qualities of his most exceptional characters: "what has been called 'consciousness' is, in the final analysis, a way — very

56. "Presentación," *Teresa*, O.C. 14: 272.
57. "La vida y la obra," O.C. 9: 937.

unsatisfactory and questionable — of recognizing that only what refuses to cease being, really is." [58] This is Unamuno's interpretation
of Spinoza's concept of *conatus*, the will to continue eternally, to
which he has added imagination and subjectivity, without which the
will-to-be withers under the weight of rationalism.

The consciousness and imagination of Unamuno's characters com-
pose the body of their struggle against annihilation, the power that
lies in the hands of their creator, just as Unamuno's struggle against
oblivion pits him against God. Their imaginative power pushes them
on in spite of their desperation and in the face of purely rational
interpretations that would dissuade such efforts. This is the one
trait that saves them from being so weak as to vanish into that feared
oblivion. They understand their peril and sense their impotence.
They are usually highly intelligent victims of life itself, like Unamuno, and react to their situations in any of the many ways that
Unamuno feels he might choose.

Unamuno's characters, though, are never truly heroic despite
their autobiographical qualities, for they ultimately lack faith in
themselves and do not believe in their power to reach any sort of
meaningful fulfillment. This is not surprising, since the hero feels
that his course of action is the only really correct one for him, and
Unamuno, who felt that he had this duty to fulfill, presents the
reader with the attitudes and ideals that he has not accepted for
his own life. Thus, the characters could be said to represent the
knowingly unheroic Unamuno and are meant to strengthen his belief in his own life. Clearly, were they heroic in their options, his
own faith would necessarily be undermined. Practically none of
them is truly creative, unlike Unamuno, who expressed his personality and attempted to develop it to its plenitude through his
creative powers. Unamuno sees his heroism as lying in his imaginative gifts in general, and especially in his ability to create people
and history: "creator, when life awoke/ I peopled my world with
my creatures [creador, al despertar la vida/ poblé mi mundo con
mis criaturas]." [59] His main impulse is a desire, or even a need, to
experience everything that he can. His curiosity is unlimited, while
the majority of his characters show an interest in knowing only

58. Ferrater Mora, *Unamuno*, p. 120.
59. *Cancionero*, no. 1748, Nov. 23, 1936.

what most directly affects them, the reason for their plight, but show little curiosity to learn how to rectify it or at least to bring forth some hope of salvation.

In some ways, then, his characters seem to be negative examples of heroism, at least insofar as Unamuno is concerned. This is deceptive, however, because every individual's needs differ and the examples, even negative ones, set before him may in some way respond to his own questioning. Julián Marías points out that Unamuno's characters have the same objective lack of reality and justification as man himself.[60] They lack the strength to support themselves in their existence and eventually fade from sight, just as mediocre man, seen from God's point of view, essentially does. He wanders through his life without specific motives and searches for an escape. Both the mediocre man and the literary character, however, have the capacity to be heroic by giving themselves faith and a deeply felt mission in life that responds to the situation in which either God or the writer has thrust them. They must account for their presence, using the few tools they have: their individuality, their consciousness, their imagination, and their spacio-temporal setting. Unamuno creates an ontological hierarchy in which the character aspires to be a reality, to put himself on an equal footing with phenomenological man (see, for example, Augusto Pérez), while man aspires to be God. The process by which each aspires to the superior state is heroism. There are, however, some characters who aspire to godliness, such as Don Quixote, and Unamuno's efforts are designed largely to keep him from falling behind such characters.

So it is that all real characters become, like all real men, agonic. Their aspirations are the same, their reality is no less, and their efforts are just as heroic. For this reason, Unamuno chooses to call all his characters, and all men who partake of a considerable degree of reality, "agonists": "A truly agonizing man is an agonist, sometimes a protagonist, other times an antagonist." [61] There are, to be sure, many characters who have no real existence, but we must limit our discussion to those who have enough reality to be capable of achieving heroism, regardless of whether they ever do.

60. Julián Marías, *Miguel de Unamuno*, p. 93 and passim.
61. "Prólogo," *La agonía del cristianismo*, O.C. 16: 457.

López Morillas has pointed out an important aspect of Unamuno's distinction between antagonists and protagonists: "while Unamuno shares with his agonists the quality of being a man, putting aside as secondary the ideological aspect, in his antagonists, on the other hand, the author makes the ideological aspect stand out, putting aside as secondary the quality of being a man." [62] Unamuno's concentration on the human aspects of his protagonists, with all their flaws and inconsistencies, is intended to make them come alive; but his antagonists do not generally represent anything that could even remotely be termed heroism because they are mere vehicles intended to collide with the protagonists and leave the imprint of their form, although seldom of their personalities. They are shadowy and show few signs of evolution or change. Just as man must spend his lifetime dealing with concepts that may deeply change his attitude about himself and his existence, so must the protagonists of the novels.

Unamuno veers away from the realistic interpenetration of characters in his novels and plays, although he does not deny its importance in life. To reveal as much as possible of his protagonists, he does not create an entire society of real people, in the manner of Balzac and Galdós, but limits himself to one person's struggle with existence and his effect on others, rather than theirs on him. To this stripping of the novel he adds a simplification of the protagonists' agony. Julián Marías sees this limited interpretation of the characters as one of the most significant aspects of Unamuno's novelistic technique: "Unamuno respects the essential *opacity* of the person. He never shows his characters, not even when he sees them 'from within,' in all their clarity and transparency, because he knows very well that the human person is never completely possessed, not even by himself, but rather that he conceals an inscrutable mystery." [63] They are rarely weighed down by many concerns, but rather by one, which, in its turn, affects their entire existence. All aspects of the protagonists' personalities are fused into this single preoccupation, so that, rather than settle for breadth, like the realists, he settles for depth in a limited facet. The protagonists become clinical cases, as Manuel Durán points out: "Idea and emotion are fused together —

62. Juan López Morillas, "Unamuno y sus criaturas: 'Antolín S. Paparrigópulos,'" *Cuadernos Americanos* 7, no. 4 (1948): 240.

63. Julián Marías, *Filosofía española actual* (Madrid, 1963), p. 65.

and this is how the intimate character of a living being operates — but it is a question of a single idea, a single emotion, which, of course, makes it possible to obtain ideal conditions of in vitro experimentation." [64]

Unamuno thereby makes a definitive break with the techniques of nineteenth-century realism and, rather than a multitude of shallow samplings, limits himself to one impressively deep vertical examination, representative of the totality of the character's being. Depth is consequently given to protagonists by the use of monologues, which Unamuno admits may seem unrealistic but which serve to get directly to the matter at hand without the need for elaborate artistic devices. The monologue is, after all, a discussion or, more often, a conflict between the various egos that make up the complex human personality, and to eavesdrop on characters' conversations obviates the need for narrative passages, which disappear almost entirely after *Paz en la guerra*. In this way, Unamuno is obviously successful at reaching the intimacy he wants. Beginning with *Niebla*, a turning point in his control of his characters, none of his protagonists dies without protest, unless it is at the hand of God himself, and this can be effective only if the writer can justify their rebelliousness by revealing — or rather by having his characters reveal — to the reader all the mechanisms that motivate their view of themselves.

The Innovations in Unamuno's Characterizations

We see, then, that despite their reality and personalities, Unamuno's characters always remain under his dominion for a number of reasons. They struggle to be free and totally independent, and this gives them vitality by lending drama to their plight, but they are always unfinished, as Unamuno deliberately does not develop their lesser aspects. Their reality is due to the act of speculation that this lack of completion permits the reader. What if the character had been different? How would this have affected the totality of his being? Unamuno gives us enough to make them believable,

---

64. Manuel Durán, "La técnica de la novela y la generación del noventa y ocho," *Revista Hispánica Moderna* 23 (1957): 23.

but not enough so that they can be freed from their dependence on him, their creator, as Don Quixote and Sancho were freed from theirs.

His control also lies in his seeing first the conflict and then creating a character who reacts to it in a meaningful, even though futile, way. For this reason he soon ceases to feel the need for elaborate physical details. The characters never become complete enough to exist for us outside that situation, and they have reality for the reader only insofar as they are examples of certain ontological struggles, just as the reader himself is, or could be. Agnes Moncy feels that they would have been more real if Unamuno had not imagined how he would have reacted in such a situation, but instead had put someone totally different into his characters. That is, if he had made them less limited by their autobiographical qualities: "If he had not transferred himself so completely to the spirit he invented, even to the point of supplanting it by filling it with himself, and if he had been more prepared to imagine the reactions of the other one, perhaps he would have managed to create beings less dependent on Unamuno's feeling and belief." [65]

Whether this would have been desirable, given the motives for his fiction, remains dubious, for, like Eugenio de Nora,[66] Moncy seems to desire greater objectivity rather than greater reality, a goal Unamuno was not attempting to reach. Instead of creating the complex, fictitious society that Nora would have desired, Unamuno strips his characters of all physical (apparential) details and leaves them with little more than their psychological (substantial) individuality to identify them and give meaning to their doubts. He is a writer of protest, whose fiction gives perspective and strength to the plight of man as an individual in the face of the dehumanizing forces of positivism and its ideological successors. Sherman Eoff explains the difficult reality of Unamuno's fiction by saying that "he is one of the most conspicuous spokesmen for the modern uneasiness that finds individual consciousness called upon to justify itself in a world view that holds the physical universe in the spotlight and

65. Agnes Moncy, *La creación del personaje en las novelas de Unamuno* (Santander, 1963), p. 31.

66. Eugenio de Nora, *La novela española contemporánea* (Madrid, 1963), 1: 15.

relegates the human self to the background." [67] His protest is on behalf of progress and demands, not a return to the social focus of Galdós, but an examination of the individual existence in its relation to both society and the cosmos. His characters do not rise to the impressive magnitude of the heroes of the earlier novels, but rather represent the extension of the mediocre protagonist of the nineteenth century toward the non-hero and anti-hero of the later existentialists and even toward the absurdity of the postexistentialist protagonists.

The realists destroyed the technique of typification of characters designed to illustrate a thesis. In Galdós, the novelist ceases to be the chronicler or secretary of reality and becomes, instead, its translator or interpreter by way of the creation of accessible characters, who form the most decisive element in his novels. For three-quarters of a century, social revolutions had changed the principles of European literature, and levels of society virtually unknown in literature of the eighteenth century emerged onto the literary scene, revealing an individuality that the realists had to recognize. The protagonist acquired a new depth and was composed partly of what men are made of and partly of what the writer's imagination made them. Ordinary people in whom the reader could see himself became protagonists, and the novelist had to underscore certain aspects of their day-to-day personalities so that the individuality necessary to maintain interest would become evident. That is to say, they were ordinary, but with a difference that would justify their position as protagonists.

As a consequence, the hero as such tended to disappear because the great distance between principal and secondary characters and between protagonists and readers could no longer be so easily maintained. Social boundaries had begun to disappear, and it was more difficult to isolate the hero and make of him a truly colossal figure. He could no longer be monolithic but had to be composed of many facets; he could no longer represent just a class or an idea, but rather the complexity of the human soul; he no longer represented a limited existence, however impressive, in a larger context, but

67. Sherman Eoff, *The Modern Spanish Novel* (New York, 1961), p. 187.

rather life itself, a single part of which was revealed in a limited framework suggesting that the life of the character transcended his novelistic function. The plot became a function of the character, and the character, a small sample of a social situation.

Unamuno dispenses with the limited social setting and places his characters in a setting without boundaries, out of place and out of time. Individuality becomes the sole preoccupation, not as a specific social problem, but as an ontological quest. The protagonist has no setting beyond one of ideas (his and others') and of responses (his). Unamuno immediately limits his scope for the creation of heroic figures because heroism is a distinctly social phenomenon and his protagonists have scarcely any society in which to exercise their will. Instead, Unamuno presents his reader with heroism's raw material, and by means of the ideas that are bounced off the protagonists by the antagonists, allows the reader to decide for himself what sort of hero the protagonist *could* have been — and more important, what type of a hero the reader believes that *he* could be. By permitting the protagonist to belong to the middle classes, the realists allowed a greater majority to identify with him through the similarity of their social settings. Unamuno, on the other hand, lets the reader identify by presenting him with various possibilities for the ego, without limiting him with an undue number of material considerations. This better reflects contemporary man's sense of alienation and leads ahead to the fiction of Sartre, Camus, Beckett, Borges, and Cela.

6. Unamuno's Concept of Heroism in His Fictional Works

In the *Diario íntimo,* we are warned: "One must go to the theory by way of the practice; this is the right road. By wanting to set off from the theory, one remains impotent." [1] And yet we must try to give some meaningful structure to Unamuno's system of fictive creations insofar as their heroic, and thus real, qualities are concerned. Any attempt to place each protagonist in a category is at best arbitrary but is intended to clarify Unamuno's own manner of bestowing or removing reality so that we may see how each protagonist reacts to the situation in which he finds himself, and to what degree Unamuno gives him the individual strength, imagination, and consciousness to overcome obstacles, impose his ego, and achieve an independent immortality.

Several attempts have already been made — with varying degrees of success — to classify the characters, all for different purposes and based on differing criteria. Agnes Moncy divides them loosely into two groups as viewed from the position of the ego, the consciousness of the strongest and most aware character: "obstacles to his being, and more infrequently, spiritual participants in his being." [2] The difficulty presented by this grouping is that it leaves no room for consideration of the overwhelming majority of Unamuno's creations — those who are indifferent to their own ego in relation to others, either through some form of spiritual blindness or through ignorance.

Manuel Durán also classifies them in two groups: those who go through some sort of psychological or, as is more often the case, spirit-

1. *Diario íntimo,* p. 315.
2. Moncy, *La creación del personaje,* p. 37.

ual evolution (Manuel Bueno, Augusto Pérez) and those who undergo virtually no change at all (Tula, Alejandro Gómez). This division shares many similarities with López Morillas's distinction between protagonists (very human) and antagonists (pure ideas).[3] In making this distinction, Durán says:

> The rectilinear character escapes the conflict through the very vigor of his progression, which nothing can stop; the agonic character, on the other hand, fully lives the conflict, but when the tremendous inner fight that consumes him is made pure, when the conflict becomes independent of the external world, and thereby stabilizes itself against any influence of circumstances, it ceases to develop on the temporal level and becomes a conflict of essences, eternal and, in a way, inhuman.[4]

The question is to examine the inner workings of these characters in their vision of themselves, and their success in fulfilling that vision, in order to try to see what failings Unamuno gives them that make them, at best, only partially heroic. Those who are *agónicos* must closely approximate the heroic ideal; but both types do reveal possibilities of being, the significance of which must be examined and weighed in order to evaluate heroism as a force for achievement.

Eleazar Huerta makes a division into four categories, which are, to a certain degree, an extension of those made by Durán:

> There will be characters who, since they are purely *superficial,* will not capture the basic truth because they are concerned about their appetites, routines, and entanglements. . . . Other deeply feeling (*entrañables*) characters capture the basic truth only vaguely, but without knowing it; they do not see it with desperate clarity. A third type, the *pedants,* sees it badly and therefore faces it falsely. Finally, there is a class of Unamunesque characters who understand the great problem and react to it in an authentic way: this is the group made up of those who reach the *tragic* level.[5]

The difficulty with this classification is that it suggests that those who are tragic are to some degree successful, which is not precisely

3. López Morillas, "Unamuno y sus criaturas," p. 240.
4. Durán, "La técnica de la novela," p. 24.
5. Eleazar Huerta, "Unamuno novelista," in *Unamuno,* ed. Mauricio Amster (Santiago de Chile, 1964), p. 123.

true. Huerta divides the characters mainly on the basis of their attitudes toward their position rather than on their success in rising to meet and, if necessary, overcome it. As heroism is also a social phenomenon and only attains its complete meaning in a specific situation, the external forces must also be examined in order to understand the complete character.

The emotional relationships must be seen in context, since Unamuno is almost exclusively concerned with spiritual points of contact. Serrano Poncela characterizes the technique as follows: "What happens is that, in order to carry out his function, he must have a minimum of aesthetic content and a maximum of thinking tension, and because of this his characters and his settings become amazingly schematic." [6] Especially in the works after *Niebla*, a particular character trait becomes the driving force for the novels and plays, and its effect on all who surround the protagonist becomes the touchstone for the protagonist's success or failure in his effort to impose his personality upon his context. We shall, then, use the principles of personal plenitude as described in previous chapters to attempt to evaluate the protagonists' efforts to conquer their situation and achieve reality, taking into consideration not only their individual characters, but also the external pressures exerted upon their efforts by others and by life itself, particularly the conflict between history and fiction, and the internal forces of the diverse parts of the ego, which are in a state of constant struggle.

The Basis: Paz en la guerra

A separate case must be made for *Paz en la guerra*; its theme is not an individual one, but rather a collective one in which the individuals are practice models for what is to come. By Unamuno's own admission, this novel is oviparous. It was published in 1897 after many years in which he collected notes, documented the work for historical accuracy, and expanded it from a short story ("Solitaña," 1889) to one of his longest single works. It served as a basis for almost everything that Unamuno did in the future, both philosophically and artistically, since it was his last truly oviparous work, and also the last fictional

6. Segundo Serrano Poncela, "Encuentros con Unamuno," in *El secreto de Melibea* (Madrid, 1959), p. 196.

work in which the protagonist was a collective one. He says in the prologue to the second edition (1923) that "here is the revelation that history was for me, and with it art." After the publication of this novel, Unamuno separated himself from the legacy of Tolstoy and the realists and moved toward the future with his "intimate dramas," a form much better adapted to his purposes and to his vision of the human situation. In the future he concentrated on the inner tensions and eliminated much of the exterior decoration, explaining that, "I did not want to distract the reader from the story of the development of human actions and passions." [7] We must see how this change came about and to what extent the seeds for the following works were sown in the years leading up to 1897.

In an extraordinary number of his works to follow, the theme was that of envy and internal conflict. This theme of inner strife became a vital force for Unamuno, and in *Paz en la guerra* he showed both sides of the problem: the civil conflict and the resulting consciousness of human brotherhood. This is indeed his only work in which a social situation is examined broadly, horizontally, with the focus on a stratum and the function of various individuals within it. The war arrives in Bilbao and brings with it a social consciousness that the populace has not yet felt, but, in accordance with his belief in intrahistory, Unamuno does not allow the individuals to disappear in their anonymity. Rather, he examines the extent to which they are affected by the events and what importance this has on the daily life — on an eternal, rather than on an immediate, scale — of the society at large. As Julián Marías illustrates: "On the one hand, everyday life becomes stronger, rises higher, and becomes more personalized; instead of feeling themselves in collectivity as if they were almost vegetably implanted in a body, men feel as though they are participants in a historical destiny, subjects of that lofty event which is developing before their very eyes, therefore, personages." [8]

Nevertheless, this feeling of individual significance within a large and apparently momentous historical context is somewhat illusory, since the waves pass while the depths are left essentially unchanged. Each man feels important as an individual, much as Pedro Antonio

---

7. "Prólogo," 2d ed. (1923), *Paz en la guerra*, O.C. 2: 73, 74.
8. Marías, *Miguel de Unamuno*, p. 83. See also chapter 1 above.

does when he recalls his participation in the first Carlist war of 1833–39, but the practical effects are few. The protagonist in an event of this magnitude is not the individual but the people, and the historical fact is something of a phantom. The individual feels that he is participating when in fact he has little or no effect and, conversely, the war may seem to have an irremediable effect on his life, as it does in the case of Pedro Antonio, but that effect does not really change the intrahistory of which he forms a part.

Unamuno discovers in this novel the impossibility of evaluating the meaning of individual effort in a historical setting in which social upheaval becomes the decisive element. His task in the future will be to find out what makes up society. We have already said that he reveals the depths of his characters through personal details, and from the outset he uses this technique in *Paz en la guerra*. The guests who take part in the gatherings in Pedro Antonio's home are described by means of the gestures which they habitually employ and which are indicative of their personalities, just as they have been of men since time immemorial. They are the deepest and most unchanging aspect of intrahistory, for they express individuality through the immutable alluvion of mankind's existence. As Blanco Aguinaga explains: "The circumstance does indeed exist, with its pains, but *if we contemplate it from outside of ourselves,* or from *within* our eternal Humanity, it turns out to be only a contingent part of a whole that is always equal to itself." [9] Thus, although these friends are symbolic as individuals partaking of a certain measure of reality, none is so centrally placed as to be the basis for the entire action.

Unamuno creates for himself two autobiographical figures who serve as alter egos: Ignacio Iturriondo and Pachico Zabalbide. Ignacio begins passively, much like his father but even more like his mother. He is given a traditional Catholic education and is an unconscious recipient of his people's traditions. His readings of the exploits of the great heroes begin to instill in him some feeling of rebelliousness, and he tries unsuccessfully to assert himself at various points in the novel, especially when the war approaches and he feels compelled to fight. He does have some heroic characteristics; but like many of Unamuno's characters, he is stifled by his environment: first at home, then in

9. Blanco Aguinaga, *El Unamuno contemplativo*, p. 62.

Bilbao, and finally in the war where action is the only certain belief: "There no one spoke of ideas or principles. Once the action of war had begun, ideas were converted into movement, spread around and reduced to movement; when they came together, they were transformed into action, pure action, sower of new ideas."

Heroism is action, but pure action leads to blindness, and this becomes Ignacio's failing. He has been brought up to believe in Carlism since birth, through his father's participation in the first Carlist war, as well as through the traditionalism of his mother and his Catholic education. No choice was made by Ignacio and his sense of duty is based on the positivistic inevitability of his environment rather than on any individually evolved will to act. Within the struggle he has no personal significance, and although he can say, "I do my duty," [10] the mission is accidental. Like his fellow soldiers, he learns the importance of fraternal unity in a common cause; but, like them, he does not understand what that cause is or whether it is really his, for it is a fight against an abstraction. The enemy means nothing and none of them can say why he is the foe: he is just "the other one."

Even Ignacio's death is of no importance to his cause. He has not made himself indispensable and his individuality has been lost. The only real effect his sacrifice has is on his father, who returns to his faith in order to find consolation. However, there is no doubt that Ignacio's reality will vanish with his father's — and that Pedro Antonio's, in turn, will disappear because his contribution to the previous war contributed little to his personality and he has even lost his son in this one, thus leaving him with virtually no hope of immortality. Social change can swamp the individual, yet without changing the structure of intrahistory.

Most of the other characters are so sketchy as to vanish into the haze of the novel. Those who do emerge with any degree of reality help principally to illustrate why Ignacio was powerless to assert himself and rise above his environment. Tío Pascual is a priest whose theology leaves no room for any sort of intellectual consideration, and he is darkly responsible for the automatic and arbitrary ideas instilled in Ignacio, which so resemble his own: "He believed in the Demon just as he believed in God, often without distinguishing the work of

10. *Paz en la guerra*, O.C. 2: 208, 218.

one from that of the other." [11] There is no need for him to make a commitment, and so Ignacio is not called upon to make one either.

Celestino, the Carlist lawyer, is a pedant of the type we shall see repeatedly in Unamuno's works. Life for him is something upon which to impose his monolithic views. With unflinching blindness and insufferable ignorance he dedicates himself to repeating the views of others in an attempt to mold those who will listen into an image so irrelevant to the needs of the individual as to be pernicious, not only to the victim but to society at large. He impresses the naïve Ignacio and, with Tío Pascual, becomes the other negative force in Ignacio's life and a principal cause of its meaningless destruction.

The other characters complete the picture of this eternal society: don Juan Arana, slave to his desk; the superstitious don Miguel Arana, who by the end of the novel seems to have merited his death when he looks back upon his life and feels "an immense sadness at not having lived and a belated repentance for that fear of happiness which had made him lose it." There is also Ignacio's father, a passive dreamer like his son. He lives in the past, which he sees as his moment of glory and personal expression, and even his vision of present events is merely a projection of his memories upon a new screen. Life presents few problems for him and he makes little effort to rise. He is the man whose life is not subject to his own will but is entrusted to luck, which almost never interferes with the regularity of all that he does: "His existence flowed like the current of a gentle river, with an unheard murmur that would not be noticed until it was interrupted." It is almost as if he had not existed at all, were it not for his son; and when Ignacio dies, for the first time in the novel Pedro Antonio begins to realize the vacuum he has made out of his life: "Pedro Antonio felt, with a feeling that was not concrete, that with his son had died the cause for which he gave his life." [12] Pedro Antonio had relived his own youth through his son, and once he was taken away from him, there was nothing left that mattered in the war. He had made no life of his own and his only creative act was his son, who was allowed to have scarcely any more success than his father. Pedro Antonio finds peace in religion, at the urging of Pascual, and his life continues its

11. Ibid., p. 146.
12. Ibid., pp. 310, 78, 377–78.

meaningless course, particularly after the death of his wife, for even if he had the will to act, there is no polarization possible now.

Josefa Ignacia is typical of many of Unamuno's women: she is serene and calm, happy in a faith that she scarcely understands. Her placidity and her husband's grayness are the background for the life of their son. They have complemented each other throughout the mediocrity of their existence, and she represents for her husband the years of heroism, 1833–39, the years in which he was a fighter and conquered her. For his wife, Pedro Antonio had been a crusader in those years. Nevertheless, she responds to the death of her son with all a mother's sorrow. She is not heroic, but Unamuno rarely expected this of his women.

The positive forces in the life of Ignacio were Juan José and Unamuno's other autobiographical character, Pachico. Juan José and Ignacio had tried to be heroic from their earliest years together, when they had conquered the mountain, and what few signs of heroism Ignacio did acquire came from these two characters — the only ones, moreover, who saw how futile his death really was. From the beginning, Juan José has a feeling for epic greatness and grandiose gestures, and he conceives of the war as a truly heroic opportunity. He wanted the war to finish with "something unexpected, heroic. Out of faith's last effort would rise the miracle." [13] Only then could the war really acquire meaning and justify its length, its resulting hardships, and its destruction. His disgust defeats him, for he abandons the cause, believing that the paralyzed will of the country should deprive it of any right to be saved. He allows himself to be destroyed by the very apathy he so hates, much as many other characters will.

Pachico Zabalbide is by far the most profound and enigmatic character in the novel. Never sufficiently complete to be real, he is a vehicle for the commentary of Unamuno in the years before he inserts himself directly into his novels. He is considered by his contemporaries to be odd, and his introspection leads him to weigh the value of becoming a saint, much as occurred with the young Unamuno. A great reader of Chateaubriand and the Catholic Romantics, he finds himself torn between the emotional pull of faith and his attempts to rationalize it; and, like Unamuno, he is deeply influenced

13. Ibid., p. 390.

by the heroic world of Shakespeare and by the writings of Ossian. Since he was intended to be a representation of Unamuno, he could safely be given greater psychological depth than the other characters. His way of expressing himself reveals him to be a complex person who deeply impresses those who come into contact with him. He is mainly concerned with instilling his listeners with doubts and new ways of thinking: "his two listeners left him with hot heads and cold feet, yes, but with a jumble of dark ideas suggested to them by the impact of that thought which was so foreign to them." [14] The conflict between all and nothingness runs throughout his thought, and will, of course, be a vital problem for some of the later characters; but he is never given a chance really to change anything in the novel. The reader is left with the feeling that here indeed is a heroic personage, but Unamuno lets him talk and contemplate without ever having much effect.

Oddly enough, Pachico has the function of Unamuno's future antagonists — he represents ideas rather than any real humanity — yet he has the character of a hero and an "agonist." He is preoccupied with the ego, and in his moments of contemplation the problem of the individual and his relationship with others becomes vivid. He feels the need for action and is quick to reject the purely contemplative or studious life because he feels that opportunities for fulfillment are fleeting. For this reason, he expresses Unamuno's desire "to be oneself and to be all": "To have to pass from yesterday to tomorrow without being able to live at the same time throughout all time!" He is moved by the anguish and consciousness that Unamuno demands in his philosophical works, and expresses the heroic fear of annihilation if life is permitted to slip away into oblivion and insignificance. Desire for immortality is his driving force: "It was a crazy terror of nothingness, of finding himself alone in empty time, a crazy terror that shook his heart into palpitations and made him dream that, without air, smothered, he was falling continuously and without rest into the eternal void, in a terrible fall." [15]

This is, of course, an expression of Unamuno's own fears, and the war merely confirms Pachico's feelings until he realizes fully the

14. Ibid., p. 137.
15. Ibid., pp. 133, 134.

need for individual heroism, based on personal initiative: "the world offers itself entirely and without reservation to whomever without reservation and entirely offers himself." The heroic mission gives meaning to the individual existence, and Pachico then decides on action and eternal war. He has retired momentarily to his solitude and has come to see more clearly what his mission must be: "Up there, serene contemplation gives him transcendent and eternal resignation, the mother of the temporal lack of resignation, of the inability ever to be content down here, of the constant asking for greater rewards, and he comes down having decided to provoke discontent in others, for this is the prime impulse of all progress and all good." [16] He has understood his position and formulated his attitudes. His mission has been determined and we know enough about his character to see in him a true hero. No other character in Unamuno's work will give such clear indications of all the necessary traits, and Pachico alone among the protagonists seems capable of succeeding completely.

Unamuno has not solved anything in this novel: the ending is merely a promise of greater struggles to come. Pachico, however, is the key to success, and perhaps for that reason will never be dealt with by Unamuno again. He is the only character who begins to find answers to his questions. Unamuno has passed through his period of apprenticeship and in all his later works will limit his focus to the individual.

The Heroic Effort

No attempt to cast light on Unamuno's theories of heroism could be based on a chronological accounting of his works, and for that reason this classification is based entirely on the success of each protagonist in achieving his goal and his reasons for aiming for it. Since none succeeds totally, the characters have been divided on the basis of that gap between the actual and the ideal, or as is often the case, between fiction and reality. Those whose personalities are rich and well-developed but who, through lack of confidence, doubt, or fear, fail to achieve completely heroic dimensions are the pathetic heroes. They are placed in and defeated by a situation of their own making

16. Ibid., pp. 415, 417.

and are victims of their own strength since, as agonizing individuals, they feel their ontological ambiguity too deeply and fall into despair rather than rise effectively to the challenge. The most nearly heroic of all the characters, theirs is a success of half measures, and much of their inspiration for the reader derives from the frustration felt at the elusive nearness of that success. The reasons for this, which are really two, have already been suggested: Unamuno protects his own position; and he wants to elicit this reaction in the reader so that he, too, will participate and thereby benefit from the failure, however partial it may be, of the protagonists. The most outstanding example of the pathetic hero is, of course, Manuel Bueno.

The Triumph of Reason: *San Manuel Bueno, mártir*

The theme of believing while doubting is a constant throughout Unamuno's writings and received its fullest theoretical treatment in 1925 with the publication of *La agonía del cristianismo*. He gave it life and new dimensions in *San Manuel Bueno, mártir,* written in 1930 and one of his most concrete works. In the latter there is no abstraction of the ego, nor is the protagonist an incarnation of a mono-mania, as is the case in most of the other novels. Don Manuel represents creative doubt. He lives with death throughout his life. It is not terror of death specifically that corrodes his strength, but rather the feeling that earthly life may have no purpose if there is no im-mortality. This is indeed a heroic concern, but, as has been said, Unamuno felt that such a sense of despair could possibly be allevi-ated by fame, as it was in part for Don Quixote, or by physical de-scendants.

Neither of these choices is open to don Manuel, however, because he is a priest whose mission is to show the significance of eternal resurrection. He cannot compromise with mere fame, nor can he count on children to re-create him through time: he can create dis-ciples, but they will be followers of what he himself does not believe in and they cannot perpetuate his intimate being, but only an image of him. Therefore, don Manuel's only hope of salvation lies in the hero's polarization — here, between the priest and his parishioners. They need him to teach them about and give them faith in eternal life, while he needs them to help him to believe, since he is incapable of believing on his own. Just as Don Quixote's flagging faith was restored by the encouragement of Sancho, so don Manuel looks for the same support from the people of Valverde de Lucerna.

The novel is yet another treatment of the problem (or what at this time Unamuno was calling the "mystery") of personality. "The other one" in this case is the parish. In don Manuel, there is not a true conflict between reason and emotion, since he has no faith and that is what the parishioners provide: they are his faith and he is their reason. They complement each other; but just as the hero cannot exist without his audience, so don Manuel finds himself on the brink of oblivion and annihilation throughout his life. He saves his parishioners from despair through his reason, but because theirs is the "collier's faith," they do not depend on him for existence in the way that he needs them for justification. Specifically, he doubts his own immortality but searches for peace for his flock.

Although he has lost his faith, he has tried to replace it with his sense of ethical responsibility. That is, he tries to fulfill his mission as he sees it even though he questions its validity. This is his weakness, of course, for if the hero must constantly re-evaluate his course of action and its relevance to his personal frame of reference, why does don Manuel continue what he feels is a lost cause? The answer is one we have already examined: that it is no more certain that there is *not* a chance for immortality than it is that there *is* a chance, and don Manuel decides that while he personally doubts, there is no reason to destroy his flock by robbing them of their simple hope. Rather than insist constantly on his own beliefs in the hope of converting someone to his cause, he has chosen to champion his followers' cause in the hope that he will be able to convert himself.

Don Manuel's position is ambivalent because he seems to equivocate in his teachings and this could be unjust, as Unamuno points out; but don Manuel feels that if there is a God and immortality, his duty is to lead his flock toward them. Don Quixote released the galley slaves because he felt that, although it was not right in secular terms, it was acceptable from the superior point of view of divine justice. Don Manuel echoes this sentiment when he says: "Human justice does not concern me." [17] Just as his mission is to indoctrinate his parishioners as if there were a God, he himself must try to live in ac-

17. *San Manuel Bueno, mártir,* O.C. 16: 588–89.

cordance with this possibility too. He must devote himself entirely to the salvation of the town, as his entire existence will become illusory and irrelevant without the immortality that can be his only through the success of these efforts.

For this reason he almost never allows himself to be alone with his fears: the people sustain him, give him justification, and are his polarization, and he admits: "I must not live alone; I must not die alone. I must live for my people, die for my people. How am I going to save my soul if I do not save my people's soul?" [18] He creates faith in the people so that they may live heroically, for without it, they could lack the strength to live at all. Manuel Bueno is a hero whose mission is inconsistent with his personality, but this is also the source of his heroism: to the best of his ability he tries to rise above this limitation and fulfill his purpose.

There is another obstacle to the total honesty of don Manuel: the town would not have believed in his lack of faith in any case. Heroism is deeds, and those of don Manuel carried far more weight than any protestations regarding his beliefs: "They would have believed in his works and not in his words, because words do not serve to support works, but rather the works are enough in themselves." [19] He was not making an intellectual or rational appeal to his parishioners, but an emotional one. They were not, and would not have been, interested in his theology because the deep spiritual crises through which he passed would have been meaningless to them. Reality is what makes people work and this is the basis of the people's belief in don Manuel's faith. They could see its positive results in their daily lives, and whether or not these good works to which he devoted himself had their basis in hypocrisy would be of no importance to them.

Obviously, this lays open the entire question of the truth of the religion that don Manuel was teaching, but he said that human justice did not concern him and he clearly felt that the religion he gave them was the most relevant to their lives: "True religion? All religions are true, as long as they cause the people who profess them to live spiritually, as long as they comfort them for having to be born

18. Ibid., p. 594.
19. Ibid., p. 628.

in order to die; and for each people the truest religion is their own, the one that has made them. And mine? Mine is to comfort myself by comforting others, even though the comfort that I give them may not be my own." [20] Religion is man's support, but not his master. Don Manuel may be providing a placebo, a fiction for his parishioners, but it enriches them and makes life more meaningful for them. This makes it truth and, as Unamuno says, don Manuel's main characteristic is "heroic saintliness," while Lázaro refers to don Manuel's "saintly cause." [21]

If don Manuel's actions had led him to faith, both in himself and in the hope of immortality, he would indeed have been a true hero; but his rational being defeated his will, or as Lázaro says, "he is too intelligent to believe everything that he has to teach." He cannot, then, pass his lifetime in contemplation because that is what has weakened him: "His life was active and not contemplative, as he fled as much as he could from having nothing to do." [22] Through his charitable activities and his complete dedication to the welfare and faith of his people, he could avoid excessive reflection on the danger of annihilation. These activities were also a possible source of faith in the sense that they brought him closer to those who did believe and might have given him some of their faith, but did not.

There are many circumstantial similarities between don Manuel, Don Quixote, and Christ. Like Don Quixote, don Manuel refused to believe in anyone's evil intentions, and like both of them, he left none of his teachings in writing. These are superficial points of contact, to be sure, but they do create a certain parallelism with other heroic figures, and Unamuno thus leads us to wonder how many others who seemed to have unshakable faith were indeed racked by doubts and fears. On his deathbed, Don Quixote renounced his faith, just as in his last mass don Manuel renounces his hope of heroism and says, "There is no eternal life other than this one." [23] After having given up all hope of faith he, too, dies; but just as Unamuno hopes

20. Ibid., p. 605.
21. Ibid., pp. 593, 605.
22. Ibid., pp. 601, 590.
23. Ibid., p. 314. Fundamental to a complete understanding of *San Manuel Bueno* is Ricardo Gullón's article, "El testamento de don Miguel," in *Autobiografías de Unamuno* (Madrid, 1964), pp. 331–55.

for the resurrection of Don Quixote, so the townspeople hope for that of don Manuel.

Don Manuel's Sancho is Lázaro, the progressive atheist who becomes a devoted disciple of Manuel's creative doubt in a deep spiritual union. Lázaro is his real triumph, much more so than the town itself, because Manuel brings him from negation and atheism to doubt and belief in a possibility. Lázaro is his spiritual son and will carry on after his death in a similar state of dynamism and tension, very much alive and very active. If Manuel managed to satisfy the town by means of a well-intentioned deceit, this was not possible with Lázaro, whom he could convert only by means of a more rationally based truth. He believed in Lázaro and put him on the road to the absolutes that he himself never found, but not by means of the blind faith of Valverde or Blas, the village idiot who mechanically repeats the things he hears, much as the parishioners do. If Blas and Valverde represent don Manuel as seen from without, Lázaro and, to a certain extent, Angela, reveal him from within. Angela is to don Manuel what Paul was to Christ and what Cervantes was to Don Quixote. She, too, eventually enters into a state of creative doubt, as she evolves within her own narrative and begins to see both sides of don Manuel's heroism: that which changed the parishioners as well as that darker side which changed Lázaro but destroyed don Manuel.

The Triumph of Faith: *El hermano Juan* and "Una visita al viejo poeta"

On October 19, 1900, Unamuno said in a letter to Pedro Jiménez Ilundain: "The fundamental concept is that the world is a theater, and that in it every one thinks only of the gallery; that while he thinks he is acting on his own, the fact is that he is reciting the part they taught him in eternity." [24] He was speaking of *Amor y pedagogía*, published two years later and, as we shall see, this aspect was later dropped. However, the idea continued throughout Unamuno's lifetime and forms the basis for his last original drama, *El hermano Juan* (1934), in the prologue to which he says:

24. Quoted by Geoffrey Ribbans, "The development of Unamuno's *Amor y pedagogía* and *Niebla*," *Hispanic Studies in Honour of J. González Llubera* (Oxford, 1959), p. 271.

Because all the ideal greatness of Don Juan Tenorio, all his eternal and universal reality — that is, all his historical reality —
consists in the fact that he is the most obviously theatrical, representative, historical character in that he is always acting — that
is to say, playing himself to himself, and not to his mistresses.
The material, the biological, aspects disappear beside this. Biol-
ogy yields to biography, the material, to the spirit.[25]

To Don Quixote's cry of "I know who I am!" Unamuno observes that
Don Juan could respond with "I know that I am performing" or "I
know what I am performing."

In *El hermano Juan,* then, Unamuno proposes to examine heroism
as a theatrical gesture, and he creates a character whose entire personality starts out as histrionics. Inés says to him: "You——, I don't
know——, but, really, it strikes me that you are always performing"
— and indeed he is. Nonetheless, at the end of the play he can
respond by pointing out: "but we are nothing less than a complete
theater! Literature made flesh." [26] This is the fate of Don Juan: he is
a product of a literary tradition and is burdened by his theatricality;
he is not what his performance would suggest and he, like so many
other characters in Unamuno's work, will find himself torn between
these two personalities. He will achieve a greater degree of heroism
than the others because he is aware of his performance and tries to
control it and to protect — or rather, discover — his personality. The
tension created within him by this dramatic conflict between his
consciousness and his lack of personality has dangerously undermined his confidence in himself: "I was born condemned to being
unable to make a woman of any woman, unable to make a man of
myself." [27] He finds himself unable truly to impose his personality
on anyone in spite of — or rather, because of — the reputation he
has developed as a reincarnation of Don Juan Tenorio.

He sees himself, then, as a joker tricked by his own cunning: "My
job. A trickster . . . tricked. How lucky I am!" The problem of personality is especially difficult for Juan, more so than for any other

    25. Prologue, *El hermano Juan,* O.C. 12: 866.
    26. *El hermano Juan,* O.C. 12: 889, 980. See also Ricardo Gullón, "The
Soul on Stage," in *Unamuno: creator and creation,* ed. J. Rubia Barcia,
M. A. Zeitlin (Berkeley, 1967), pp. 139–55.
    27. Ibid., p. 886.

character who agonizes in Unamuno's work with the exception of Manuel Bueno, who at least found that he could live with the personality he projected, whereas Juan finds that he has no personality whatever beyond that which he must portray. Antonio advises him to give up his life as a shadow of Tenorio and become a real man:

> *Antonio:* Pull yourself together and think about starting a new life, about being yourself.
> *Juan:* Myself! That's easy to say! That's the snag!

Rather than create himself as a true hero, he has satisfied himself with a myth, largely of his own invention, and then discovers that he is nothing more than that myth. He has played his part so long that he sees all life as a theater in which the passions he is supposed to embody are the strings pulled by a greater force, which treats him — and therefore, he supposes, all men — as puppets: "nothing less than a complete God of Love amuses himself, I mean, re-creates himself by playing with us." [28] Only by withdrawing and indulging in charitable works can he give himself some reality. This is how he escapes from the image with which he has lived and tries to find or create his true self.

Juan's greatest act of heroism is his decision to retreat and form himself in truth, and he expresses the truest part of his mission just before his death. He has brought together everyone he has hurt and whom he wished to save by his retreat. Now, with his passing, he knows that he will relieve them of the burden of unhappiness he brought upon them: "I must die, for otherwise you would not have become one. . . . I must die that you may live." [29] He dies in a final act of self-assertion. Seeing himself as a negative force, he fulfills himself through withdrawal and, ultimately, death. In essence, his heroism lies in his rejection of heroic aspirations, and indeed of fame or immortality. He succeeds in understanding his position in life and in making it as beneficial as possible, even though the damage may already have been done. Manuel Bueno could not reconcile his inner and outer selves, while Juan tries to re-create himself from within, by rejecting his outer self completely and starting anew.

28. Ibid., pp. 930, 948, 954.
29. Ibid., p. 981.

The women should play a crucial part in any discussion of Don Juan, but in Unamuno's works they are generally either very schematic or very similar, since Woman usually represents the same basic concepts: "But the fact is that the women in my fictional works, my female creatures — and at the same time creators — are not completely developed. They pass through my works, almost always in silence, at the most whispering, praying, speaking softly in their men's ears — the ears of their hearts — , anointing them with the dew of their deeply felt humanity." [30] In the interpretation of the Don Juan problem, however, this could scarcely serve, given the personality crisis faced by the protagonist.

Elvira appears to be the strongest person in the play, although she lacks the inner depth that Juan eventually reveals. She is far more egotistic than he and, like the few women in Unamuno's works who do seem clear, wants to triumph at all costs, at the expense of everyone and for the benefit of only herself. She expresses this when she says to Juan: "I have brought you to make a man of you and, above all, to make a woman of myself. And I shall get my way, I swear." She is very much aware of herself and her own continuity. She sees in her relationship with Juan the possibility of motherhood that she desires, and her consciousness of her own personality makes it clear very early that this is her only concern: "The more they trample me, the more I shall spring back . . . , erect! I am I, Elvira, I!" At times this confidence and determination are disconcerting and leave the reader wondering which of the two characters is more heroic. Especially when Elvira can say to Juan: "I seek to wound you the better to cure you." [31] Nevertheless, there can be little doubt that her motives are to perpetuate herself, and that no desire to enrich either Juan or humanity moves her.

Juan is partially heroic, then, because of his final attempt at grandeur, his realization of the lack of direction and purpose in his existence and of the transparency of his rôle. Instead of playing to the gallery, he plays to himself and eventually reaches the point where he sees death as his greatest contribution. Whether his assessment was accurate is a difficult judgment to make, for he is at best

30. *El hermano Juan,* Prologue, p. 879.
31. Ibid., pp. 922, 903, 913.

an enigmatic character, and even his death is theatrical. Nevertheless, he inspires admiration and respect in the reader because, like Manuel Bueno, he can resolve the mystery of his personality only in death. Manuel Bueno, however, can be sure that if there is immortality, he has warranted it through his actions, while Juan can only hope to have warranted it through the very act of dying.

In "Una visita al viejo poeta" (1899), Unamuno treats a similar personality problem in which the protagonist reacts much as Juan does. The narrator pays a visit to the old poet, who has withdrawn to a religious retreat in order to immerse himself in life and find and maintain his true personality. He rejects any idea of mere fame, emphasizing the superiority of his concrete self over any idea that others may have of him. He admits that his name is no longer mentioned as often as it once was, but adds that he may only now be enjoying his greatest influence. Fame, then, is not the only form of immortality. By living unto himself alone he has stripped himself of the apparential, much as Juan did, and is able to approach God with more success than he could before, when he only succeeded in getting close to God's image projected upon the Infinite. Juan found that he had no real self because it had vanished behind what he portrayed, but he re-created it by withdrawing into himself; and the old poet expresses an identical approach to a situation that is only slightly different in essence: "No, I do not want my personality, what men of letters call personality, to smother my person (and he touched his chest while saying it.)" [32]

This is an agonizing dilemma to which both protagonists react with a deep understanding of their own missions. The poet is more directly concerned with the problem of immortality than Juan, but is willing to renounce fame, an apparential benefit, if this will allow him to approach true immortality, both in spirit on earth and near God. For this reason he can hope that his personality will continue to influence mankind even after his name has become less frequent upon their lips: "It usually happens that when they talk least about a writer is when he has his greatest influence." [33]

32. "Una visita al viejo poeta," O.C. 2: 748.
33. Ibid., pp. 747–48.

We have seen that Juan's salvation lies partly in a return to the ideals of childhood. This was a constant preoccupation for Unamuno, who felt that children alone have the innocence to believe without the trammels of reason. Consequently, throughout his work there are references to his own childhood, that of his characters, that of their children, and particularly to the mother as a link with that lost innocence. The old poet has also found much of his consolation in these memories as, like the hero, he tries to recapture that youth and the goodness it implies which is necessary for both heroism and the Kingdom of Heaven. Says the old poet: "This house reminds me of the one of my childhood, the one that was razed by the inevitability of progress. It had a little garden like this. Here my soul is bathed in my memories of childhood; here I renew my gentle wakefulness after years of sleep." [34] Any approach to God must pass through childhood because only then can one truly believe with innocence in both man and God. The poet's rejection of fame is partly an effort to regain that period and its values.

The Heroic Woman: *Raquel encadenada*

The last protagonist who finds herself in conflict between what she seems to be and what she feels she should be, is Raquel (1921), a woman of deep inner strength, and consequently the only one of near heroic proportions in Unamuno's fiction. From the beginning it is obvious that she is a woman of iron will and, as the play progresses, she becomes stronger — and indeed nearly obsessed. She is beyond all sense of social propriety and will do whatever seems necessary, regardless of the possible consequences, to achieve her goal. In this respect she is like Tía Tula, in that both women are searching for their fulfillment in some form of motherhood, yet their situations and resulting attitudes are quite distinct.

Like her namesake in *Dos madres*, Raquel is, above all, conscious of her lack of fulfillment. She feels no satisfaction in the success of her musical career, into which she has been thrust by Simón, and she rebels: "I am missing everything ——! You are missing everything, Simón!" [35] Her husband seeks his fulfillment, an entirely financial

34. Ibid., p. 746.
35. *Raquel encadenada*, O.C. 12: 680.

one, in his wife, and no spiritual, or even carnal, plenitude forms part of his concept of himself. He grows weaker as the play progresses and Raquel, more heroic, as she becomes firmer in her determination to have the child to whose life and development she feels she can contribute. Simón has tried to persuade her to continue her career, and yet he makes no attempt to support her emotionally. He effectively abandons her even though it is she who leaves. Raquel cries out to him on many occasions and shows her desire to continue to devote herself to her marriage as well as to a child; yet he refuses adamantly. Raquel has no choice but to cease performing her music, since it is her only weapon against her husband. She has heroic aspirations, but all her efforts to perform are vitiated by Simón's usury: "I have resolved never to play again. I cannot free souls with music so that you may enslave them. . . . And I am not working any more!" She has considered her position and has agonized in her realization of its futility. She goes to the aid of Aurelio's child and evaluates her total potential — all before making the final break with Simón. We do not see her yet as a hero, but merely in her first heroic gestures, which lead her to change her polarization to a mission that is closer to her heart: "Now, yes, I will work . . . for my child!" [36] Tula alleviates her frustrated sense of motherhood by usurping other women's children; Raquel, on the other hand, chooses to demand her own liberty rather than take someone else's.

The four protagonists discussed in this section are the most nearly heroic in Unamuno's gallery. They have little in common with each other except a determination to understand, develop and reassess their own personalities. They are all "agonists" and decide in favor of a successful completion of their missions. Manuel Bueno continues the task with which he started, Juan withdraws in search of himself, the old poet shields himself from destruction by his external personality, and Raquel rebels against annihilation by the selfish whim of another; but all four fail to some extent. Manuel Bueno's heroism lies in the external image which he has projected and which will be the salvation of his followers. The most pathetic of all, he fails because he cannot satisfy himself or even convert himself to the causes he

36. Ibid., pp. 708, 728.

champions. Juan fails because his greatest realization is his own lack of substance and reality. The old poet has retired from the fight in a search for peace, and his only followers are those who believe in his external self and know nothing about what he calls his concrete self. Raquel, like Pachico Zabalbide, is only on the threshold of heroism when Unamuno removes her from view. These are the heroes who might have been.

The Heroic Potential

If evaluations must be made, the following are the protagonists who would appear in the second circle of Unamuno's creative ontology. They are the characters with nearly as much personality as those discussed but who are defeated in their goals more from without than from within. They are tragic because their defeat seems more clearly predestined than that of the pathetic heroes, and one often feels that they were not given the same opportunities as the others. The clearest example is Unamuno's conception of Phaedra.

Victims of Life: Fedra and Soledad

As with almost all of Unamuno's women, the problem of *Fedra* (1910) is partially that of frustrated motherhood, although this play involves some rather bizarre twists on that theme. In keeping with the original concept of Euripides, Unamuno has made Fedra the victim of fate, and this theme is repeated throughout the play. She herself is fully aware of this and admits to Hipólito: "This is fate, Hipólito, which one cannot, which one must not resist." [37] Because she is married to Hipólito's father Fedra finds herself trapped by life itself. She loves Hipólito but her duty is to Pedro, and she cannot leave him in order to escape the temptations of the situation. In any case, her passion is so strong, it is unlikely that she could forget her stepson. She is by no means a placid woman and everything she does screams life at the reader. Unamuno has allowed her to agonize through the reader's mind with a vehemence and a desperation probably unequalled in his work. She lives, and will not give that aspect of herself up to circumstances, no matter how compelling.

37. *Fedra*, O.C. 12: 423.

Hipólito and no one else can make her complete: in him lies all her fulfillment as a woman, as a mother, as an individual, and as a personality. She has no choice but to compromise her stepson, even though no one in the drama is more aware of the evil and danger in such a move than she. Without love she cannot transcend herself, and her love is for the man who, except for circumstances, is her ideal polarization. Every requirement for her fulfillment has been met, but she is married to Pedro, whom she cannot abandon under any circumstances. Without love she is not a person; yet life has not allowed her to consummate this passion, which is indeed heroic in all aspects but one.

As Iris M. Zavala mentions, Hipólito is perhaps the key. He is strangely unreal in the play, and yet his limited strength — his virtue — destroys Fedra completely: "He is like Tula, the saint who made sinners with her inhuman idea of virtue." [38] Fedra finds no effective support in the play, for Pedro is at first ignorant of the truth and finally is destroyed too. The nurse is able to offer no solutions, and Marcelo is only another side of Hipólito: they complete each other in a relationship that is almost ironical. Fedra needs Hipólito to fulfill her, but he finds his fulfillment in Marcelo, the logical friend who is as incapable as he of understanding the enervating vitality of Fedra. She stands alone in this play, surrounded by weak characters lacking in grandeur. This accentuates her isolation and the impossibility of her life.

In the collection, *El espejo de la muerte* (1913), Unamuno includes a story entitled "Soledad," in which the protagonist finds herself in a situation somewhat analogous to that of Fedra. Soledad suffers the indifference of her father and older brother and is abandoned by her lover, who says that she needs someone who can make her happier than he could. Her brother leaves home, her father dies, and she then retreats to a farm in the country and lives by herself. Unamuno makes a plea for the woman, who does not have the outlets of a man when left alone. It is a touching and compassionate tale of despairing love in a woman who lives amputated from society because she cannot escape from the solitude and isolation imposed

38. Iris M. Zavala, *Unamuno y su teatro de conciencia* (Salamanca, 1963), p. 57.

upon her by circumstances — in this case, society. The moral, Unamuno observes, is that: "Man in our societies has areas in which to
forget about his solitude; but a woman who does not want to lock
herself up in a convent, what is she going to do among us as a woman
alone?" [39] Like Fedra, Soledad finds herself overwhelmed and defeated by her love in relation to circumstances against which she is
powerless, although innocent.

The Defeat of Fiction: Niebla

In 1914 Unamuno published what was to be his most provocative
novel, Niebla, an extremely contemporary work in which the problem of fiction and reality, and which is stronger, reaches full flower,
yet is only temporarily resolved. In the "Historia de Niebla," he explains the foundations upon which this extraordinary work was built.
Speaking of the fictional and real worlds, he says: "And beneath
these two worlds, holding them up, is another world, a substantial
and eternal world, in which I dream myself and those who have
been — many still are — flesh of my spirit and spirit of my flesh, a
world of consciousness with neither space nor time, a consciousness in
which, like a wave in the sea, lives the consciousness of my body." [40]
We have already discussed this problem in chapter 5, but now we
shall see to what degree it can affect the personality of an individual,
either fictive or historical.

As Joseph Gillet has demonstrated, the autonomous character has
a strikingly long history, and a comment appearing in Kierkegaard's
Journal seems to parallel exactly the climax of *Niebla*. The entry is
from July 1837: "The hero in a novel was just going to make a re-
mark when the author takes it out of his mouth, whereupon the hero
gets angry and says that it is his, and shows that it suits him alone
and that 'if things go on like this I won't be the hero at all.'" [41] In

39. "Soledad," O.C. 2: 690.
40. "Historia de Niebla," O.C. 2: 802.
41. Gillett, "The Autonomous Character in Spanish and European Literature," p. 182. See also Ruth House Webber, "Kierkegaard and the Elaboration of Unamuno's Niebla," *Hispanic Review* 32 (1964): 118–34; Alexander
A. Parker, "Interpretation of Niebla," in *Unamuno: creator and creation*, ed.
Rubia Barcia and Zeitlin, pp. 116–38; Geoffrey Ribbans, "La evolución de la
novelística unamuniana: *Amor y pedagogía y Niebla*" and "Estructura y
significado de Niebla," in *Niebla y soledad* (Madrid, 1971), pp. 83–107 and
108–42.

Niebla, Unamuno does in the novel what Pirandello was doing in the theater but what Unamuno himself never dared to do in his dramas: he allows the protagonist to become independent of his creator. The implications are far-reaching.

Augusto Pérez is an overindulged young man who has been spoiled by his mother and has really had no opportunity to develop his own personality. What saves him from being a totally superficial character is his gradual realization of the vacuity of his existence. He lacks all sense of motivation, and is torn by the doubts that arise from his intelligence coupled with his hollowness: "And this life of mine, is it a novel, is it a *nivola* — what is it? All of this that happens to me and that happens to those who are around me, is it reality or fiction? Is all this not perhaps one of God's dreams, or of whomever it may be, that will vanish as soon as he awakens, and for this reason we pray to him and raise hymns and songs to him, to make him drowsy, to rock him to sleep?" [42]

Augusto, says Franck, is a sort of foreshadowing of T. S. Eliot's J. Alfred Prufrock, "too sensitive for mediocrity, too kind for villainy, yet too indecisive for heroism." [43] He enters the novel out of his mist and seems scarcely more substantial than mist himself. He has no direction and is suffering from crushing boredom, ennui. He reveals no self-assertion whatever: "Augusto was not a walker, but rather a stroller through life." [44] Even as the novel progresses and he passes through his abortive love affair with Eugenia, he reverts to his original character at every defeat, rising only momentarily above his limitations:

> He barely set foot on the street when he found himself with the sky overhead and the people going and coming, each according to his business or his taste, and they were not noticing him, involuntarily of course, nor did they pay attention to him, undoubtedly because they did not recognize him, and he felt that his ego, that ego that said "I am I!" was getting smaller and

42. *Niebla,* O.C. 2: 897. Sonnet 61 of *De Fuerteventura a París* recalls *Niebla* in many ways. See O.C. 14: 542.

43. R. Franck, "Unamuno, Existentialism and the Spanish Novel," *Accent* 4 (1948–49): 87.

44. *Niebla,* O.C. 2: 805. Like Don Quixote, Augusto manages to polarize his energy only when freed of the influence of his family.

smaller and was doubling up into his body, and even when it was
in there was looking for a tiny corner in which to snuggle so that
it wouldn't be seen.[45]

He is *involuntarily* ignored by those in the street, in other words,
he has utterly no reality for them. This is the horrible realization he
must face. Only in his solitude does he regain any self-confidence;
yet in total solitude it has no practical value. He protects himself by
becoming a lonely man so that there is no concrete proof of his unreality. He wants to exist fully but seems forced to be unreal, and
only by continuing persistence in all his efforts (his attempt to conquer Eugenia, his rebellion against death) does he succeed in acquiring a real existence. He realizes that he is only apparential, and
the struggle between this realization and a desire to be substantial
motivates him, as it motivated Don Quixote and Segismundo before
him.

Chance does join with Augusto's will on one occasion, though, to
introduce him to Eugenia. He sees her in the street during one of
his witless wanderings in which he plans to follow a dog — any dog,
a decision recalling Don Quixote's plan to follow Rocinante. He falls
in love with her at once, new Dulcinea, even without knowing her,
and converts her into his purpose in life. This is what we must pro-
saically call his "polarization": "This Eugenia of mine is a blessing
from God. She has already given a purpose, an aim, to my wanderings through the streets. Now I have a house that I can roam near;
I have a concierge-confidant." He has found someone to whom he
can dedicate his efforts and who will indeed be the goal he is attempting to reach: "Now my life has a purpose; now I have a conquest to carry out." [46] Love and purpose have come combined in one
person, and Augusto can see beyond himself for once.

He immediately converts his love into a semimystical experience
and an important ontological justification: "Love is ecstasy; it lifts
us out of ourselves." Indeed, his supposed love for Eugenia makes him
more certain of his existence until, in a theatrical declaration of personality, comparable in his mind to those cries of Don Quixote and
Don Juan, he can state emphatically: *"Amo, ergo sum!"* The gap

45. Ibid., p. 908.
46. Ibid., pp. 812, 814.

that he has not yet managed to bridge, and that will eventually be one of the causes of his defeat, is that between the possession of Eugenia in his own mind and possession in her mind. It is true that Dulcinea was never aware of Don Quixote's love for her, but his love grew out of a genuine emotion, while the authenticity of Augusto's passion will always be held in suspicion by all who know him. His friend Víctor Goti says to him: "you have been in love *ab origine,* ever since you were born; your infatuation is inborn." [47] Víctor remains unconvinced by Augusto's attitude and feels that he is in love with Woman, perhaps, but that Eugenia is only the accidental object of his affection.

Augusto tries to disprove this accusation by both asserting his own personality and completing the conquest of Eugenia. When he decides to take over her mortgage, he refers to it somewhat grandly as "a heroic resolution" and finds a great deal of moral support in the simple-minded anarchy of don Fermín, who declares: "my anarchism consists . . . in the idea that everyone should sacrifice himself for others, that everyone should be happy by making others happy." This is heroic advice indeed, at least on the surface, but it does little to conquer Eugenia, who is unsympathetic to Augusto's crisis and, like Víctor, suspects the authenticity of his heroism. She confesses to her aunt: "I don't want heroes. That is, those who try to be heroes. When heroism comes of its own accord, naturally, that's fine, but when it comes through planning?" [48] She is more impressed by the straightforward indolence of Mauricio than by the contrived grandeur of Augusto.

There is still something unreal about Augusto that preoccupies and disturbs all his acquaintances. He is more real physically than spiritually, but is mystified by the means to solve this: "I have too much body because I am lacking soul. Or isn't it rather, that I am lacking soul because I have too much body?" He is able to feel his lacks and inadequacies, but he has not managed to clarify them enough to be able to fill them. He lives conscious of his insufficiency, but seems incapable of passing beyond that stage to plenitude. Víctor has told him that the first birth of a man is to love, and Augusto feels he has

47. Ibid., pp. 824, 837, 816.
48. Ibid., pp. 850, 860, 879.

experienced that; but it is only when he is rejected by Eugenia that he is made aware of the enduring pain that real man must face: "the second birth, the real one, is to be born through pain to the consciousness of never-ending death, to the fact that we are always dying." [49] First, man is conscious and then he begins to suffer with the realization that he is threatened by annihilation and that he must always struggle under the agony of imagining himself as not existing. Augusto, then, begins to feel even more certain of his own existence after Eugenia's elopement than he did when he first felt love for her, for his anguish becomes real.

There are, then, four stages in Augusto's development. He begins as a virtual nonentity, devoid of aim or purpose. He then sees Eugenia and devotes himself to her, withdrawing to Liduvina and Rosario to reevaluate his true feelings. Eugenia abandons him completely and he becomes deeply aware of the pain of existence and becomes a true agonist. Unamuno brings on the fourth stage in person when he begins to emphasize his own part in Augusto's suffering. He places himself outside his characters and makes himself visible to the reader, explaining: "Therefore, when we look for reasons to justify ourselves, we are, strictly speaking, simply justifying God. And I am the God of these two *nivolistic* devils." In an ingenious attempt to give greater depth to his character while still maintaining himself on a superior level, he makes himself a character and appears in the novel as his own creator. Augusto visits him in Salamanca, and when Unamuno announces that he plans to kill him, Augusto sees himself on the edge of the abyss and rebels completely, with a true expression of the heroic will: "I want to live, live . . . , and to be me, me, me." [50]

It is this refusal to bow down before the novelist that gives Augusto his dignity and his reality. He has gradually acquired existence in the novel and now he is being asked to relinquish it at the whim of the man who gave him life in the first place. Augusto does not see the justice of the situation, and even Víctor has told him that the novelist is not the person upon whom his reality depends:

49. Ibid., pp. 878, 969.
50. Ibid., pp. 950, 981.

Víctor: The soul of a character in a play, a novel, or a *nivola*
           has nothing inside except what is given to him by——
Augusto: Yes, his author.
Víctor: No, the reader.[51]

Augusto begins to add new dimensions to his reality through this realization that he now has powers Unamuno cannot take away from him. As long as he can continue to live in the minds of the readers, he cannot die; Unamuno is far more vulnerable than he:

> And if I live like this in the fantasies of several people, is it not perhaps true that what belongs to several is true and not what belongs to just one? And why, rising out of the pages of the book in which is deposited the story of my fictitious life, or rather, out of the minds of those who may read it — you, the ones who are reading it now —, why can I not live as an eternal and eternally suffering soul? Why? [52]

The reader is caught in a curious play of mirrors as Augusto begins to stride uncontrollably off the pages. Unamuno does, of course, eventually manage to kill him in a God-like way, but it is inescapable that he does so because he is afraid Augusto will overpower him. Unamuno leads himself into a situation similar to that of Cervantes; but he protects himself by inserting himself directly into the novel so that he is guaranteed to have no less reality for the reader than Augusto, who achieves no small victory when he succeeds in coming back to haunt his creator in his dreams. He then exemplifies the independence an idea or concept can have after the creator is through with it, and also shows the precise relationship that exists between any "real" character and the reader. A character may be able to exist without his creator, but he cannot exist without a reader.

Unamuno defeats Augusto with life, or history, by imposing his phenomenological personality upon Augusto's fictive one. It is a Pyrrhic victory at best, since he had to become fictional himself in order to do it, but he does succeed in keeping Augusto largely within the bounds of the printed page. All distinctions become arbitrary at this point, since Unamuno has moved us entirely into a spiritual mist

51. Ibid., p. 971.
52. Ibid., p. 983.

in which no dividing lines are clear. As Víctor Goti points out in his prologue to the novel, the question of independence and, we may suppose, heroism, is not easily solved between author and character: "I am, at least, firmly persuaded that I lack what psychologists call free will, although it comforts me to think that don Miguel lacks it too." [53] This is undeniable, for in *Niebla* it becomes impossible to make any significant assertions regarding who is totally fictional or who is completely historical, since both Unamuno and Augusto cross those limits.

Unamuno delighted in adding to the reader's doubts by reaffirming that it was not his intention that his protagonist should become so strong: "A plan is made for a novel, too, just as it is for an epic or a play; but afterwards the novel, epic, or play imposes itself upon the one who thinks he is its author." [54] This is an exaggeration, but it does serve to illustrate the strength fictional man can acquire and the degree of reality he can achieve. As mentioned in chapter 5, the roots for this technique can be found in Cervantes and in Galdós's *El Amigo Manso,* particularly the concept of suffering as a route to genuine existence. Augusto's greatest failing is, perhaps, his rather mechanical intellect, but he does have a charm that attracts even if it does not convince. He upsets the traditional equilibrium between fiction and reality though he seems too often to be a transparent mask for Unamuno's trickery.

The Triumph of Fiction: *Cómo se hace una novela*

The triumph of history over fiction is easily understood, as it seems to fit into man's normal concept of himself in relation to his environment; but since we have seen that Unamuno believed fiction could be just as powerful, it is not surprising to find works in which the hero is destroyed, not by his inability to impose a fictional situation upon society, but rather by his inability to conform to a fictional frame of reference. The most striking example of this is *Cómo se hace una novela* (1927).

The novel to which the title refers is life, and Unamuno presents an example of how to make a novel, that is to say, how to create one's

53. Ibid., "Prólogo," p. 783.
54. "Historia de *Niebla,*" O.C. 2: 797. Cf. chapter 5, n. 34, above.

own life. As Armando F. Zubizarreta has demonstrated, the work contains three novels: first, "the novel of an autobiographical-romantic confession"; second, "the process of reading this novel is the thread of the plot in the novelistic essay"; and finally, "the sum total of Jugo de la Raza's novel — autobiography — plus the documentary memoirs in which it is immersed . . . the work *Cómo se hace una novela.*" [55] This strange effect, not unrelated to that seen in *Niebla,* immediately brings to mind again the second part of *Don Quijote,* in which Cervantes used a surprisingly similar technique to give depth to his characters and set the reader's mind to work and participate in the creation of the novel. E. C. Riley makes a valid analogy between Cervantes's technique and that of Velásquez, in a comparison that helps to shed light on Unamuno's work as well. Speaking of the *Quijote* and its relationship to *Las meninas,* Riley says:

> It is full of tricks. There in the picture is the painter at work on his own painting, the largest figure in the scene, but dark and unobtrusive. There too is the back of the very canvas we are looking at. . . . And the viewer realizes with a shock that he is looking at the picture from the spot, close to the watchful monarch and his wife, from which the picture was painted in effect. One all but glances over one's shoulder. . . . [Velásquez] has contrived to be simultaneously outside and inside his subject, and what is more, to draw the outside spectator into it too.[56]

We know that this was exactly what Unamuno had in mind, and it is this technique that makes the work so spectacular.

The protagonist, U. Jugo de la Raza, reads novels so that he may live in them and in their characters, but Unamuno insists he also has deeper motives much nobler than that: "in reality he looks for novels with the aim of discovering himself, with the aim of living in himself, of being himself." Like so many of the protagonists we have already examined, Jugo de la Raza is in search of his own personality and he looks for the reality of it in novels. His defeat and the theme of the entire book come to be expressed in the sentence he finds in a mysterious novel that he buys, which dominates, and

55. Zubizarreta, *Unamuno en su 'nivola,'* p. 214.
56. E. C. Riley, *Cervantes's Theory of the Novel.* (Oxford, 1962), p. 48.

apparently conquers, his entire existence: "When the reader reaches the end of this painful story he will die with me." [57] The fictional character can dominate and exercise greater reality than the supposedly historical one, and in fact can ultimately bring about his destruction.

Unamuno did indeed create Jugo de la Raza as his most autobiographical character and, through him, sought his own unity. Jugo tries to become part of the characters he reads about in order to give substance to his own life. He does not exist until he finds the fatal novel that gives his life conflict and reveals his danger and fleeting mortality. He must make the decision to defeat the uncertainty of life and conquer the fictional element so as to conquer death itself. The novel that Unamuno is writing and the novel that Jugo de la Raza is creating are both attempts to create one's own personality, to make out of oneself a real character, and to base around him the novel of life. The imagery is distressingly trite, but Unamuno gives it immediacy by involving the reader through threats to his own reality. The very conventionalism of the idea of life as a novel grants him the liberty to concentrate on the prime purpose of showing to what extent this is true, and to what extent its truth portends defeat for the unwary.

It must be understood that Unamuno scarcely creates a protagonist in this work, much less a heroic figure. He presents nothing more than a sketch of a character with a few stage directions that illustrate his thesis. What we do know about Jugo de la Raza makes of him a rather melodramatic personage faced with a highly emotional and pathetic conflict, which does, however, serve as a definite example of self-assertion and gives the reader firm directions to take in the development of individual personality and meaningful accomplishments. Jugo de la Raza is not real, but rather a problem, a hypothesis designed to concern the reader as directly as possible and provide an outlet for Unamuno to test the tensions he feels within his own life. Jugo de la Raza does not succeed in freeing himself from either of the fictional forces with which he struggles as a creation in a novel or as a reader of a novel. If the reader wishes to be real, he must fight similar forces and free himself into a degree of inde-

57. *Cómo se hace una novela* (Buenos Aires, 1927), pp. 73, 74.

pendence that permits clear progress as an actively participating individual in the creation of life.

The Triumph of Fiction: *Tulio Montalbán* and *Sombras de sueño*

In these two works, which are essentially the same and, for our purposes will be treated as such, Unamuno shows another facet of the rebellion of the historical man against the fictional entity. Jugo de la Raza failed, and Julio Macedo fails too, but not in the same way. The question in both the novel (*Tulio Montalbán y Julio Macedo*, 1920) and the drama (*Sombras de sueño*, 1926) is which of the two men, Julio Macedo or Tulio Montalbán, is the more real? For those with whom he must deal, it turns out that his former ego is.

Tulio Montalbán converted his love for the first Elvira into action on behalf of his homeland, and this is the start of his heroism. When he commits spiritual suicide and becomes Julio Macedo, he is giving preeminence to the inner, meditative man who wants to find peace in a different part of himself (cf. "Una visita al viejo poeta"). He has attempted to abandon the apparential world of revolution and heroics in order to retreat into what he hopes will be a substantial world that will bring him tranquillity. This conflict is underscored by his relationship with both the second Elvira and her father. The old man lives only in his history books and Elvira lives only in the biography of Tulio Montalbán, written by his father-in-law, who hoped to share the immortality of his heroism by writing a commentary. At the end of the play and the story, both men have had their values upset, as Solórzano finds out that his world is false and Macedo discovers that he cannot defeat his fictional self.

The problem, then, is unique in that, rather than fight the influence of a fictional hero of someone else's creation, as in *Cómo se hace una novela*, Macedo must conquer the other half of his own ego. All heroes live in a perpetual state of tension, but they opt for one dominant factor in their personality and use it as their foundation. As Tulio Montalbán, this protagonist did that; but in order to prevent himself from being drawn into tyranny, and to maintain the purity of his mission, he was forced to convert himself into another hero with another mission. The second Elvira was to become his new polarization, and he was to replace a heroism of action with a hero-

ism of meditation. He tells her: "Now I want to live! Now I want
to live again! I want to know what is it that they call life and that
others enjoy." [58] Like Don Quixote, he becomes a man without history who has abandoned one of the factors within his ego in favor
of another.

He wants to be remade by Elvira so that his new personality will
be complete and deeply motivated. Within himself, he is certain
that he is now more real than his former self, especially since Tulio
Montalbán would have no reality for Elvira were it not for the biography she possesses. In fact, Julio Macedo senses what Unamuno
maintains throughout his work: that history need be no more real
than fiction, nor fiction any more real than life itself: "I do not believe that any type that appears in books is real, regardless of whether
they are history books or novels." [59] Unamuno makes a subtle point,
for Macedo does not believe in the absolute reality of history over
fiction any more than Unamuno does; but, on the other hand, he
does not recognize that either form can be more powerful and real
than life in certain circumstances, the very type of circumstances of
which he will be a victim. He totally underestimates that reality,
and when Elvira discovers that he is her lifelong idol, she faces the
problem of Damiana and Laura in *El otro*: she discovers that she
loves the other one.

For this reason, neither "El otro" nor Julio Macedo can conquer
himself because they are both defeated by the other one. In Macedo's
case, however, the other is a complex individual since Unamuno has
once more obscured all boundaries. Julio Macedo is the descendant
of a now fictional entity who was a historical figure, and his former
biography was a historical work, which has become fictional, with
more power than the man of flesh and blood. Tulio Montalbán's
heroism would have been defeated by his own ambition, which he
conquered, and he was thus immortalized. The defeat of Julio
Macedo's heroism is brought about by the fictional creature he created and his reluctance to sever all ties with it by continuing his de-
nials to Elvira. He realizes his error when he tells her: "Those of
us who seem to be flesh and blood are merely fictional entities, shades,

58. *Tulio Montalbán y Julio Macedo*, O.C. 9: 391.
59. Ibid., p. 395.

phantasms, and those who appear in pictures and books, and those of us who appear on the stages of the theater of history, are the real ones, the lasting ones." [60] He is, in a way, the victim of his own immortality.

A somewhat similar problem is encountered in the short story, "Al correr los años" (1913), in which Juana discovers herself excluded from her husband's affections because of his renewed love for her as she was at the age of twenty-three. She becomes isolated temporarily by an immortalization (in this case a photograph) of an aspect of her personality that no longer exists and that otherwise would no longer have any reality.

Victims of Self: "El que se enterró," "Artemio, heautontimoroumenos," and *El otro*

In several works Unamuno examined the problem of warring factions within the ego of an individual. In the preceding subdivision we saw the conflict between fiction and history, including past aspects of the ego and their effect on present aspects. In 1908, Unamuno published a short story in which a man witnesses his own death and actually buries his own body. In "El que se enterró," Emilio has changed completely, and he tells the narrator that one night when he was terrified by the fear of annihilation (cf. the 1897 crisis of Unamuno), a man entered the room. Emilio was confronted by himself. He lost consciousness and "died," but upon awakening he felt different and saw his old body still in the chair. He had become "the other one" and proves it by digging up the body for the narrator to see. He claims that truth is what has a practical effect and that, since he had experienced death, he must indeed have died, especially since he felt himself to be different than before. The fragmentation of his ego is irrevocable.

In 1918, Unamuno added another dimension to the conflicts within the ego in another short story, "Artemio, heautontimoroumenos." Artemio is engaged in a constant and self-destroying struggle between his ambition and envy, which push him on at all costs, and his pride, which makes him draw back. Since neither half triumphs, he loses both in a single ego that has no distinctive character. In

60. *Sombras de sueño,* O.C. 12: 789.

many ways this could be an early sketch for *Abel Sánchez,* but it seems to cast even more light on the play, *El otro,* written in 1926.

The connection can best be described in the desperate cry of "El otro," who says: "Ah, being born double is a horrible torture! Not being always one and the same!" [61] This problem links the play with the two short stories mentioned and yet separates it from *Tulio Montalbán,* in which the conflict is not within the individual, but is, rather, a conflict between two selves that takes place and is effectively resolved in society, virtually without the active participation of the main character.

In *El otro* society confused the twins even though they tried to have their own personalities. The conflict had to lead to the triumph of one over the other, and one had to die as a result of this duality. In effect, they were not two people, personae, but two facets, possibly identical ones, of the same being. Since each conscious individual aware of the danger of oblivion must strive "to be himself and to be all," it is inevitable, says Unamuno, that one should kill the other, and it makes no difference which is the murderer or which the victim. This is, of course, the Cain and Abel theme, but there are basic differences between the effects of the conflict in this play and in *Abel Sánchez.* In this play, the conflict is between two indistinguishable men who meld into one being, also amazingly lacking in distinguishing traits. Neither of the brothers has any heroic qualities as far as the reader can tell, and the only significance of each is in relation to the other one. One does not and, as it turns out, cannot, exist without the other. In *Abel Sánchez,* on the other hand, the crisis is between two highly individual personalities, and it becomes a question of jealousy and injustice rather than a simple attempt to define oneself. There is tragedy in the novel because of the inherent value of the protagonist.

In *El otro,* it is conflict and the desire for totality that drives the protagonist to kill his brother. He must be the other one without ceasing to be himself. This leads to the attempt to conquer the affections of both wives and, finally, to the loss of all personality.

61. *El otro,* O.C. 12: 789. See also Ricardo Gullón, "¿Quién soy yo?" in *Autobiografías,* pp. 152–77; "Imágenes de *El otro*" in *Spanish Thought and Letters in the Twentieth Century,* ed. Germán Bleiberg and E. Inman Fox (Nashville, 1966), pp. 257–70; "Imágenes del otro," *Revista Hispánica Moderna* 35 (1965): 210–21.

The truth is that he had more significance when his brother was alive. With him dead, the living brother becomes nothing but the murderer and the one who suffers the pain of that crime. He does appear to win the love of both women, but it is false because they are in love with what he represents: the one who suffers and their own continuity as women and mothers. "El otro" says to Laura: "What you want is to know what the other's kisses taste like, you want Cain and not Abel, whom he killed." Whereas Elvira was in love with the man who no longer existed, Laura and Damiana love the one who remains, whoever he may be. The Ama says: "A woman who is a woman, that is, a mother, falls in love with Cain and not Abel, because it is Cain who suffers and feels pain." [62] She might also have added that Cain is the only one left. She alone could distinguish between the brothers, but refuses to do so, thus effectively sealing them in their own oblivion. "El otro's" attempts to find out which one each woman was in love with reveal to him that his crime has failed; he has not succeeded in imposing himself except as a physiological entity. What little personality he had, vanished with that of his brother.

The points made in this play are complex and tie it to many other works, as we have indicated. It is most often considered as yet another example of the Cain and Abel theme, and is often linked with both *Tulio Montalbán* and *Abel Sánchez*. There are, indeed, strong thematic parallels, and the crises faced by all the protagonists are not dissimilar, but the resolution of the conflicts, based upon the personality of each protagonist is different in each case. For that reason we have chosen to deal with *El otro* as a play in which the protagonist enters into a conflict with his own duality and loses both aspects of it. Julio Macedo made a strong decision and was defeated by it; Joaquín Monegro is a man of strongly defined character. Both these men have heroic roots; but "El otro" is an individual who does not succeed in developing a personality.

Victims of Self: *Abel Sánchez*

In *Abel Sánchez* (1917), Joaquín Monegro is another highly capable and individualistic man. His downfall is precipitated by another, whose entire life exerts such an influence upon his own that

62. Ibid., pp. 836, 858.

Joaquín loses almost all sense of being if he cannot refer back to his hatred for Abel Sánchez. As we have said, in some ways the theme resembles that of *El otro*; but here Unamuno is dealing with two men who are as different as they could be. They are never confused in social contacts and each has a speciality, talent, or mission highly peculiar to him as an individual. Of the two, indeed, Joaquín is probably the deeper and more productive, and he does succeed in leaving behind at least one disciple. Like Artemio, he is his own victim, but only insofar as he is reflected in another. He sees all of Abel's actions as part of his own perdition, to such an extent that he displaces his ego into Abel and lives only in his hatred for him. Thus he has polarized his actions and made it impossible to exist without the coordinate existence of the object of this passion. For this reason, he cannot allow Abel to die.

Joaquín is a clearly and perceptively delineated character who does not possess any of the static qualities that appear in other protagonists. His existence is one of dynamism and tension between his desire to free himself from the influence of Abel and his inability to sever himself from the hatred that has become the motivating force in his life. Many characters in Unamuno's work fight to free themselves from an aspect of their personality they did not choose, but Joaquín struggles to free himself from an ego that is in another person but that is nothing more than an extension of his own. By killing Abel he will destroy himself as a personality because he will have lost his motivation; but by permitting him to live he renders himself incapable of acting independently and of following his own beliefs.

His lack of faith in himself, of course, is the basis for his envy and resulting hatred. Abel seems to represent fulfillment and immortality through art, while Joaquín's work will die with him. Even Abelín is small consolation for that awareness. Joaquín suffers the silence of God and agonizes, while Abel is the embodiment of complacency and an irritating self-sufficiency that breeds nothing but further discontent in Joaquín. This dissatisfaction with Abel's attitude toward life, with his unquestioning acceptance of all his good fortune, with his lack of suffering, worry, or agony, leads Joaquín to a frustration that defeats his own possible aspirations and implants in him a competitive trait that irrevocably binds him to another. He

fails to be able even to devote himself properly to his disciple because of this link with Abel.

The progression in Joaquín's personality leads him from a mere
retreat into studies after losing Helena to Abel, to an active participation in the competition in which he is the only contestant. He
tries to find his goals in another woman, but he cannot; even she
realizes that her husband is doomed to live out his hatred, because
he is not his own man, and more and more cannot direct his own
emotions. He effectively turns against her, too, by convincing himself
that she married him only out of compassion. He becomes incapable
of realizing his dreams and feels inferior because he cannot give immortality to his patients as Abel gave it to Helena in her portrait.
He cannot be free, because first he must believe that he is free.

Joaquín is neither entirely his own victim nor the victim of another, but the victim of a personality from which he cannot escape
because of his lack of faith in his own strength. He becomes motivated instead by a spirit of envy and vengeance. He displays all the
marks of a hero except the belief in his own ability, "because Joaquín
thought that he was an exceptional spirit and, as such, tortured and
more capable of pain than the others, a soul marked by God with
the sign of those great ones who are predestined." [63] This lack of
faith blinds him to the possibility that one of the reasons for his
apparent rejection by all who know him could be precisely his superiority, for he is obviously warmer and more human than his
enemy. An awareness of his own qualities would ultimately have
made him the victor, but Unamuno believed that, then, Abel would
have killed Cain. Nevertheless, from the viewpoint of heroism alone,
the potential lay in Joaquín.

Victims of Self: *La esfinge*

Unamuno's first major drama was written in 1898 and concerns
another protagonist who rejects his course of action because of a
belief in the necessity for a different mission. Unlike Juan and the
old poet, Angel seems by the end definitely to have failed in his
attempt to raise himself by rejecting the temptations of power and
fame, because the passivity that we can really only suspect in "Una
visita al viejo poeta" is explicit in this drama.

63. *Abel Sánchez*, O.C. 2: 1099.

Angel is a revolutionary leader who rejects his position in a desire to live as an individual with only his own interests in mind. He wants to withdraw like the old poet, but his motives are never entirely satisfactory because they are unclear to others and leave him open to accusations of cowardice and weakness by his wife and friends. Unamuno explains the theme in a letter to Ganivet dated November 20, 1898: "It is the struggle of a conscience between the attraction of glory, of living in history, of passing on its name to posterity, and the charm of peace, calm, of living in eternity." [64] It seems from the very outset that Angel's motives are somewhat cloudy even to himself and, like Juan, he finds himself playing a part in which he represents himself without having any deep intuition as to what that self is. He explains his situation to Felipe, probably the only person in the play who begins to understand him: "I am just playing a part, Felipe; I spend life contemplating myself, being a theater for myself." [65] This is the same problem of fragmentation of the ego that Manuel Bueno, Juan, and the old poet have tried to resolve.

Angel searches for a justification of himself that he has been unable to find in his revolutionary activities. He finds himself as far removed from the people he is trying to help as Manuel Bueno, for there is a gap of ignorance between them. The people are basically ignorant of their goals and purposes, while Angel, who knows what he wants to do, does not believe in those aims any longer because they demand too much of him: "Poor people! They don't know what they want, but they want something, while we know what we want, but don't want. Liberty, liberty! Saintly word!" [66] He feels he may be doing an injustice by imposing his ideals upon those who blindly accept them because they are the only ones offered. He feels that the people could be more heroic if they did not fight in ignorance for what he wishes to achieve, and that they should formulate their own purposes based on their own will: "The instinct of the multitudes is very great when it isn't bastardized with things imposed from outside." [67] These words will acquire a tragic ring when Angel is killed by the people's hands.

64. Quoted by Manuel García Blanco in prologue, O.C. 12: 11.
65. *La esfinge,* O.C. 12: 228.
66. Ibid., p. 218.
67. Ibid., p. 219.

Angel's ideals express many of the aims of heroism, and the purity of his intentions seems quite evident throughout; yet his sudden death ends his chance of fulfilling himself in a different way. He is in search of a spiritual honesty among men that is one of the prime reasons for his sudden decision to change. Felipe feels that, whatever Angel decides to do, it must include fulfillment of himself without which he could contribute nothing, and advises him to start with himself before he attempts to help mankind: "Cowardice is when each does not give in to his own nature, ignoring the voice of his conscience. . . . What's the point of wanting to redeem your neighbour if you yourself are so in need of redemption? If each one were to regenerate himself, we would all regenerate ourselves." This sounds like the first step toward heroism, but Angel is more interested in abandoning all effort and merely living for tranquillity. His lack of faith in himself lies at the root of this desire, for he no longer believes in his value as a force for change. This loss of self-confidence leads to his abandoning his plans, as he longs to eradicate rather than to redeem himself: "I am no one. I am going to cancel myself out, lose myself in the crowd. By renouncing myself and finding myself at the end, I will find that peace that I cannot reach. . . . I am nothing!" [68]

Angel's potential is misguided and stifled, and rather than renew himself, he asks for deliverance from his own personality. He buckles under the weight of his mission: "I wish I could unburden myself of this self, which is smothering me."[69] This entirely negative approach to himself and his position is what most weakens his influence with those surrounding him, and finally, of course, with those he has led:

Angel: I don't want to . . . , I don't want to!
Joaquín: That's all you know: not to want! [70]

Does this make him a hero of "the will-not" (*noluntad*)? Perhaps to a certain extent, but the complete failure of his life would suggest otherwise: his decision implies cowardice rather than courage. Angel decides in favor of "not wanting to be," rather than "wanting not to be," and this leaves him with no inner strength whatever.

68. Ibid., pp. 228, 229.
69. Ibid., p. 310.
70. Ibid., p. 247.

The other motivating influence and potential polarization in
Angel's life is his wife, Eufemia, who bears a strong resemblance to
Elvira in *El hermano Juan* and often tries to exert the same influence.
From the beginning she was a surprise to Unamuno's friends, who
found her to be unreal and out of place in the play. A letter from
Jiménez Ilundain written after having read the play is typical:

> Angel's wife — where the devil have you seen such a woman?
> Does this mean that lately radical feminism has been introduced
> into Spain? . . . The opposite would really be dramatic and sug-
> gestive, that is, a woman who, at any time and with any motive,
> looks for a pretext to rein in her husband, the dreamer, to make
> him come down to real life, to misfortunes, to petty things.[71]

At both ends of his theatrical career, then, Unamuno found himself
creating women who were scarcely typical of his other works. Eufemia and Elvira both make an attempt to convert their men into
images of their own ambition. Eufemia says of Angel: "I must make
the ultimate effort to save him; it's my work! Poor me!" [72] Juan, however, really resists Elvira whereas Angel does so only out of a feeling
of rebellion. Eufemia has had a much deeper influence on the forma-
tion of his personality than Elvira had on that of Juan, and Angel
has found himself incapable of resisting it until he makes a grandiose
gesture rather devoid of meaning: he resigns his post in order to
escape the conflict he is too weak to dominate.

Joaquín considers Angel to be Eufemia's creation: "And you,
Eufemia, you are the one who must be congratulated above all —
you who are this man's soul, his support, his sense of reality." [73]
Angel realizes that he has become a tool in her hands, and that alone
he means nothing: she has made him great so that she may attain
immortality through him. She is not a mother, but she is searching
for glory through her husband's accomplishments. For this reason
she must abandon him when he rebels. He wishes to be his own man
but he fails. His attempt at genuine heroism was ambivalent and
defeated him. He rejected his place in society because he rejected
his relationship with his wife, but he replaced it with surrender in-

71. Quoted by García Blanco, prologue to vol. 12, O.C., p. 24.
72. *La esfinge*, O.C. 12: 263.
73. Ibid., p. 217.

stead of a renewed struggle. Eufemia moves on to a new search for glory while Angel falls prey to his own uncertainty.

Others who find themselves victimized either by an inner conflict or by a disparity between what they misguidedly desire and what they achieve, include: "El lego Juan" (1898), whose total sense of being is altered by his feeling that he has caused his master to sin (cf. *La Tía Tula*); "De águila a pato" (1900), an allegory in which the eagle is destroyed by interrupting his own continuity and trying to achieve someone else's goals; Serafín in "Principio y fin," who is weakened by his vacillation and the uncertainty of his aims, which may be due either to a genuine spiritual crisis or to a basic indecisiveness in his character; and the schoolmaster of "Razón de ser," who spends a lifetime of regret until he realizes, when it is all over, that perhaps he really was right but lacked the strength of faith and the perceptiveness to see it while young enough to benefit further from it. In "Los hijos espirituales" (1916), the young couple are self-destructive in their unwillingness to fulfill their obligations to each other, and the senseless friction that develops between them is based on adamant characteristics in each of them which have no significance in their concept of themselves beyond a puerility that eventually leaves both of them with nothing. In the story "Don Martín, o de la gloria" (1900), the obverse of the coin seen in "Una visita al viejo poeta" is revealed. Martín has devoted his life to achieving fame; yet when it finally comes, he finds it is not satisfying. The story is a study in self-deception and the disillusionment that can be the result of goals ill-conceived for a particular personality.

The Victims of Others

In this grouping we come into contact with characters who reveal a lack of initiative that makes them, not the victims of circumstances or of deep inner conflicts they cannot successfully resolve, but merely of those who are stronger than they. Often they are misguided because of someone else's intentions, but often it is through their own inertia. This is a large category, and the two most striking examples are probably Agustín (*Soledad*, 1921 — drama) and Apolodoro (*Amor y pedagogía*, 1902), both of whom have strong personality traits that are stifled by someone else's will. Unlike many of those we shall see, they are not nonentities from the beginning, for Unamuno permits us to see their potential, which the more dominant Soledad and Avito bend to their own vision of the character.

Agustín is relatively unconcerned by their childless marriage because he can achieve his immortality in the theater, but Soledad is a picture of frustrated motherhood relieved only when Agustín, aware of his error in changing careers, reverts to childhood and permits his wife to assume the wife-mother rôle. Agustín could have achieved his goals by creating drama out of the deep inner conflicts which, while tearing him apart, seem to his wife nothing more than yawns. Feeling himself to be a creator and knowing that he introduces doubts and worries to his viewers in the theater, he has an audience and is successful at reaching them in his plays. His God-like declarations reflect many of those made by Unamuno in his own name. He could not have succeeded in politics because he is concerned with immortality and eternity, not the here and now; but the influence of his wife leads him into politics and then, when his failure there becomes apparent, back into himself, where she can once more contribute to his inner world. She had wanted him to create a people, but not one of dreams and ideals; her aim was concrete, temporal, and possibly even heroic, and her husband's aspirations were even more so, yet were cut off. It is easier to examine the effective annihilation of Apolodoro Carrascal through discussing the character of his father. The child's true personality shows, however, that in a far more extreme way he suffers from misdirection much as Agustín does.

In the two versions of *La venda* (1899 and 1900), María is forced by her family to abandon her reliance upon her former blindness and is made to face her father on their terms, without her blindfold. The point is, of course, that while blind she is able to see the substantial world and is not distracted by the merely apparential. She is a symbol of faith, but her family forbids her reversion to blindness, despite the greater authenticity it offers her. The conflict is between reason and faith, as symbolized in the drama (but not in the short story) by two secondary characters. Nevertheless, María is defeated in her effort to concentrate exclusively on the substantial world as she perceives it because, robbed of her blindness, she loses an essential part of her individuality, and is for that reason no longer accorded the right to depend exclusively upon faith and intuition. She is forced into the universal crisis, which suits neither her mission nor her personality.

In "La locura del Doctor Montarco" (1917), the protagonist is also defeated, but by the demands of others to which he does not feel inclined to conform and which he resists. He expresses himself in extravagant fiction. Considered mad and locked up by society, he chooses an existence of his own creation, given form by an alter ego, Herr Schmarotzender (*schmarotzen* is the German verb meaning to be parasitical). In spite of his obvious intellectual and imaginative superiority, Montarco, like Joaquín Monegro, is inevitably crushed beneath the weight of his social surroundings. The story is largely allegorical, but the defeat of the protagonist is brought about less by his own weakness than by the apparential strength of his patients and society at large.

In several other short stories, Unamuno examines deeply, albeit briefly, the problem of external domination as the root of the destruction of the ego. They can only be mentioned here. In "El dios pavor" (1892), "Abuelo y nieto" (1902) and "La beca" (1913), the protagonists are controlled — either because of youth and inferior position, or because of age and supposed uselessness — so that they can benefit others exclusively, or so that, at the very least, they do not present obstacles. No sense of involvement is indicated between those in control and those who are stifled, nor is there any sense of family fidelity or responsibility. "Ramón Nonnato" (1913), on the other hand, is the victim of the guilt he feels for his father's nefarious business dealings, even though he himself is blameless. In that sense, he is also a victim of himself. In "El abejorro" (1900), the main character is haunted throughout life by the memory of his father's death, the bee that bothered them both at that moment, and his father's last question, asking the boy if he would always be good. The traumatic experience has robbed him of the ability to think about anything else.

In "El secreto de un sino" (1913), Noguera is the victim of Perálvarez's hypocrisy and in "Las tijeras" (1889), the two men have found their polarization in their supposed hatred for each other, and when one dies the other finds himself dominated by his memory and unable to restore any sense to his own life, much as the narrator in "La sombra sin cuerpo" (1921) finds that the suicide of his father has made a void of his own life. In "La carta del difunto," Juana finds herself and her aims in marriage without strength or resilience after receiving the posthumous letter of her former fiancé. All these characters are to some extent controlled by a personality other than their own; yet while we include them in a separate category, it must be remembered that, given Unamuno's ideas of self-fulfillment, much of the blame must ultimately be laid at the victims' feet.

The Heroic Progression

There is another group of protagonists who eventually reveal at least a minimal measure of heroism through some change occurring in the work in which they appear. Almost all of them achieve some polarization or sense of mission through love for another person, whereas the others must develop greater inner strength, and therefore, greater potential, through some realization about their own personalities.

Self-realization

There are two characters who fall into this category and both of them are in short stories. Toribio, in "Del odio a la piedad" (1913), visits Madrid while thinking of his enmity with Campomanes. There he begins by hating a total stranger, Rafael, until he comes to know him. They then become close friends, and when he returns to his home he finds that Campomanes reminds him of the stranger and he ceases to hate him. Through his friendship with Rafael, Toribio has matured in his attitudes and has risen above the folly of his hatred for Campomanes, seeing the pettiness the entire dispute revealed in his own soul.

In "Redondo, el contertulio" (1912), Unamuno examines the upward progression of Redondo, who returns to his village after years in America and becomes a member of the tertulia that is successor to the one in which he used to participate when young. He confronts his own image and develops a possessive attitude toward the gathering which causes him to dislike a certain new member. Eventually, however, he realizes his blindness when another dies, showing him the need to hold on to all he can and to reject no one foolishly. He rises above his own image of himself, which is merely his idea of the legend the younger man had of him, and becomes a more mature man with a greater realization of the true part he was called upon to play in the group.

In the drama *El pasado que vuelve* (1910), Víctor 1° finds his justification in his grandson, whom he manages to imbue with similar ideas of independence and moral conviction. After a lifetime of criticism and doubt as to the wisdom of his rupture with his father, he finds his strength in Víctor 2°, who will follow his path.

The Polarization of Love

This includes an exceptionally large group of lesser characters each of whom finds his justification, after a somewhat mediocre or meaningless existence, in a deep love for another who complements him. Until the moment of realization of that love, generally very pure in feeling regardless of its physical manifestations, the protagonists have usually wandered through their lives with some sort of a superficial motivation, as in the cases of "El sencillo don Rafael" (1912), "El padrino Antonio" (1915), and the protagonists of "Cruce de caminos" (1912), who were, at least unconsciously, searching for just the polarization they found, albeit temporarily, "Ver con los ojos" (1886), "Poema vivo de amor" (1889), "Don Bernardino y Doña Etelvina" (1916), and "Querer vivir." Others were led from a somewhat unwise course of action to one that more exactly corresponded to their situations and attitudes — see, for example, "En manos de la cocinera" (1912). These cannot strictly be referred to as heroic figures, but they are brought to greater fulfillment, or at least such a fulfillment is implied through their newly discovered love for one who can respond to their sense of self. Individuals whose solitary value is relatively minor or whose aims are undetermined can approach completeness together, and this, in turn, can lead to strength alone.

The Anti-heroes

The Dominators

One of Unamuno's most distinctive types of protagonist is the person who shows signs of a well-defined personality at the service of a misguided mission. These characters direct and control the personalities of others in such a way that the dominated character cannot develop. The degree to which the aim is false varies greatly, but it is this poor choice of motive that deprives the protagonist of his true greatness and often makes him a negative influence. Many of these are women whose fanaticism about motherhood causes them to destroy those in their path and to use others as instruments for their own fulfillment.

In 1920, the volume *Tres novelas ejemplares y un prólogo* was published, containing two novels in which this type of person appears: "Dos madres" and "El marqués de Lumbría." The cunning Raquel of the first gave much besides her name to the protagonist of the play *Raquel encadenada,* but she is a far less altruistic person, although no less real for being so. She is the only strength that her lover, don Juan, has, and their relationship works, says Unamuno, only because "don Juan needed a will to make up for the one he was lacking." This is to say that he lacks personality because of Raquel, or at least that any he might have had has been crushed under the weight of her strong will. There is no real question of love, and certainly none of polarization, since don Juan seems incapable of doing anything on his own initiative: "Was he, don Juan, in love with Raquel? No, rather absorbed by her, submerged in her, lost in the woman and in her widowhood." Just as Cosme was nothing without Damián, so is don Juan insignificant without the will of Raquel to which he so readily responds. He is a man whose weakness as an individual extends even to his thoughts of immortality. He has no interest in children, either spiritual or physical because his sense of defeat does not let him imagine that they could be any stronger than he: "But he had no appetite for fatherhood! . . . Why should he leave in the world another one like himself?" [74] This is a sound point, but it is of no concern to Raquel, whose only interest is in having children, regardless of whom they resemble or what their character may be. If they were to be similar in spirit to Juan, they would be more compliant with her wishes.

Juan is not stupid, however, and it is this awareness of his plight that gives pathos to his character and emphasizes the strength of character in Raquel. Juan knows full well what part he plays in his mistress's life, but has been so emasculated that he is unable to resist: "He felt that for Raquel he was just an instrument, a means. A

---

74. "Dos madres," O.C. 9: 430, 424, 431.

means for what? For satisfying an excessive hunger for motherhood? Or rather a strange vengeance, a vengeance from other worlds?" There is a parallel to be drawn between Juan and the Raquel of *Raquel encadenada*. Both of them are victimized in similar ways, but whereas Raquel sacrifices everything to free herself from her chains and devote herself to children, Juan permits himself the complacency that Unamuno so often railed against. Even when he agrees to marry Berta, it is with the secret hope that she will give him the will to rebel; that becomes impossible, however, when Berta, in her way, falls as much under the domination of Raquel as Juan: "The one with whom Berta was madly in love was Raquel, Raquel was her idol." By allowing Raquel to take over her children with no moral justification whatsoever, she too becomes enslaved. No one believes that it is possible to succeed against Raquel's wishes and no effort is made — either by Juan, or by the parents of Berta, or by Berta herself, who possibly benefits from the situation more than anyone besides Raquel herself because she learns what her own weakness is through her relationship with the woman: "And she let herself be absorbed by Juan's mistress and kept discovering herself through the other woman." [75] In fact, all the secondary characters learn of their ineptness as individuals through their dealings with and defeat by Raquel.

Unamuno does more to give Raquel depth by describing those who wallow in her wake than he does by describing her directly. She does know her own mind and is capable of exerting her will so that she may be herself and be all — but she is tyrannical. The closer she comes to motherhood, however apparential it may be, the more despotic she becomes. Like the other characters in this category, she is something of a monomaniac, with her own benefit as her only goal. She is defeated in her ambition to have a child only by her sterility. Her strength of character and determination are basically heroic, but she spurs no one on to greater fulfillment.

The situation presented in "El marqués de Lumbría," is not dissimilar. Carolina, with her iron will, conquers and annihilates Tristán, a weak man throughout, and becomes a mother by dint of that will. Like Raquel, she allows herself to be stopped by nothing.

75. Ibid., p. 451, 432, 441.

Her character makes her capable of anything, but again her goal is beneficial only to herself and is unjust for all.

The most complete development of the theme is to be found in the novel *La Tía Tula*, published only one year later, in 1921. The central motivation, however, is slightly different. Rather than concentrate merely on the business of acquiring a child, Unamuno shows in this work what could be called the essence of being a mother. "Dos madres" and "El marqués de Lumbría" deal with creating a concrete mother-child relationship through whatever means seem necessary; but in this novel he goes one step further, as he examines how a woman can impose herself on her "children" in a truly spiritual sense. These are the psychological aspects of maternity.

The hero must fulfill a need; he must show or prove the possibility of greater development by bringing to the fore the inherent weaknesses in one's character. Tula, however, weakens her audience (Ramiro and the children) first and then fills the need she has created. In many ways she resembles Alejandro Gómez ("Nada menos que todo un hombre") in this; for her heroism, if it may momentarily be called that, is false in that it has its greatest effect where it should have been least necessary. There is something frightful about Tula and her methods. She lacks the purity of purpose that we saw in Manuel Bueno, for example, but is not as nefarious as Raquel ("Dos madres") or Carolina. She shows, however, no respect for anyone else's will. On the surface she is the model of motherhood and purity, but as Ramiro realizes: " 'You're a saint, Gertrudis,' Ramiro told her, 'but a saint who has made sinners.' " There is a perversion in her efforts and in her view of purposes. Only when Manuela dies does Tula finally begin to feel some of the guilt that is rightfully hers. Devoting herself almost entirely to the children of Manuela and Ramiro, she cries: "They are the children of my sin! Yes, of my sin!" [76] She is the founder of a family that eventually becomes a community representing her personal fulfillment and immortality. It has been formed, however, through a dedication to the principle of broadening her own position as spiritual mother. There is a lack of evolution in her personality, as her function as mother is never threatened, and is indeed reinforced, by these people who

76. *La Tía Tula*, O.C. 9: 590, 598.

seem born to live together, subject to her domination, and participating as members of the family group.

The remarkable thing about this community, aside from its cohesiveness, is its solitude. Virtually no interpenetration of characters is possible in the novel, since each person lives in almost complete isolation. The justification for their existence as a group is a kind of spiritual inbreeding in which each member gives meaning to the mother. The children give Tula her fulfillment as a mother, and she in turn emasculates and eliminates Ramiro. He is the producer of children in any woman not worried, as Tula is, by the preservation of her virginity; then, like Raquel, she takes control of the fruit of this union. She is necessary to Ramiro because she is his refuge and continuity, not as an individual woman but symbolically. Like most of Unamuno's women, she represents the intrahistory of man. The importance to her of the children's attitude toward her is evidenced by her eagerness to be called "mother" and reluctance to be referred to as "step-mother," and thus be relegated to a secondary position in their ill-defined personalities. This is a deliberate technique used by Unamuno to show the children's individuality but lack of inner development at Tula's hand. The only one who emerges is Manolita, since she is designated as Tula's follower, her Sancho. What we have learned about Tula is assumed to apply to Manolita as well: "through her, the spiritual eternity of the family continued. She inherited the family's soul, rendered spiritual in the Aunt." [77] Tula succeeds in achieving some degree of immortality, even though it is done through shadows instead of personalities. She has felt a sense of mission throughout her life and has resolved to die with the thought that she must have completed that mission. Like all heroes, she vacillates and entertains certain doubts about herself — "But do I understand myself? Do I understand myself?" — but she does not interrupt the continuity of her course of action. Her entire life has been centered around an activity limited to her immediate family: "But she had passed through the world outside the world." The blame must be shared, however, with Ramiro, who resigned himself to the situation. He alone could have prevented it, but his reaction was somewhat like that of Juan in "Dos madres." For example, after his marriage to

77. Ibid., p. 627.

Manuela he abandons himself completely: "Ramiro lived deep in resigned despair and more subjected than ever to Gertrudis's will." [78] Tula only accepted the opportunities that she caused to come about. Her actions were destructive to many, but no one had the stronger will necessary to stop her, and she believed that her motives were just.

One of the most direct representations of the effects of a despotic personality is the theatrical novella "Nada menos que todo un hombre" (1916), in which the protagonist has a brutal will dominated completely by the image it has formed of itself. Alejandro Gómez is scarcely human, nor is he intended to be; yet he dominates Julia with every breath. There is something intentionally grotesque about him, and his absurd attempts at Nietzschean heroism show him to be without substance or viable motivation. His sense of mission is limited to the perpetuation of himself through the son whom he claims he inevitably had to father; yet beneath the image there is the destructive void of a desperate will without justification beyond that which he demands from others. His barbarity is mitigated only at the end when he sinks into a realization of his crimes and of his true love for Julia.

His influence is not heroic in any sense of the word since it is founded on fear and not on exemplary conduct: he is pure egotism and wants to better himself at the cost of his wife. His vaunting is false and his claims that he is unlike others are tricks sustained by his lack of a past. Like Don Quixote and Julio Macedo, he claims to be reborn, but he does not reinforce this rebirth with new vital content. His wife thus becomes an object, an instrument to give him a justification that he cannot achieve alone. When she finally discovers the truth about him, he is without force and the outcome of the story is inevitable. He finishes without having transcended himself at all, since he did not follow up his claims and declarations of uniqueness with authentic actions. He is essentially as Eugenio de Nora pictures him: "No, Alejandro is not, strictly speaking, a man, not even a *being*; he is a blind *wanting*, an exclusive and brutal will projected on his surroundings." [79] He is designed to reveal the neces-

78. Ibid., p. 582, 614, 588.
79. Eugenio de Nora, *La novela española contemporánea*, p. 29.

sary authenticity of the heroic ego and the self-destruction incurred by deception. The house built on sand must inevitably fall under the weight of its own superstructure.

No protagonist other than Alejandro reveals such violent domination of another, yet various do succeed in imposing themselves falsely. Some of them, like Abel Sánchez, do so almost out of ignorance; others do it out of vengeance and with no idea of profiting by such an action, like Jorge in "La carta del difunto"; others do it out of selfishness and blindness, like the father in "Un cuentecillo sin argumento." Still others are cynical about it, and the fraud is due more to the stupidity of the victim than to the efforts of the perpetrator. This is best exemplified in two short stories on political themes: "¡Viva la introyección!" (1913), a case of causing people to believe out of ignorance; and "El redondismo" (1914), in which people are allowed to believe what they want, as long as they are lulled in their complacency.

The Pedants

This group is obvious and is one of Unamuno's prime concerns in the human spiritual framework. It consists of those who, in a manner not unlike that used by Alejandro Gómez, impose themselves without possessing the underlying substance in their personalities to justify their influence. They are not necessarily stupid, for they are aware of their own vacuity and resort to a total reliance on ideas — either their own or others' — to express whatever personality they hope eventually to achieve. The most striking example of this is, of course, don Avito Carrascal of Unamuno's pedagogical novel, *Amor y pedagogía* (1902). It is Unamuno's wish to lash out against the excesses of reason, and particularly the advances made by the positivism of the nineteenth century, and to reestablish emotion and humanity as viable forces in human achievement. In a discussion with Avito, don Fulgencio stresses the importance of heroism: "And in this theater the extraordinary thing is the hero . . . , the one who takes his part seriously and doesn't think about the gallery, and doesn't care a bit about the audience, but rather makes his performance alive, truly alive, and in the duel scene really kills the one who plays the part of his adversary." [80] Unamuno, in keeping with

80. *Amor y pedagogía,* O.C. 2: 480.

the times (Baroja was to write *El árbol de la ciencia* in 1911, and Pérez de Ayala's *Prometeo* appeared in 1916), opposes exalted intellectualism at the expense of civilization and culture, which is nothing less than the manifestation of a collective individuality that can be suffocated by false science and pedantic or restrictive educational values.

Carrascal is the man who feels that love and pedagogy (in this case, the attempted breeding of a new Nietzschean superman) are mutually exclusive. His ideas are combatted principally by don Fulgencio, who feels that a little madness is a healthy trait indeed, for it is natural and therefore right. Unamuno is setting up Carrascal as the embodiment of the theories of development he most despises. He wishes, through Carrascal's example, to prove that it is necessary to live first before formulating theories, that personalities cannot be formed on the basis of abstract theories blindly applied to a situation torn out of all context. Carrascal, like most of Unamuno's pedants, is an atrocious puppet devoid of humanity, who trips and rises to trip again, until finally he dashes himself against the wall of rationality he has been constructing. He is partially redeemed only at the end of the novel, when the suicide of his son makes him recognize the futility of his pedantry and he must resign himself to the irrationality that is humanity and that is far more potent than the abstractions with which he has lived for so long.

There are a startling number of pedants in Unamuno's work. In the story "Juan-María" lies the seed of *Amor y pedagogía,* and in "El diamante de Villasola" (1898) a more successful version of Apolodoro Carrascal is described: one so carefully polished by his schoolmaster that he shines brilliantly in Madrid, but whose defeat comes when it is realized that, like a diamond, his light is merely reflected. Any native gifts he might have had, have been corroded by the insistent pedantry of his master. In "Gárcia, mártir de la ortografía fonética" (1923), the protagonist is somewhat more likeable because his obsession, however pedantic, is more appealing and less pernicious than that of the others; yet he is defeated in the end because he has to conform like everyone else. Other pedants are "Don Catalino, hombre sabio" (1915) and "Don Silvestre Carrasco, hombre efectivo" (1917). Because of their monomania and insistence upon trivialities of meaningless consistency, the protagonists of "La caridad bien ordenada"

(1898) and "La revolución de la biblioteca de Ciudámuerta" (1917)
would also have to be included.

The Non-heroes:

This is certainly the least influential yet one of the most important
categories, because it contains all the mediocrities and nonentities
produced by Unamuno's imagination: those characters who fumble
their way through their stories by the grace of either God or Unamuno, but never through any awareness or imagination of their own.
Most of them are innocuous, but nothing is less complimentary. They
are the least heroic of all since they believe in nothing, feel nothing,
and consequently do not agonize or care about anything. Life is something to pass through as painlessly and effortlessly as possible, and
for them Unamuno was fond of saying, "The question is to pass time
without getting seriously involved." A decided majority of Unamuno's
secondary characters would be included in this category, led by
Tristán ("El marqués de Lumbría"), Juan ("Dos madres"), and
Ramiro (*La Tía Tula*), whose situations we have already seen.
Interestingly enough, Unamuno devoted at least three of his best
short novels to various types of mediocrity, in which he gives depth
to the seriousness of such a characteristic and its external influences.

In "La novela de don Sandalio" (1930), he showed with great perception the effect an almost nonexistent man can have on another,
in this case an apparently intelligent and well-informed man who is
bored with mediocrity and its consequent foolishness. The narrator
takes the figure of don Sandalio, with his lack of personality, and
in his own mind converts this emptiness into a person of fascination,
mystery, and deep personal crisis. As time passes and he feels more
comfortable with don Sandalio — although it can hardly be said that
he knows him any better — he feels the need to possess him and
make him his own. Inherently, don Sandalio has no existence in any
meaningful sense, either for the narrator or for the other members
of the casino; but the narrator takes refuge in his own vision of the
man and thus gives him reality — yet always just the desired amount.
The process is much the same as that employed by Unamuno with
his own characters. He finally dies as proof that he lived. As Ricardo
Gullón illustrates, the process is a game of mirrors: "for if Unamuno

is reflected in the narrator and the narrator in don Sandalio, don Sandalio is duplicated in his first playing partner, who in turn will be reflected in another, and the other in someone else, and so on into infinity." [81]

The implications of this are serious and important for an understanding of the "mystery of the personality," as the question of absolute reality reaches a degree of complexity we have not dealt with before. Although a person's reality does depend upon his effect on others, how far does this duplication extend, to what degree does it originate in others, and what is the reality of the initial image that is reflected to infinity? The problem is particularly significant for the light it casts on the reality a person can achieve involuntarily, without displaying any heroic characteristics whatever. Indeed, don Sandalio's life centers around his chess games, which are his way of deliberately avoiding involvement and passing the time. There is no communication between don Sandalio and the narrator, and the consequent feeling of frustration is what causes the narrator to convert his chess partner into a completely fictitious character and a focus of his own life.

This narrator is an important element in his own right, for he could represent any of several people, as Gullón points out. He could be don Sandalio himself in a process of introspection and self-duplication such as we have seen in "El que se enterró" and *Tulio Montalbán*, in which case the character might represent a definite attempt at heroism through his efforts to surpass his own feeling of mediocrity; or, don Sandalio could be the person to whom the letters are written, the enigmatic Felipe, in which case the process is one of helping someone else to overcome his mediocrity. Thirdly, the narrator could be Felipe, who is writing about himself in the person of don Sandalio, and then the introspection and fragmentation of the personality becomes the product of a heroic figure filled with the deepest feeling of agony. It would be foolhardy to attempt to give a concrete solution to the story, however appealing the choices may be, for Unamuno is presenting us with various possibilities of being, all of which he recognizes. He said on many occasions that he would

81. Ricardo Gullón, "Don Sandalio o el juego de los espejos," *Papeles de Son Armadans,* 30: 319. This article was republished in *Autobiografías de Unamuno,* pp. 312–30.

like to write a story in two columns, so that the reader could choose the outcome. He has done at least as much here and, through the apparently hollow figure of don Sandalio, has offered the reader an ontological monster to which he cannot remain indifferent. In any case, the characters are a reflection of Unamuno's ego, and as he must represent the initial image, the resulting personalities are his responsibility.

None of the other characters in this middle ground of Unamuno's work stimulates the reader with such force. Many inspire a feeling of emptiness and frustration because of their lack of inner motivation, such as Ricardo and Liduvina in "Una historia de amor" (1911), whose attempts to express themselves through their flight and furtive passion lack any sense of conviction, and who fail dismally because of their confusion about what they themselves represent. Although the problem is treated with great insight, the protagonists are condemned by the novelist to suffer a common pain for having sealed themselves up in a solitude that makes them both unreachable. Rather than personality as such, this is really the problem of their destiny, or mission, which leaves in their mouths nothing but the bitter aftertaste of sin predicated on a reluctance to commit themselves. Emeterio of "Un pobre hombre rico" (1930) also passes through life in a state of constant noninvolvement until it seems too late for him to rectify the waste. Whether that is indeed true is a vital question, but one he does not care to ask, for he is safer not allowing himself to be assaulted by too many tardy doubts.

In "El amor que asalta" (1912), Unamuno describes two mediocrities who find their one moment of commitment when they finally consummate the love that has been lying dormant for so many years. It is not a heroic decision and has no serious consequences, as the moment of commitment kills them both.

There is also a long list of uninspired characters who can scarcely be referred to as protagonists because life is a passive experience for all of them. They are perhaps exemplified by Juan Manso (1892) who is refused admission into heaven because he is not willing to keep his place in line. They all feel, like Bonifacio (1913), that they will be able to extricate themselves by pulling on their ears. The withering of personality is examined in "¿Por qué ser así?" (1898), which is almost identical to "Nerón tiple" (1890), "Sueño" (1897),

"El alcalde de Orbajosa" (1921), "La promesa," "Solitaña" (1889), out of which probably grew *Paz en la guerra,* and "El espejo de la muerte" (1911). All the situations are by no means identical; the reasons for this wasting away vary greatly except for the fact that it is always due to some manifestation of the character's reluctance to act with conviction — or indeed to act at all in some cases.

Others try to save themselves through a totally false method of action that is intended solely to deceive with as little effort as possible. This is seen in "¡Cosas de franceses!" (1893), "Una rectificación de honor" (1913), where the satire is farther-reaching than this comment may suggest, and "Un caso de longevidad" (1917). In all of these cases, however, there is also a deliberate effort to caricature certain aspects of society, and this is more truly the basis of the stories than any specific attempt to unravel the mysteries of self-fulfillment.

In at least four stories, the protagonists live out lives based upon a false notion of themselves or of the importance of certain trivialities. Perhaps these could also be called the lesser pedants: "La redención del suicidio" (1901), "El misterio de iniquidad" (1913), and "La manchita de la uña" (1923). In "Robleda el actor" (1920) we are confronted by a man who is a hero in reverse. His concept of fulfillment is to make his own personality vanish entirely behind the character he is supposed to represent. The theme is the diminution of the ego.

In summary, then, Unamuno's protagonists may be divided into some five main groups after the experience of *Paz en la guerra:*

1. Those who, despite a strongly felt mission and a true heroic potential, fail to achieve fulfillment, either because of Unamuno's strong control or because of their inability to overcome successfully the doubts racking their spirits.

2. Those who have or develop a great number, if not all, of the qualities of the hero, but ultimately fail because they are the victims of any one of several factors: the circumstances of life itself; the relative strength of either historical reality or fiction; their own misconceptions about themselves and the mission they are called upon to fulfill; the inescapable domination of a personality stronger than their own.

3. Those who, although always ineffectual, move toward a greater degree of heroism and immortality through the polarization of love or a deeper realization of their own value as individuals.

4. Those whose stronger or more frankly self-centered will permits them to exert a weakening influence upon others through cunning, an exaggerated interpretation of their own rôles, or an inordinate reliance upon the brittleness of fixed ideas that serve them as a base.

5. Those who quite simply show no development of the raw material of their individuality nor the sense of agony necessary to convert their basic selves into the heroic potential. They are the unconscious masses.

These divisions are necessarily arbitrary and were not intended by Unamuno; yet they serve to illustrate the variety of approaches he used to plumb and reveal the depths and immensity of the human potential in order to see what it can achieve, how it can achieve it, and what the many possibilities for individual fulfillment are.

Conclusion

One of the main purposes of this work has been to investigate Unamuno's prose fiction as a concrete expression of his most fundamental preoccupations, which we have related under the concept of the heroic will. Unamuno formed no part of the dehumanizing trends of the middle and late nineteenth century, and much of his work is a violent rejection of the principles of positivism. In many ways, viewed within his historical context, he represents a reversion to the Romantic ideals of man as a suffering individual, and his link with Kierkegaard shows the Dane and the Spaniard to have been close in many of their attitudes.

Unamuno was also influenced by and occasionally close to the ideas of Nietzsche, as expressed in *Also sprach Zarathustra*, but his belief in the aspirations of each individual separates them decisively. His constant struggle to return to the faith of his childhood, lost in the years as a student in Madrid and culminating in March of 1897, and his belief that this could be accomplished through a return to innocence or a deep commitment to the ideal of Woman as Mother, underlie his preoccupation. Religion itself was a sublime effort of the will, and there is a crucial distinction to be made between the man who will not believe, through a conscious effort, like Nietzsche, and the man who cannot believe, despite a conscious effort, like Unamuno. Thus it is that, more than any other Spanish writer, Unamuno had an immeasurable influence upon, not merely his contemporaries, but also succeeding generations, who find in him the expression of anguish that characterizes the existential crisis into which they have been thrust.

No study has yet been made that examines in depth the reverberations of Unamuno's thought; yet in Spanish literature written since the last decade of the last century, one finds his imprint like a watermark in fine paper. His concepts of heroism and personal fulfillment link him to the Romantics, for he faces the anguish with optimism and an unshakable faith in the potential of humanity through the efforts of the individual. However, he is also Spain's first twentieth-century writer. Armando Zubizarreta calls him "the first contemporary man,"[1] because he points the way to the new ontological crises of man. His thinking represents a remarkable transition, and in many ways, one leaves the nineteenth century forever when one leaves Unamuno and his confidence in the hope of social and personal regeneration. On the one hand, this confidence now seems to ring hollow in its apparent simplicity and naïveté, while, on the other, he is certainly contemporary as he anticipates and suffers the same doubts as the intellectuals who will follow him throughout Europe. His solutions are much more closely related to the nineteenth century of Kierkegaard than are his problems. His strident cries continue to possess an immediacy that demands attention as a note of optimism among the torturous concerns that close over the late existentialists and postexistentialists.

Unamuno breaks away from the realist tradition when he presents Spain with her first truly metaphysical novels, in which the novel is its own problem. In an attempt to vulgarize philosophical concerns and give them form, he turned to the novel and the theater as means of spreading ideas. He may never be recognized as truly colossal in either of these genres; yet in his examination of the crisis of self he provides the transition from Kierkegaard to Heidegger and from Balzac to Beckett. Heidegger admits his influence,[2] as do Camus and Sartre, and the very term "tragic sense of life" is taken directly into their work, which does, in large part, presuppose the doubts of Unamuno. He concentrates on the problem of man with a precision that brings philosophy and metaphysics into literature in a way hitherto unknown in Spain; yet his technique of stripping

---

1. Zubizarreta, *Unamuno en su 'nivola,'* p. 322.
2. Miguel Cruz Hernández, "La misión socrática de don Miguel de Unamuno," *Cuadernos de la Cátedra Miguel de Unamuno,* 3 (1952): 46. See also Mario James Valdés, *Death in the Literature of Unamuno* (Urbana, Ill., 1966), p. 12.

characters and situations until they have no vestiges of life and are mere vehicles for his own doubts, tends to give much of his work an artificiality that is deeply deceptive.

Unamuno was a didactic writer in that a thesis was always implicit in his work; yet unlike almost any other thinker of this century, he sees everything and everyone as only a reflection of an aspect of his own soul. His question into the mysteries of being was in many ways original, but his impact is limited by the fact that he succeeded in casting more light upon himself than upon the problems. Let us not be misled, however, for this was, after all, his objective. His immortality and his heroism are due to the ever-present immensity of his own personality and the conflicts it suffers, rather than to his success in changing the structure of European philosophy. For this reason his effect is incalculable. He strove to evince heroism in his readers and in himself through a clarification and expansion of each man's character. His influences should not imply anonymity; he feels that he will be recognized as a great force even though succeeding generations may not be able to point to his track, since individuality does not permit copying and heroism is ultimately unique. Unamuno the hero must show the way and be remembered in that context; but when each man continues, he does so in his own right.

There is, then, a fundamental duality in his lasting effect. He must vanish into the successful life of his followers, who succeed in creating their own unique personalities; yet he, too, will stand out as a personality and live, as he hoped, not as an amalgam of mere ideas, but as a man of flesh and blood. Thus he becomes highly characteristic of his time and the decades that follow, when intellectuals shall know what Victor Brombert refers to as the "crisis of Humanism." [3] Heroism represents a reevaluation of man in the face of that crisis and a possible justification of his existence whether there be a God or not. God may ensure immortality for man, but some form of perpetuation is possible without him. Unamuno proves this by his own example.

It is, then, up to the individual to harmonize the conflicts between the desire for peace and the need for strife, the temptation of fame

3. Victor Brombert, *The Intellectual Hero* (Chicago, 1964), p. 18.

and the promise of immortality, the excitement of facility and the responsibility of sincerity. His fulfillment is his purpose and his justification; his fellow men are his strength and his inspiration; society and humanity, his beneficiaries and his reflection; God, his hope and his perpetuation. No man feels more deeply than he the tragedy of life without expansion or the impossibility of heroism without faith; yet no man more than he struggles to overcome a fear of nothingness by means of a hope in his ability to regain his innocence. There is no chance of respite for either Unamuno or his followers; there is no promise of ease or security. His heroism is most arduous, for the burden is squarely upon the individual and, once accepted, cannot be shirked. The onus of responsibility must fall on each man with a finality that staggers the intellect while giving encouragement to the soul. Reason has been surpassed, and man is projected into the infinity of his emotions and the endlessness of his capabilities.

Bibliography

1. Texts of Unamuno

Cómo se hace una novela. Buenos Aires, 1927.
Diario íntimo. Edited by P. Félix García. Madrid, 1970.
Ensayos. Edited by Bernardo G. de Candamo. 2 vols. Madrid, 1964.
Obras completas. Edited by Manuel García Blanco. 16 vols. Madrid, 1952–58.

2. Texts of Other Authors

Carlyle, Thomas. *Correspondence between Goethe and Carlyle.* London, 1887.
———. *On Heroes, Hero-Worship and the Heroic in History.* Lincoln, Nebraska, 1966.
———. *The French Revolution: A History.* 2 vols. London, 1907.
———. *Past and Present.* London, 1938.
James, William. *Psychology.* Cleveland, 1948.
———. *Pragmatism.* New York, 1914.
———. *Selected Papers in Philosophy.* London and New York, 1947.
———. *The Varieties of Religious Experience.* New York, 1902.
Nietzsche, Friedrich. *Thus Spoke Zarathustra.* Translated by R. J. Hollingdale. Baltimore, 1961.
———. *The Will to Power.* Translated by Walter Kaufmann. New York, 1967.
Senancour, Etienne Pivert de. *Obermann.* Paris, 1912.
Spinoza, Baruch. *Ethics.* London, 1967.
Tolstoy, Leo. *War and Peace.* Translated by Constance Garnett. New York: Modern Library, n.d.

3. Critical Works

Abellán, José Luis. "Influencias filosóficas en Unamuno." *Insula* 16, no. 181 (1961): 11.

218   BIBLIOGRAPHY

―――. *Miguel de Unamuno a la luz de la psicología.* Madrid, 1964.
Aja, Pedro V. "Unamuno y la inmortalidad del hombre concreto." *Revista cubana de filosofía* 2, no. 8: 25–29.
A. L. "The Life of Don Quixote and Sancho." *Bulletin of Spanish Studies* 5 (1928): 97–98.
Albérès, René M. *Miguel de Unamuno.* Paris and Brussels, 1957.
Alberich, José. "El obispo Blougram y San Manuel Bueno." *Revista de Literatura* 15 (1959): 90–94.
―――. "Sobre el positivismo de Unamuno." *Cuadernos de la Cátedra Miguel de Unamuno* 9 (1959): 61–75.
―――. "Unamuno y la duda sincera." *Revista de Literatura* 14 (1958): 210–25.
Albornoz, Aurora de. *La presencia de Miguel de Unamuno en Antonio Machado.* Madrid, 1968.
Allen, Gay Wilson. *William James.* New York, 1967.
Alonso, Dámaso. *Poetas españoles contemporáneos.* Madrid, 1965.
Altolaguirre, Manuel. "Don Miguel de Unamuno." *Revista Hispánica Moderna* 6 (1940): 17–24.
Alvar, Manuel. *Acercamientos a la poesía de Unamuno.* Tenerife, 1964.
Amster, Mauricio, ed. *Unamuno.* Santiago de Chile, 1964.
Aranguren, José Luis. "El talante religioso de Miguel de Unamuno." In *Catolicismo y protestantismo como formas de existencia.* Madrid, 1963.
―――. "Personalidad y religiosidad de Unamuno." *La Torre* 9, no. 35–36 (1961): 239–49.
Armas Ayala, Alfonso. "Unamuno en Canarias: capítulos de un libro." *Cuadernos de la Cátedra Miguel de Unamuno* 10 (1960): 69–99.
Ayala, Francisco. "El arte de novelar en Unamuno." *La Torre* 9, no. 35–36 (1961): 329–59.
Ayllón, Cándido. "Experiments in the Theatre of Unamuno, Valle-Inclán and Azorín." *Hispania* 46 (1963): 49–56.
Azaola, José Miguel de. "Las cinco batallas de Unamuno contra la muerte." *Cuadernos de la Cátedra Miguel de Unamuno* 2 (1951): 33–109.
―――. *Unamuno y su primer confesor.* Bilbao, 1959.
"Azorín." *La generación del 98.* Salamanca, 1961.
Badanelli, Pedro, ed. *Cartas inéditas de Miguel de Unamuno a Alberto Nin Frías.* Buenos Aires, 1962.
Balseiro, José Agustín. *Blasco Ibáñez, Unamuno, Valle-Inclán y Baroja: cuatro individualistas de España.* Chapel Hill, N.C., 1949.
―――. *El Quijote de la España contemporánea: Miguel de Unamuno.* Madrid, 1935.
―――. *El vigía.* Vol. 2. Madrid, 1928.
―――. "The Quixote of Contemporary Spain: Miguel de Unamuno." *PMLA* 49 (1934): 645–56.

Baquero, Gastón. "Monólogo con Don Quijote (Preámbulo de introduc-
ción al pensamiento de Unamuno)." *Revista Cubana* 14 (1940):
143–60.
Baráibar, Carlos de. "En torno a las novelas de Unamuno." *Atenea* 27,
no. 301 (1950): 5–21.
Barea, Arturo. *Unamuno*. New Haven, 1952.
Baring, Maurice. *Landmarks in Russian Literature*. London, 1960.
Baroja, Pío. *Memorias*. Vol. 3. Madrid, 1951.
Baroja, Ricardo. *Gente de la generación del 98*. Barcelona, 1969.
Basave, Agustín. *Miguel de Unamuno y José Ortega y Gasset: un
bosquejo valorativo*. México, 1950.
Basdekis, Demetrios. *Unamuno and Spanish Literature*. Berkeley, 1967.
Baudoin, Charles. *Le Triomphe du héros*. Paris, 1952.
Bayley, John. *Tolstoy and the Novel*. New York, 1966.
Benardete, Mair José. "Personalidad e individualidad en Unamuno."
Revista Hispánica Moderna 1 (1934): 1.
Benavides Lillo, Ricardo. "Para la genealogía de Augusto Pérez." In
Unamuno, edited by Mauricio Amster. Santiago, 1964.
Benítez, Hernán. *El drama religioso de Unamuno*. Buenos Aires, 1949.
Benito y Durán, Angel. *Introducción al estudio del pensamiento de
Unamuno*. Granada, 1953.
Bentley, Eric. *A Century of Hero-Worship*. Boston, 1957.
Berkowitz, H. Chonon. "Unamuno's Relations with Galdós." *Hispanic
Review* 8 (1940): 321–38.
Berlin, Isaiah. *The Hedgehog and the Fox*. New York, 1957.
Bertrand, J. J. A. "Seconde mort de don Quichotte." *Cuadernos de la
Cátedra Miguel de Unamuno* 1 (1948): 71–74.
Blanco Aguinaga, Charles. *El Unamuno contemplativo*. Mexico, 1959.
———. "Interioridad y exterioridad en Unamuno." *Nueva Revista de
Filología Hispánica* 7 (1953): 686–701.
———. "Sobre la complejidad de *San Manuel Bueno, mártir*, novela."
Nueva Revista de Filología Hispánica 15 (1961): 569–88.
———. "Unamuno, don Quijote y España." *Cuadernos Americanos*
11, no. 6 (1952): 204–16.
———. "Unamuno's *Niebla*: Existence and the Game of Fiction." *MLN*
79: 188–205.
———. "Unamuno's *yoismo* and Its Relation to Traditional Spanish In-
dividualism." In *Unamuno Centennial Studies*, edited by Ramón
Martínez López. Austin, 1966.
Bleiberg, Germán, and Fox, E. Inman, eds. *Spanish Thought and
Letters in the Twentieth Century*. Nashville, 1966.
Bousoño, Carlos. *Teoría de la expresión poética*. Madrid, 1966.
Bowra, C. M. *Heroic Poetry*. London, 1964.
Brion, Marcel. "Miguel de Unamuno et le quichottisme." *La Revue*
(1950), p. 529.

Brombert, Victor. *The Intellectual Hero*. Chicago, 1964.
Brooks, Van Wyck. *The Malady of the Ideal: Obermann, Maurice de Guérin, and Amiel*. London, 1913.
Butt, J. W. "Determinism and the Inadequacies of Unamuno's Radicalism, 1886–1897." *Bulletin of Hispanic Studies* 46, no. 3 (1969): 226–40.
Campbell, Joseph. *The Hero with a Thousand Faces*. Cleveland and New York, 1956.
Cannon, Calvin. "The Mythic Cosmology of Unamuno's *El Cristo de Velázquez*." *Hispanic Review* 28 (1960): 28–39.
Caravia, Pedro. "Espejo de la muerte y espejo de Unamuno." *Escorial* 9 (1942): 151–57.
Cardenal de Iracheta, Manuel. "Unamuno y su drama religioso." *Cuadernos Hispanoamericanos* 15 (1950): 576–80.
Castro, Américo. "Cervantes y Pirandello: un estudio comparativo." *La Nación* (Buenos Aires), April 16, 1924.
———. "Incarnation in *Don Quixote*." In *Cervantes Across the Centuries*, edited by Angel del Río. New York, 1947.
Cazamian, Louis. *Carlyle*. Translated by E. K. Brown. Hamden, Conn., 1966.
Chaves, Julio César. *Unamuno y América*. Madrid, 1964.
Clavería, Carlos. *Temas de Unamuno*. Madrid, 1953.
———. "Unamuno y Carlyle." *Cuadernos Hispanoamericanos* 10 (1949): 51–87. (Reprinted in above.)
Collado, Jesús-Antonio. *Kierkegaard y Unamuno*. Madrid, 1962.
Corominas, Pedro. "La trágica fe de Miguel de Unamuno." *Atenea* 46 (1938): 101–14.
Cranstone, Maurice. *Philosophy and Language*. Toronto, 1969.
Cruz Hernández, Miguel. "La misión socrática de don Miguel de Unamuno." *Cuadernos de la Cátedra Miguel de Unamuno* 3 (1952): 41–53.
Curtius, Ernst Robert. *European Literature and the Latin Middle Ages*. New York, 1953.
Del Río, Angel. "Las *Novelas ejemplares* de Unamuno." *Revista de la Universidad de Buenos Aires* 5, no. 1 (1960): 22–34.
Díaz, Elías. *Revisión de Unamuno*. Madrid, 1968.
Díaz Plaja, Guillermo. *Modernismo frente a Noventa y ocho*. Madrid, 1951.
———. "Unamuno, antimodernista." *Insula* 19, no. 216–17 (1964): 18.
Durán, Manuel. "El 'otro Unamuno' y la labor de investigación de Carlos Blanco." *Revista Hispánica Moderna* 27 (1961): 156–58.
———. *La ambigüedad en el Quijote*. Xalapa, Mexico, 1960.
———. "La técnica de la novela y la generación del 98." *Revista Hispánica Moderna* 23 (1957): 14–27.
———. "Los últimos días de Unamuno." *Revista de la Universidad de México* 14, no. 2 (1959): 16–18.

———. "Unamuno y 'El Gran Inquisidor.'" *Revista de la Universidad de México* 10, no. 7 (1955–56): 13–15.

———. "Unamuno y su 'Elegía en la muerte de un perro.'" *Insula* 19, no. 216–17 (1964): 3 and 32.

Durant, Will. *The Story of Civilization*. Vol. 2. New York, 1939.

Earle, Peter G. "El evolucionismo en el pensamiento de Unamuno." *Cuadernos de la Cátedra Miguel de Unamuno* 14–15 (1964–65): 19–28.

———. *Unamuno and English Literature*. New York, 1960.

Ehrenbourg, Ilya. *Duhamel, Gide, Malraux, Morand, Romains, Unamuno, vus par un écrivain d'U.R.S.S.* Translated by Madeleine Etard. Paris, 1934.

Eliade, Mircea. *Le Mythe de l'éternel retour*. Paris, 1949.

Elton, Oliver. *A Survey of English Literature: 1830–1880*. London, 1948.

Emmanuel, Pierre. "La théologie quichottesque d'Unamuno." *Esprit* 24 (1956): 345–55.

Enguídanos, Miguel. "Unamuno frente a la historia." *La Torre* 9, no. 35–36 (1961): 251–63.

Enjuto, Jorge. "Sobre la idea de nada en Unamuno." *La Torre* 9, no. 35–36 (1961): 265–75.

Eoff, Sherman H. *The Modern Spanish Novel*. New York, 1961.

Esclasans y Folch, Agustín. *Miguel de Unamuno*. Buenos Aires, 1947.

Fabian, Donald L. "Action and Idea in *Amor y pedagogía* and *Prometeo*." *Hispania* 41, no. 1 (1958): 30–34.

Farré, Luis. "Unamuno, William James y Kierkegaard." *Cuadernos Hispanoamericanos* 20 (1954): 279–99; 21: 64–88.

Fasel, Oscar A. "Observations on Unamuno and Kierkegaard." *Hispania* 38 (1955): 443–50.

Fernández, Pelayo H. "Más sobre *San Manuel Bueno, mártir* de Unamuno." *Revista Hispánica Moderna* 29 (1963): 252–62.

———. *Miguel de Unamuno y William James*. Salamanca, 1961.

———. *El problema de la personalidad en Unamuno y San Manuel Bueno*. Madrid, 1966.

Ferrater Mora, José. "Miguel de Unamuno et l'idée de la réalité." *Revue de Métaphysique et de Morale* 63 (1958): 468–73.

———. *Unamuno: a Philosophy of Tragedy*. Translated by Philip Silver. Berkeley, 1962.

Ford, Boris, ed. *The Pelican Guide to English Literature: From Dickens to Hardy*. Vol. 6. London, 1966.

Forster, E. M. *Aspects of the Novel*. London, 1966.

Franck, R. "Unamuno: Existentialism and the Spanish Novel." *Accent* 4 (1948–49): 83–88.

Fuster, Joan. *Maragall y Unamuno frente a frente*. Santiago, 1964.

Garagorri, Paulino. *Unamuno, Ortega, Zubiri en la filosofía española*. Madrid, 1968.

García Blanco, Manuel. *América y Unamuno*. Madrid, 1964.
———. *"Amor y pedagogía*, nivola unamuniana." *La Torre* 9, no. 35–36 (1961): 443–78.
———. *En torno a Unamuno*. Madrid, 1965.
García Morejón, Julio. *Unamuno y el Cancionero*. São Paolo, 1966.
———. *Unamuno y Portugal*. Madrid, 1964.
Gibian, George. "The Forms of Discontent in Dostoevsky and Tolstoy." In *Comparatists at Work*, edited by Stephen G. Nichols, Jr. and Richard B. Vowles. Waltham, Mass., 1968.
Gifford, Henry. *The Novel in Russia*. New York, 1964.
Gil, Ildefonso Manuel. "Sobre la novelística de Unamuno." *Cuadernos Hispanoamericanos* 57: 323–26.
Gillet, Joseph E. "The Autonomous Character in Spanish and European Literature." *Hispanic Review* 24 (1956): 179–90.
Gómez de Ortega, R. "Don Miguel de Unamuno y su ensayo 'El sepulcro de don Quijote.' " *Bulletin of Spanish Studies* 1 (1923): 43–48.
Gómez-Moriana, Antonio. *Über den Sinn von 'congoja' bei Unamuno*. Meisenheim am Glan, 1965.
González, José Emilio. "Algunas observaciones sobre tres novelas de Unamuno." *La Torre* 9, no. 35–36 (1961): 427–42.
———. "Joaquín Monegro, Unamuno y *Abel Sánchez*." *La Torre* 10, no. 40 (1962): 85–109.
González Arrili, B. "Las novelas de Unamuno." *Caras y Caretas*, February 9, 1929.
González Caminero, Nemesio. *Unamuno: trayectoria de su ideología y de su crisis religiosa*. Comillas, 1948.
González Ruano, César. *Vida, pensamiento y aventura de Miguel de Unamuno*. Madrid, 1954.
Granjel, Luis S. *Retrato de Unamuno*. Madrid, 1957.
Grau, Jacinto. *Unamuno, su tiempo y su España*. Buenos Aires, 1946.
Gullón, Ricardo. "Aspectos de Unamuno." *Insula* 178 (1961): 3.
———. *Autobiografías de Unamuno*. Madrid, 1964.
———. "Imágenes de *El otro*." In *Spanish Thought and Letters in the Twentieth Century*, edited by Germán Bleiberg and E. Inman Fox. Nashville, Tenn., 1966.
———. "Imágenes del otro." *Revista Hispánica Moderna* 31 (1965): 210–21.
Guy, Alain. "Miguel de Unamuno, pélerin de l'absolu." *Cuadernos de la Cátedra Miguel de Unamuno* 1 (1948): 75–102.
Hook, Sidney. *The Hero in History*. Boston, 1955.
Hoyos, Antonio de. *Unamuno escritor*. Murcia, 1959.
Huerta, Eleazar. "Unamuno novelista." In *Unamuno*, edited by Mauricio Amster. Santiago, 1964.
Huertas-Jourda, José. *The Existentialism of Miguel de Unamuno*. Gainesville, Fla., 1963.

Huizinga, J. *The Waning of the Middle Ages*. New York, 1954.

Ilie, Paul. *Unamuno: an Existential View of Self and Society*. Madison, Wisc., 1967.

———. "Unamuno, Gorky and the Cain Myth: Toward a Theory of Personality." *Hispanic Review* 29 (1961): 310–23.

Johnson, W. D. "Vida y ser en el pensamiento de Unamuno." *Cuadernos de la Cátedra Miguel de Unamuno* 6 (1955): 9–50.

Jung, Carl G. *Psyche and Symbol*. New York, 1958.

———. *Psychological Types*. Translated by H. Godwin Baynes. London, 1923.

Kail, Andrée. "Unamuno and Gide's Concept of the Novel." *Hispania* 45 (1962): 200–04.

Kirsner, Robert. "Galdós and the Generation of 1898." *Hispania* 33 (1950): 240–42.

———. "The Novel of Unamuno: a Study of Creature Determinism." *Modern Lauguage Journal* 37 (1953): 128–29.

Kock, Josse de. *Introducción al Cancionero de Miguel de Unamuno*. Madrid, 1968.

Kretschmer, Ernst. *The Psychology of Men of Genius*. Translated by R. B. Cattell. New York, 1931.

Lacy, Alan. "Censorship and *Cómo se hace una novela*." *Hispanic Review* 34 (1966): 317–25.

———. *Miguel de Unamuno: the Rhetoric of Existence*. The Hague and Paris, 1967.

Laín, Milagro. *La palabra en Unamuno*. Caracas, 1964.

Laín Entralgo, Pedro. *La espera y la esperanza*. Madrid, 1957.

———. *La generación del noventa y ocho*. Madrid, 1945.

Landsberg, P. L. *Reflexiones sobre Unamuno*. Santiago, 1963.

Lavrin, J. "A Note on Nietzsche and Dostoevsky." *Russian Review* 28: 160–70.

Lázaro, Fernando. "El teatro de Unamuno." *Cuadernos de la Cátedra Miguel de Unamuno* 7 (1956): 5–29.

Lázaro Ros, Armando. "Unamuno, filósofo existencialista." In Marjorie Grene, *El sentimiento trágico de la existencia*. Madrid, 1952.

Leal, Luis. "Unamuno y Pirandello." *Italica* 29 (1952): 193–99.

Lebois, A. "Le révolte des personnages: de Cervantès à Raymond Schwab." *Revue de Littérature Comparée* 43 (1949): 482–576.

Lehman, B. H. *Carlyle's Theory of the Hero*. Durham, Eng., 1928.

Levi, A. W. "The Quixotic Quest for Being." *Ethics* 46, no. 2 (1956): 132–36.

Levin, Harry. *The Gates of Horn*. New York, 1966.

Lewis, C. Day. *The Poetic Image*. New York, 1947.

Livingstone, Leon. "Interior Duplication and the Problem of Form in the Modern Spanish Novel." *PMLA* 73 (1958): 393–406.

————. "Unamuno and the Aesthetic of the Novel." *Hispania* 24 (1941): 442–50.

López Estrada, Francisco. *Métrica española del siglo XX.* Madrid, 1969.

López Ibor, Juan José. *El español y su complejo de inferioridad.* Madrid, 1961.

López Morillas, Juan. "Unamuno y sus criaturas: 'Antolín S. Paparrigópulos.'" *Cuadernos Americanos* 7, no. 4 (1948): 234–49.

Lubbock, Percy. *The Craft of Fiction.* London, 1966.

Luby, Barry J. *Unamuno a la luz del empirismo lógico contemporáneo.* New York, 1969.

Lukács, Georg. *The Historical Novel.* Boston, 1962.

————. *La Théorie du roman.* Translated by Jean Clairevoye. Lausanne, 1963.

————. *Realism in our Time.* New York and Evanston, 1964.

————. *Studies in European Realism.* New York, 1964.

Madariaga, Salvador de. "Miguel de Unamuno." In *De Galdós a Lorca.* Buenos Aires, 1960.

Manyá, Joan B. *La teología de Unamuno.* Barcelona, 1960.

Marcilly, C. "Unamuno et Tolstoï: de *La Guerre et la paix* à *Paz en la guerra.*" *Bulletin Hispanique* 67 (1965): 274–313.

Marías, Julián. *La filosofía española actual.* Buenos Aires, 1948.

————. *Miguel de Unamuno.* Buenos Aires, 1960.

Marrero, Vicente. *El Cristo de Unamuno.* Madrid, 1960.

Martínez Blasco, Angel. "Existencialismo en la poesía de Unamuno." *Insula* 181 (1961): 17.

Martínez López, Ramón, ed. *Unamuno Centennial Studies.* Austin, Tex., 1966.

Matlaw, Ralph E., ed. *Tolstoy: a Collection of Critical Essays.* New York, 1967.

Meyer, François. *La ontología de Miguel de Unamuno.* Translated by Cesáreo Goicoechea. Madrid, 1962.

Moeller, Charles. *Literatura del siglo XX y cristianismo.* Vol. 4. Translated by Valentín García Yerba. Madrid, 1960.

Moncy, Agnes. *La creación del personaje en las novelas de Unamuno.* Santander, 1963.

————. "Un puñado de Niebla." *Insula* 216–17 (1964): 12 and 26.

Monner Sans, José María. "Unamuno, Pirandello y el personaje autónomo." *La Torre* 9, no. 35–36 (1961): 387–402.

Morales, José Ricardo. "Don Miguel de Unamuno, persona dramática." In *Unamuno,* edited by Mauricio Amster. Santiago, 1964.

Morón Arroyo, Ciriaco. "*San Manuel Bueno, mártir* y el 'sistema' de Unamuno." *Hispanic Review* 32 (1964): 227–46.

Mounier, Emmanuel. *Introduction aux existentialismes.* Paris, 1962.

Nora, Eugenio G. de. *La novela española contemporánea.* Vol. 1, Madrid, 1963.

Nuez, Sebastián de la. *Unamuno en Canarias.* La Laguna, 1964.
————. "Unamuno y Galdós en unas cartas." *Insula,* 216–17 (1964): 26.
Olaso, Ezequiel de. *Los nombres de Unamuno.* Buenos Aires, 1963.
O'Leary, J. E. "Voltaire y Unamuno, Don Quijote y San Ignacio de Loyola." *Repertorio Americano* 8 (1924): 377–80.
Oostendorp, H. Th. "Los puntos de semejanza entre *La Guerra y la Paz* de Tolstoy y *Paz en la guerra* de Unamuno." *Bulletin Hispanique* 69 (1967): 85–105.
Oromí, Miguel. *El pensamiento filosófico de Miguel de Unamuno.* Madrid, 1943.
Ortega y Gasset, Eduardo. *Monodiálogos de don Miguel de Unamuno.* New York, 1958.
Padín, J. "El concepto de lo real en las últimas novelas de Unamuno." *Hispania* 11 (1928): 418–23.
Papini, Giovanni. *El crepúsculo de los filósofos.* Translated by José Sánchez Rojas. Madrid, 1918.
París, Carlos. *Unamuno: estructura de su mundo intelectual.* Barcelona, 1968.
Paucker, Eleanor Krane. *Los cuentos de Unamuno, clave de su obra.* Madrid, 1965.
————. "Unamuno's 'La venda': Short Story and Drama." *Hispania* 39, no. 3 (1956): 309–12.
Pérez de la Dehesa, Rafael. *Política y sociedad en el primer Unamuno.* Madrid, 1966.
Predmore, Richard L. "Flesh and Spirit in the Works of Unamuno." *PMLA* 70, no. 4 (1955): 587–605.
Putnam, Samuel. "Unamuno y el problema de la personalidad." *Revista Hispánica Moderna* 1 (1935): 103–10.
Regalado, Antonio. *El siervo y el Señor.* Madrid, 1968.
Ribbans, Geoffrey. *Niebla y soledad.* Madrid, 1971.
————. "The Development of Unamuno's *Amor y pedagogía* and *Niebla.*" In *Hispanic Studies in Honour of J. González Llubera.* Oxford, 1959.
Riso, Norma Olga. *La paradoja de la existencia en don Miguel de Unamuno.* Mexico, 1965.
Rivera de la Vega, Herminia. "Unamuno novelista." Master's thesis, University of Puerto Rico, 1946.
Roca, Alberto. "Cartas religiosas de Unamuno y Machado." *Islas* 2, no. 2–3 (1960): 639–42.
Romera Navarro, M. *Miguel de Unamuno: novelista, poeta, ensayista.* Madrid, 1928.
Rudd, Mary Margaret. *The Lone Heretic.* Austin, 1964.
Salamanca, University of. *Unamuno a los cien años.* Salamanca, 1967.
Salcedo, Emilio. *Vida de Don Miguel.* Madrid, 1970.

Salinas, Pedro. "El 'héroe' literario y la novela picaresca española." In *Ensayos de literatura hispánica*. Madrid, 1967.

Sánchez Barbudo, Antonio. *El misterio de la personalidad en Unamuno*. Buenos Aires, 1950.

———. *Estudios sobre Galdós, Unamuno y Machado*. Madrid, 1968.

Sánchez Trincado, J. L. "Criaturas de Unamuno: Elvira." *Repertorio Americano*. June 11, 1938, pp. 347–48.

———. "Teatro: arte y juego." *Repertorio Americano*. December 25, 1937.

Schürr, Friedrich. "Miguel de Unamuno, romancier et dramaturge existentialiste." *Langue et Littérature* 6: 281.

Sedwick, Frank. "Unamuno and Pirandello Revisted." *Italica* 33 (1956): 40–51.

———. "Unamuno and Womanhood: His Theater." *Hispania* 43 (1960): 309–13.

Sender, Ramón. *Los noventayochos*. New York, 1961.

Serrano Poncela, Segundo. *El pensamiento de Unamuno*. Mexico, 1953.

———. "Encuentro con don Miguel." In *El secreto de Melibea*. Madrid, 1959.

———. "Eros y la generación del 98." In *El secreto de Melibea*. Madrid, 1959.

———. "Unamuno y los clásicos." *La Torre* 9, no. 35–36 (1961): 505–35

Shestov, Lev. *Dostoevsky, Tolstoy and Nietzsche*. Athens, Ohio, 1969.

Sobejano, Gonzalo. *Forma literaria y sensibilidad social*. Madrid, 1967.

———. *Nietzsche en España*. Madrid, 1967.

Steiner, George. *Tolstoy or Dostoevsky*. New York, 1959.

Stevens, Harriet S. "Los cuentos de Unamuno." *La Torre* 9, no. 35–36 (1961): 403–25.

Torre, Guillermo de. "Triedro de Unamuno." In *La difícil universalidad española*. Madrid, 1965.

———. "Unamuno y Ortega." *Cuadernos Americanos* 2, no. 2 (1943): 157–76.

———. "Unamuno y su teatro." *Papeles de Son Armadans* 36: 13–44.

Torretti, Roberto. "Unamuno, pensador cristiano." In *Unamuno*, edited by Mauricio Amster. Santiago, 1964.

Troyat, Henri. *Tolstoy*. New York, 1967.

Ugarte, Francisco. "Unamuno y el quijotismo." *Modern Language Journal* 35 (1952): 18–23.

Uriarte, Fernando. "Lo prefilosófico en Unamuno." In *Unamuno*, edited by Mauricio Amster. Santiago, 1964.

Vaisman, Gladys. *Un ensayo sobre Miguel de Unamuno*. Santa Fe de la Argentina, 1965.

Valdés, Mario James. "*Amor y pedagogía* y lo grotesco." *Cuadernos de la Cátedra Miguel de Unamuno* 13 (1963): 53–62.

———. *Death in the Literature of Unamuno.* Urbana, Ill., 1966.

———. "El residuo spenceriano en Unamuno." *Insula* 18, no. 200–01 (1963): 32.

Villar, Arturo del. "La poesía en Unamuno." *Insula,* no. 216–17 (1964): 17 and 24.

Vivanco, Luis Felipe. "Unamuno, poeta lírico." *Insula,* no. 216–17 (1964): 11.

Wahl, Jean. *A Short History of Existentialism.* New York, 1949.

Wardropper, Bruce. "Unamuno's Struggle with Words." *Hispanic Review* 12 (1944): 183–95.

Webber, Ruth House. "Kierkegaard and the Elaboration of Unamuno's *Niebla.*" *Hispanic Review* 32 (1964): 118–34.

Willey, Basil. *Nineteenth-Century Studies.* London, 1964.

Wills, Arthur. *España y Unamuno.* New York, 1938.

Zavala, Iris M. *La angustia y la búsqueda del hombre en la literatura.* Xalapa, 1965.

———. *Unamuno y su teatro de conciencia.* Salamanca, 1963.

Zubizarreta, Armando F. *Tras las huellas de Unamuno.* Madrid, 1960.

———. *Unamuno en su 'nivola.'* Madrid, 1960.

Index